☆ A BROOKLANDS ☆
'ROAD TEST' LIMITED EDITION

FORD ESCORT
RS & MEXICO
1970-1979

Compiled by
R.M.Clarke

ISBN 1 85520 407X

BROOKLANDS BOOKS LTD.
P.O. BOX 146, COBHAM,
SURREY, KT11 1LG. UK

Brooklands Books

MOTORING

BROOKLANDS ROAD TEST SERIES

Abarth Gold Portfolio 1950-1971
AC Ace & Aceca 1953-1983
Alfa Romeo Giulietta Gold Portfolio 1954-1965
Alfa Romeo Giulia Coupés 1963-1976
Alfa Romeo Giulia Coupés Gold Port. 1963-1976
Alfa Romeo Spider 1966-1990
Alfa Romeo Spider Gold Portfolio 1966-1991
Alfa Romeo Alfasud 1972-1984
Alfa Romeo Alfetta Gold Portfolio 1972-1987
Alfa Romeo Alfetta GTV6 1980-1986
Allard Gold Portfolio 1937-1959
Alvis Gold Portfolio 1919-1967
AMX & Javelin Muscle Portfolio 1968-1974
Armstrong Siddeley Gold Portfolio 1945-1960
Aston Martin Gold Portfolio 1948-1971
Aston Martin Gold Portfolio 1972-1985
Aston Martin Gold Portfolio 1985-1995
Audi Quattro Gold Portfolio 1980-1991
Austin A30 & A35 1951-1962
Austin-Healey 100 & 100/6 Gold Port. 1952-1959
Austin-Healey 3000 Ultimate Portfolio 1959-1967
Austin-Healey Sprite Gold Portfolio 1958-1971
BMW 6 & 8 Cyl. Cars Limited Edition 1935-1960
BMW 1600 Collection No. 1 1966-1981
BMW 2002 Gold Portfolio 1968-1976
BMW 6 Cylinder Coupés & Saloons Gold P. 1969-1976
BMW 316, 318, 320 (4 cyl.) Gold Port. 1975-1990
BMW 320, 323, 325 (6 cyl.) Gold Port. 1977-1990
BMW 3 Series Gold Portfolio 1991-1997
BMW 5 Series Gold Portfolio 1981-1987
BMW 5 Series Gold Portfolio 1988-1995
BMW 6 Series Gold Portfolio 1976-1989
BMW 7 Series Performance Portfolio 1977-1986
BMW Alpina Performance Portfolio 1967-1987
BMW Alpina Performance Portfolio 1988-1998
BMW M Series Gold Portfolio 1976-1997
BMW Z3 & Z3M Limited Edition
Borgward Isabella Limited Edition
Bricklin Gold Portfolio 1974-1975
Bristol Cars Gold Portfolio 1946-1992
Buick Automobiles 1947-1960
Buick Muscle Cars 1965-1970
Cadillac Allanté 1986-1993
Cadillac Automobiles 1949-1959
Cadillac Automobiles 1960-1969
Checker Limited Edition
Chevrolet 1955-1957
Impala & SS Muscle Portfolio 1958-1972
Corvair Performance Portfolio 1959-1969
El Camino & SS Muscle Portfolio 1959-1987
Chevy II & Nova SS Muscle Portfolio 1962-1974
Chevelle & SS Muscle Portfolio 1964-1972
Caprice Limited Edition 1965-1976
Chevrolet Muscle Cars 1966-1971
Chevy Blazer 1969-1981
Camaro Muscle Portfolio 1967-1973
Chevrolet Camaro & Z-28 1973-1981
High Performance Camaros 1982-1988
Chevrolet Corvette Gold Portfolio 1953-1962
Chevrolet Corvette Sting Ray Gold Port. 1963-1967
Chevrolet Corvette Gold Portfolio 1968-1977
High Performance Corvettes 1983-1989
Chrysler 300 Gold Portfolio 1955-1970
Imperial Limited Edition 1955-1970
Valiant 1960-1962
Citroen Traction Avant Gold Portfolio 1934-1957
Citroen 2CV Gold Portfolio 1948-1989
Citroen DS & ID 1955-1975
Citroen DS & ID Gold Portfolio 1955-1975
Citroen SM 1970-1975
Cobras & Replicas 1962-1983
Shelby Cobra Gold Portfolio 1962-1969
Cobras & Cobra Replicas Gold Portfolio 1962-1989
Crosley & Crosley Specials Limited Edition
Cunningham Automobiles 1951-1955
Daimler SP250 Sports & V-8 250 Saloon
Ultimate Portfolio 1959-1969
Datsun Roadsters 1962-1971
Datsun 240Z & 260Z Gold Portfolio 1970-1978
Datsun 280Z & ZX 1975-1983
DeLorean Gold Portfolio 1977-1995
De Soto Limited Edition 1952-1960
Charger Muscle Portfolio 1966-1974
Dodge Viper Performance Portfolio 1990-1998
ERA Gold Portfolio 1934-1994
Excalibur Collection No.1 1952-1981
Facel Vega 1954-1964
Ferrari Limited Edition 1947-1957
Ferrari Limited Edition 1958-1963
Ferrari Dino 1965-1974
Ferrari Dino 308 & Mondial Gold Portfolio 1974-1985
Ferrari 328 348 Mondial Gold Portfolio 1986-1994
Fiat 500 Gold Portfolio 1936-1972
Fiat 600 & 850 Gold Portfolio 1955-1972
Fiat Pininfarina 124 & 2000 Spider 1968-1985
Fiat X1/9 Gold Portfolio 1973-1989
Fiat Abarth Performance Portfolio 1972-1987
Ford Consul, Zephyr, Zodiac Mk. I & II 1950-1962
Ford Zephyr, Zodiac, Executive Mk. III & IV 1962-1971
Ford Cortina 1600E & GT 1967-1970
High Performance Capris Gold Portfolio 1969-1987
Capri Muscle Portfolio 1974-1987
High Performance Fiestas 1979-1991
Ford Escort RS & Mexico Limited Edition 1970-1979
High Performance Escorts Mk. I 1968-1974
High Performance Escorts Mk. II 1975-1980
High Performance Escorts 1980-1985
High Performance Escorts 1985-1990
High Perf. Sierras & Merkurs Gold Port. 1983-1990
Ford Automobiles 1949-1959
Ford Fairlane Performance Portfolio 1955-1970
Ford Ranchero Muscle Portfolio 1957-1979
Edsel Limited Edition 1957-1960
Falcon Performance Portfolio 1960-1970
Ford Galaxie & LTD Limited Edition 1960-1973
Ford Thunderbird 1955-1957
Ford Thunderbird 1958-1963
Ford GT40 Gold Portfolio 1964-1987
Ford Torino Limited Edition 1968-1974
Ford Bronco 4x4 Performance Portfolio 1966-1977
Ford Bronco 1978-1988
Goggomobil Limited Edition
Holden 1948-1962
Honda S500 • S600 • S800 Limited Edition 1962-1970
Honda CRX 1983-1987
Hudson Limited Edition 1946-1957
International Scout Gold Portfolio 1961-1980
Isetta Gold Portfolio 1953-1964
ISO & Bizzarrini Gold Portfolio 1962-1974
Jaguar and SS Gold Portfolio 1931-1951
Jaguar C-Type & D-Type Gold Portfolio 1951-1960
Jaguar XK120, 140, 150 Gold Portfolio 1948-1960
Jaguar Mk. VII, VIII, IX, X, 420 Gold Port. 1950-1970
Jaguar Mk. 1 & Mk. 2 Gold Portfolio 1959-1969
Jaguar E-Type Gold Portfolio 1961-1971
Jaguar E-Type V-12 1971-1975
Jaguar S-Type & 420 Limited Edition
Jaguar XJ12, XJ5.3, V12 Gold Portfolio 1972-1990
Jaguar XJ6 Series I & II Gold Portfolio 1968-1979
Jaguar XJ6 Series III Perf. Portfolio 1979-1986
Jaguar XJ6 Gold Portfolio 1986-1994
Jaguar XJS Gold Portfolio 1975-1988
Jaguar XJS Gold Portfolio 1988-1995
Jaguar XK8 Limited Edition
Jeep CJ5 & CJ6 1960-1976
Jensen Interceptor Gold Portfolio 1966-1986
Jensen - Healey Limited Edition 1972-1976
Kaiser - Frazer Limited Edition 1946-1955
Lagonda Gold Portfolio 1919-1964
Lancia Aurelia & Flaminia Gold Portfolio 1950-1970
Lancia Fulvia Gold Portfolio 1963-1976
Lancia Beta Gold Portfolio 1972-1984
Lancia Delta Gold Portfolio 1979-1994
Lancia Stratos 1972-1985
Land Rover Series I 1948-1958
Land Rover Series II & IIa 1958-1971
Land Rover Series III 4x4 Perf. Portfolio 1971-1985
Land Rover 90 110 Defender Gold Portfolio 1983-1994
Land Rover Discovery 1989-1994
Land Rover Story Part One 1948-1971
Fifty Years of Selling Land Rover
Lincoln Gold Portfolio 1949-1960
Lincoln Continental 1961-1969
Lincoln Continental 1969-1976
Lotus Sports Racers Gold Portfolio 1953-1965
Lotus Seven Gold Portfolio 1957-1973
Lotus Caterham Seven Gold Portfolio 1974-1995
Lotus Elan Gold Portfolio 1962-1974
Lotus Elan & SE 1989-1992
Lotus Europa Gold Portfolio 1966-1975
Lotus Elite & Eclat 1974-1982
Marcos Coupés & Spyders Gold Portfolio 1960-1997
Matra Limited Edition 1965-1983
Mazda Miata MX-5 Performance Portfolio 1989-1997
Mazda RX-7 Gold Portfolio 1978-1991
McLaren F1 Sportscar Limited Edition
Mercedes 190 & 300 SL 1954-1963
Mercedes G-Wagen 1981-1994
Mercedes S & 600 1965-1972
Mercedes S Class 1972-1979
Mercedes 230 • 250 • 280SL Gold Portfolio 1963-1971
Mercedes SLs & SLCs Gold Portfolio 1971-1989
Mercedes SLs Performance Portfolio 1989-1994
Mercury Limited Edition 1947-1959
Mercury Comet & Cyclone Limited Edition 1960-1970
Mercury Muscle Cars 1966-1971
Cougar Limited Edition 1967-1973
Messerschmitt Gold Portfolio 1954-1964
MG Gold Portfolio 1929-1939
MG TA & TC Gold Portfolio 1936-1949
MG TD & TF Gold Portfolio 1949-1955
MGA & Twin Cam Gold Portfolio 1955-1962
MG Midget Gold Portfolio 1961-1979
MGB Roadsters 1962-1980
MGB MGC & V8 Gold Portfolio 1962-1980
MGB GT 1965-1980
MGC & MGB GT V8 Limited Edition
MG Y-Type & Magnette ZA/ZB Limited Edition
MGF Limited Edition
Mini Gold Portfolio 1959-1969
Mini Gold Portfolio 1969-1980
Mini Gold Portfolio 1981-1997
High Performance Minis Gold Portfolio 1960-1973
Mini Cooper Gold Portfolio 1961-1971
Mini Moke Gold Portfolio 1964-1994
Morgan Three-Wheeler Gold Portfolio 1910-1952
Morgan Plus 4 & Four 4 Gold Portfolio 1936-1967
Morris Minor Collection No. 1 1948-1980
Shelby Mustang Muscle Portfolio 1965-1970
High Performance Mustang IIs 1974-1978
Mustang 5.0L Muscle Portfolio 1982-1993
Nash & Nash-Healey Limited Edition 1949-1957
Nash-Austin Metropolitan Gold Portfolio 1954-1962
NSU Ro80 Limited Edition
Oldsmobile Automobiles 1955-1963
Oldsmobile Muscle Portfolio 1964-1971
Cutlass & 4-4-2 Muscle Portfolio 1964-1974
Oldsmobile Toronado 1966-1978
Opel GT Gold Portfolio 1968-1973
Opel Manta Limited Edition 1970-1975
Packard Gold Portfolio 1946-1958
Pantera Gold Portfolio 1970-1989
Panther Gold Portfolio 1972-1990
Barracuda Muscle Portfolio 1964-1974
Pontiac Limited Edition 1949-1960
Pontiac Tempest & GTO 1961-1965
GTO Muscle Portfolio 1964-1974
Firebird & Trans-Am Muscle Portfolio 1967-1972
Firebird & Trans-Am Muscle Portfolio 1973-1981
High Performance Firebirds 1982-1988
Pontiac Fiero 1984-1988
Porsche 356 Gold Portfolio 1953-1965
Porsche 912 Limited Edition
Porsche 911 1965-1969
Porsche 911 1970-1972
Porsche 911 1973-1977
Porsche 911 SC & Turbo Gold Portfolio 1978-1983
Porsche 911 Carrera & Turbo Gold Port. 1984-1989
Porsche 911 Gold Portfolio 1990-1997
Porsche 924 Gold Portfolio 1975-1988
Porsche 928 Performance Portfolio 1977-1994
Porsche 944 Gold Portfolio 1981-1991
Porsche 968 Limited Edition
Porsche Boxster Limited Edition
Railton & Brough Superior Gold Portfolio 1933-1950
Range Rover Gold Portfolio 1970-1985
Range Rover Gold Portfolio 1986-1995
Reliant Scimitar 1964-1986
Renault Alpine Gold Portfolio 1958-1994
Riley Gold Portfolio 1924-1939
R. R. Silver Cloud & Bentley 'S' Series Gold P. 1955-65
Rolls Royce Silver Shadow Ultimate Portfolio 1965-80
Rolls Royce & Bentley Gold Portfolio 1980-1989
Rolls Royce & Bentley Limited Edition 1990-1997
Rover P4 1949-1959
Rover 3 & 3.5 Litre Gold Portfolio 1958-1973
Rover 2000 & 2200 1963-1977
Rover 3500 & Vitesse 1976-1986
Saab Sonett Collection No.1 1966-1974
Saab Turbo 1976-1983
Studebaker Gold Portfolio 1947-1966
Studebaker Hawks & Larks 1956-1963
Avanti 1962-1990
Suzuki SJ Gold Portfolio 1971-1997
Vitara, Sidekick & Geo Tracker Perf. Port. 1988-1997
Sunbeam Tiger & Alpine Gold Portfolio 1959-1967
Toyota Land Cruiser Gold Portfolio 1956-1987
Toyota Land Cruiser 1988-1997
Toyota MR2 Gold Portfolio 1984-1997
Triumph TR2 & TR3 Gold Portfolio 1952-1961
Triumph TR4, TR5, TR250 1961-1968
Triumph TR6 Gold Portfolio 1969-1976
Triumph TR7 & TR8 Gold Portfolio 1975-1982
Triumph Herald 1959-1971
Triumph Vitesse 1962-1971
Triumph Spitfire Gold Portfolio 1962-1980
Triumph 2000, 2.5, 2500 1963-1977
Triumph GT6 Gold Portfolio 1966-1974
Triumph Stag Gold Portfolio 1970-1977
Triumph Dolomite Sprint Limited Edition
TVR Gold Portfolio 1959-1986
TVR Performance Portfolio 1986-1994
VW Beetle Gold Portfolio 1935-1967
VW Beetle Gold Portfolio 1968-1991
VW Beetle Collection No.1 1970-1982
VW Karmann Ghia 1955-1982
VW Bus, Camper, Van 1954-1967
VW Bus, Camper, Van 1968-1979
VW Bus, Camper, Van 1979-1989
VW Scirocco 1974-1981
VW Golf GTI 1976-1986
Volvo PV444 & PV544 1945-1965
Volvo Amazon-120 Ultimate Portfolio 1956-1970
Volvo 1800 Gold Portfolio 1960-1973
Volvo 140 & 160 Series Gold Portfolio 1966-1975
Forty Years of Selling Volvo
Westfield Limited Edition

BROOKLANDS *ROAD & TRACK* SERIES

Road & Track on Alfa Romeo 1964-1970
Road & Track on Alfa Romeo 1971-1976
Road & Track on Aston Martin 1962-1990
R & T on Auburn Cord and Duesenburg 1952-84
Road & Track on Audi & Auto Union 1952-1980
Road & Track on Audi & Auto Union 1980-1986
Road & Track on Austin Healey 1953-1970
Road & Track on BMW Cars 1966-1974
Road & Track on BMW Cars 1975-1978
Road & Track on BMW Cars 1979-1983
R & T on Cobra, Shelby & Ford GT40 1962-1992
Road & Track on Corvette 1953-1967
Road & Track on Corvette 1968-1982
Road & Track on Corvette 1982-1986
Road & Track on Corvette 1986-1990
Road & Track on Ferrari 1975-1981
Road & Track on Ferrari 1981-1984
Road & Track on Ferrari 1984-1988
Road & Track on Fiat Sports Cars 1968-1987
Road & Track on Jaguar 1950-1960
Road & Track on Jaguar 1961-1968
Road & Track on Jaguar 1968-1974
Road & Track on Jaguar 1974-1982
Road & Track on Jaguar 1983-1989
Road & Track on Lamborghini 1964-1985
Road & Track on Lotus 1972-1983
R & T on Mazda RX-7 & MX-5 Miata 1986-1991
Road & Track on Mercedes 1952-1962
Road & Track on Mercedes 1963-1970
Road & Track on Mercedes 1971-1979
Road & Track on Mercedes 1980-1987
Road & Track on MG Sports Cars 1949-1961
Road & Track on MG Sports Cars 1962-1980
R & T on Nissan 300-ZX & Turbo 1984-1989
Road & Track on Pontiac 1960-1983
Road & Track on Porsche 1951-1967
Road & Track on Porsche 1968-1971
Road & Track on Porsche 1972-1975
Road & Track on Porsche 1975-1978
Road & Track on Porsche 1979-1982
Road & Track on Porsche 1985-1988
R & T on Rolls Royce & Bentley 1950-1965
R & T on Rolls Royce & Bentley 1966-1984
Road & Track on Saab 1972-1992
R & T on Toyota Sports & GT Cars 1966-1984
R & T on Triumph Sports Cars 1953-1967
R & T on Triumph Sports Cars 1967-1974
R & T on Triumph Sports Cars 1974-1982
Road & Track on Volkswagen 1951-1968
Road & Track on Volkswagen 1968-1978
Road & Track on Volkswagen 1978-1985
Road & Track on Volvo 1957-1974
Road & Track on Volvo 1977-1994
Road & Track - Henry Manney at Large & Abroad
Road & Track - Peter Egan's "Side Glances"
Road & Track - Peter Egan "At Large"
Road & Track - Best of PS

BROOKLANDS *CAR AND DRIVER* SERIES

Car and Driver on BMW 1955-1977
Car and Driver on Corvette 1978-1982
Car and Driver on Corvette 1983-1988
C and D on Datsun Z 1600 & 2000 1966-1984
Car and Driver on Ferrari 1955-1962
Car and Driver on Ferrari 1963-1975
Car and Driver on Ferrari 1976-1983
Car and Driver on Mopar 1956-1967
Car and Driver on Mustang 1964-1972
Car and Driver on Pontiac 1961-1975
Car and Driver on Porsche 1955-1962
Car and Driver on Porsche 1963-1970
Car and Driver on Porsche 1970-1976
Car and Driver on Porsche 1977-1981
Car and Driver on Porsche 1982-1986
Car and Driver on Volvo 1955-1986

RACING

Le Mans - The Bentley & Alfa Years - 1923-1939
Le Mans - The Jaguar Years - 1949-1957
Le Mans - The Ferrari Years - 1958-1965
Le Mans - The Ford & Matra Years - 1966-1974
Le Mans - The Porsche Years - 1975-1982
Le Mans - The Porsche & Jaguar Years - 1983-91
Mille Miglia - The Alfa & Ferrari Years - 1927-1951
Mille Miglia - The Ferrari & Mercedes Years - 1952-57
Targa Florio - The Ferrari & Lancia Years - 1948-1954
Targa Florio - The Porsche & Ferrari Years - 1955-1964
Targa Florio - The Porsche Years - 1965-1973

A COMPREHENSIVE GUIDE

BMW 2002

BROOKLANDS *PRACTICAL CLASSICS* SERIES

PC on Austin A40 Restoration
PC on Land Rover Restoration
PC on Metalworking in Restoration
PC on Midget/Sprite Restoration
PC on MGB Restoration
PC on Sunbeam Rapier Restoration
PC on Triumph Herald/Vitesse

BROOKLANDS *HOT ROD* 'MUSCLECAR & HI-PO ENGINES' SERIES

Chevy 265 & 283
Chevy 302 & 327
Chevy 348 & 409
Chevy 350 & 400
Chevy 396 & 427
Chevy 454 thru 512
Chrysler Hemi
Chrysler 273, 318, 340 & 360
Chrysler 361, 383, 400, 413, 426 & 440
Ford 289, 302, Boss 302 & 351W
Ford 351C & Boss 351
Ford Big Block

BROOKLANDS RESTORATION SERIES

Auto Restoration Tips & Techniques
Basic Bodywork Tips & Techniques
BMW '02 Restoration Guide
Classic Camaro Restoration
Chevrolet High Performance Tips & Techniques
Chevy Engine Swapping Tips & Techniques
Chevy-GMC Pickup Repair
Chrysler Engine Swapping Tips & Techniques
Engine Swapping Tips & Techniques
Land Rover Restoration Tips & Techniques
MG 'T' Series Restoration Guide
MGA Restoration Guide
Mustang Restoration Tips & Techniques

MOTORCYCLING

BROOKLANDS ROAD TEST SERIES

AJS & Matchless Gold Portfolio 1945-1966
BMW Motorcycles Gold Portfolio 1950-1971
BMW Motorcycles Gold Portfolio 1971-1976
BSA Singles Gold Portfolio 1945-1963
BSA Singles Gold Portfolio 1964-1974
BSA Twins A7 & A10 Gold Portfolio 1946-1962
BSA Twins A50 & A65 Gold Portfolio 1962-1973
BSA & Triumph Triples Gold Portfolio 1968-1976
Ducati Gold Portfolio 1960-1973
Ducati Gold Portfolio 1974-1978
Ducati Gold Portfolio 1978-1982
Harley-Davidson Sportsters Perf. Port. 1965-1976
Harley-Davidson Super Glide Perf. Port. 1971-1981
Harley-Davidson FXR Series Perf. Port. 1982-1992
Honda CB750 Gold Portfolio 1969-1978
Honda CB500 & 550 Fours Perf. Port. 1971-1977
Honda Gold Wing Gold Portfolio 1975-1995
Honda CBX 1000 Gold Portfolio 1978-1982
Laverda Gold Portfolio 1967-1977
Moto Guzzi Gold Portfolio 1949-1973
Norton Commando Gold Portfolio 1968-1977
Suzuki GT750 Performance Portfolio 1971-1977
Triumph Bonneville Gold Portfolio 1959-1983
Vincent Gold Portfolio 1945-1980

BROOKLANDS *CYCLE WORLD* SERIES

Cycle World on BMW 1974-1980
Cycle World on BMW 1981-1986
Cycle World on Ducati 1982-1991
Cycle World on Harley-Davidson 1962-1968
Cycle World on Harley-Davidson 1978-1983
Cycle World on Harley-Davidson 1983-1987
Cycle World on Harley-Davidson 1987-1990
Cycle World on Harley-Davidson 1990-1992
Cycle World on Honda 1962-1967
Cycle World on Honda 1968-1971
Cycle World on Honda 1971-1974
Cycle World on Husqvarna 1966-1976
Cycle World on Husqvarna 1977-1984
Cycle World on Kawasaki 1966-1971
Cycle World on Kawasaki Off-Road Bikes 1972-1979
Cycle World on Kawasaki Street Bikes 1972-1976
Cycle World on Norton 1962-1971
Cycle World on Suzuki 1962-1970
Cycle World on Suzuki Off-Road Bikes 1971-1976
Cycle World on Suzuki Street Bikes 1971-1976
Cycle World on Triumph 1967-1972
Cycle World on Yamaha 1962-1969
Cycle World on Yamaha Off-Road Bikes 1970-1974
Cycle World on Yamaha Street Bikes 1970-1974

MILITARY

BROOKLANDS MILITARY VEHICLES SERIES

Allied Military Vehicles No. 2 1941-1946
Complete WW2 Military Jeep Manual
Dodge Military Vehicles No. 1 1940-1945
Hail To The Jeep
Military & Civilian Amphibians 1940-1990
Off Road Jeeps: Civilian & Military 1944-1971
US Military Vehicles 1941-1945
US Army Military Vehicles WW2-TM9-2800
VW Kubelwagen Military Portfolio 1940-1990
WW2 Jeep Military Portfolio 1941-1945

15019

CONTENTS

ACKNOWLEDGEMENTS

For more than 35 years, Brooklands Books have been publishing compilations of road tests and other articles from the English speaking world's leading motoring magazines. We have already published more than 600 titles, and in these we have made available to motoring enthusiasts some 20,000 stories which would otherwise have become hard to find. For the most part, our books focus on a single model, and as such they have become an invaluable source of information. As Bill Boddy of *Motor Sport* was kind enough to write when reviewing one of our Gold Portfolio volumes, the Brooklands catalogue "must now constitute the most complete historical source of reference available, at least of the more recent makes and models."

Even so, we are constantly being asked to publish new titles on cars which have a narrower appeal than those we have already covered in our main series. The economics of book production make it impossible to cover these subjects in our main series, but Limited Edition volumes like this one give us a way to tackle these less popular but no less worthy subjects. This additional range of books is matched by a Limited Edition - Extra series, which contains volumes with further material to supplement existing titles in our Road Test and Gold Portfolio ranges.

Both the Limited Edition and Limited Edition - Extra series maintain the same high standards of presentation and reproduction set by our established ranges. However, each volume is printed in smaller quantities - which is perhaps the best reason we can think of why you should buy this book now. We would also like to remind readers that we are always open to suggestions for new titles; perhaps your club or interest group would like us to consider a book on your particular subject?

Finally, we are more than pleased to acknowledge that Brooklands Books rely on the help and co-operation of those who publish the magazines where the articles in our books originally appeared. For this present volume, we gratefully acknowledge the continued support of the publishers of *Autocar, Autosport, Car, Cars & Car Conversions, Car South Africa, Custom Car, Modern Motor, Motor, Motor Sport* and *Wheels* for allowing us to include their valuable and informative copyright stories.

R.M. Clarke.

Two other books in our 'Road Test' series - *High Performance Escorts Mk.1 1968-1974* and *High Performance Escorts Mk.11 1975-1980* are currently available.
No articles from these books are duplicated in this Limited Edition.

The 1600 RS is a saloon with racing car characteristics.

Formula 2-based power in an Escort

The Ford Escort 1600 RS has the same chassis modifications—such as bigger wheels and radius arms to the rear axle—as the existing twin-cam Escort. Where it differs is in having the Cosworth BDA 16-valve engine, with belt-driven overhead camshafts. This is a competition engine in road tune, with a potential 200 bhp when modified for racing, but as supplied it has only about 10 bhp advantage over the eight-valve twin-cam, and is perhaps scarcely the equal of the older engine at low and medium revs.

Obviously the unit is immensely sturdy and is completely unstressed at normal road speeds. It is therefore difficult to understand why an ignition cut-out is fitted that operates at a mere 6500 rpm, or a bit less in the case of the one I was unlucky enough to pick. As a result the engine cut out at 116 mph and that was that, though I am sure that an honest 120 mph should be available. Similarly, a 0-60 mph acceleration figure of well under 9 sec should have been in the bag, but that

damned cut-out prevented my exceeding 57 or 58 mph in second gear. As cheap little push-rod engines run at 7000 rpm as a matter of course these days, and Italian ones run up to a smooth 8000 rpm, I do feel that Mr Ford is being a bit over-cautious with his beautiful 16-valve near-racer !

Apart from that, the engine is a sheer delight. It starts at once if you follow the instructions, is smooth for a fairly big four-cylinder, and cruises very easily indeed between 100 and 110 mph. It does not do so quietly, of course—indeed, it is fairly deafening at the sort of revs it enjoys—but the kind of people who will buy it would not have it otherwise.

There is less vibration of the body panels than in the first twin-cam Escorts, but I believe that some refinement took place in the 8-valve model after I tested it. Curiously enough, there is a high whine—for all the world like a Roots supercharger—but this apparently comes from the belt that drives

the camshafts, though I have never heard any sound from a cogged belt before. Once again, it's all part of the fun, and the acceleration is really fierce.

Though this is one of the most sporting cars ever offered to the public, the body is a normal saloon, with ample passenger and luggage space. The driving position is very comfortable and one has an excellent all-round view. The high-speed stability is much better than that of the original twin-cam Escort, and the roadholding gives immense confidence. The little machine can be fairly flung into corners, and there always seems to be just a little extra cornering power to get you out of trouble.

The steering gives plenty of feel and the back axle hops very little over bumps, causing only the slightest deviation. On slower corners it is possible to hang out the rear end very decisively under power, and the traction is impressive on loose surfaces. The roadholding is amply good enough to allow full use

A small badge on the side is the only distinguishing mark from the familiar twin-cam Escort.

to be made of the power of the 16-valve engine. The ride is frankly hard and choppy, as would be expected.

The servo-assisted brakes are extremely powerful and progressive and the car remains completely steady when they are applied. The combination of brakes, acceleration, and quick, responsive steering makes this car an incredibly rapid means of negotiating winding roads, and a most enjoyable one.

No doubt the main market for the 1600 RS will be in the competition world. Regarded as an everyday car, it has the enormous advantage that it retains the full interior accommodation of the saloon from which it was derived. Whether the enthusiastic song of the engine would eventually become wearisome depends on the temperament of the owner, who is also the only person to decide if the fun is worth the price. This car has the great superiority over most of its kind of having no decoration to make it conspicuous. Only those little "1600 RS" plates give the game away, and they are difficult to spot. Nevertheless, I was twice pursued by the cops on the first day I drove the car, so I paid extra attention to my driving mirror thereafter.

Even in the heaviest traffic the engine does not foul its sparking plugs. Its flexibility is more than reasonable for such a unit, though some transmission snatch would be experienced if the revs were allowed to fall too low. The exhaust note does not attract unwelcome attention, the noise from the valve gear and air intakes being also more noticeable to the occupants of the car than to passers-by. No doubt the engine could easily be further refined if it were decided that the demand warranted it.

The engine proved completely reliable and I would have had no hesitation in driving it even faster if the ignition cut-out had not prevented me. The rest of the car was less exemplary in its behaviour, for first the starter failed and then a major gearbox derangement brought the test to a premature close. This may well have been due to hard usage by previous drivers, and we know that the box normally stands up to racing stresses without complaint. No saloon could be more like a racing car to handle or more fun to drive.

SPECIFICATION AND PERFORMANCE DATA

Car tested: Ford Escort 1600 RS two-door saloon, price £1,447 including tax.
Engine: Four cylinders, 80.97 mm x 77.6 mm, 1601 cc. Twin belt-driven camshafts operating 16 valves. Compression ratio 10 to 1. 120 bhp (net) at 6,500 rpm. Two Weber twin-choke carburetters.
Transmission: Single dry-plate diaphragm-spring clutch. 4-speed all-synchromesh gearbox with central remote control, ratios 1.0, 1.40, 2.01 and 2.97 to 1. Open propeller shaft. Hypoid level rear axle, ratio 3.77 to 1.
Chassis: Combined steel body and chassis. Independent MacPherson front suspension with anti-roll bar. Rack and pinion steering. Rigid rear axle on semi-elliptic springs with radius arms and telescopic dampers. Disc front and drum rear brakes with vacuum servo. Bolt-on pressed steel wheels fitted 165-13 radial ply tyres.
Equipment: 12-volt lighting and starting with alternator, speedometer, rev counter, oil pressure, water temperature, and fuel gauges. Ammeter, heating, demisting and ventilation system. Windscreen wipers and washers. Flashing direction indicators. Radio (extra).
Dimensions: Wheelbase 7 ft 10½ ins; Track (front) 4 ft 3¾ ins (rear) 4 ft 4 ins. Overall length 13 ft 4 ins. Width 5 ft 2 ins. Weight 17 cwt.
Performance: Maximum speed 116 mph. Speeds in gears; third 82 mph, second 57 mph, first 38 mph. Standing quarter-mile 16.5 s, acceleration: 0-30 mph 3.8 s, 0-50 mph 7.1 s, 0-60 mph 9.6 s, 0-80 mph 16.7 s, 0-100 mph 25.7 s.
Fuel consumption : 20 to 25 mpg.

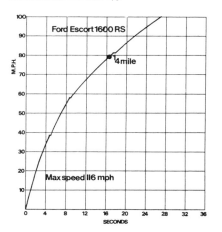

The excellent roadholding enables full use of the available power at all times.

The road-tuned Formula 2-based engine fits neatly under the bonnet (above); the comfortable seats and well laid-out dashboard provide an excellent driving position (below).

A fine road/rally compromise

Ever since they entered motor sport on a big scale back in the early 1960s, Ford have really made great strides in capitalising on their racing and rallying successes, which have been many, with respect to their road cars. Almost the very first Ford to have a major impact on the international motor sporting scene for Ford was the Lola-inspired GT40, which was a product of a Ford subsidiary, Ford Advanced Vehicles. It is a recently formed development of this Ford operation, Ford Advanced Vehicles Operations, that has produced the latest Ford, the new Mexico Escort. The Mexico is a typical example of Ford's bright attitude towards competition and motor sport " improving the breed," for the new car is a development of the Escort which carried off one of Ford's greatest victories, that of Hannu Mikkola/ Gunnar Palm in this year's *Daily Mirror* World Cup Rally.

For that event, many people in motor sporting circles were somewhat surprised to see that the backbone of Ford's attack was a fleet of works Escort TC bodies, but with specially built pushrod engines based closely on the production Kent-series 1600 cc cross-flow unit. The move was in the interests of realiability and Ford's confidence in the engine certainly proved justified with their subsequent win. Now, with the notion of passing on all information learned to the public, FAVO have produced the Mexico, the ultimate compromise for the club rallyman, and an ideal vehicle for the enthusiast for either day to day town travel or for quick road motoring.

Basis of the Mexico is the normal Escort Twin-Cam/RS1600-Type 49 Heavy Duty body. Into this the Kent-series 1600 cc engine is placed. This unit in its 1971-uprated form produces a healthy 98 bhp at 6000 rpm with 92 ft/lb torque at 4000 rpm, and so, combined with the relatively lightweight body, the car has a very lively and useful performance, and is absolutely without temperament. Basic price of the car is £881, and so with tax

the total is a reasonable £1150. The car will appear with British dealers immediately, and in left-hand-drive form next March.

Apart from the engine, the Escort is in most respects a fairly normal one, combining the usual GT-type trim and comprehensive instrumentation, which is quite adequate for most buyers, with the 1600 engine. A lot of performance and other equipment is available for the Mexico and so a very well-equipped machine can be built up for a none-too-exorbitant price by buying optional accessories from Ford Rallye Sport Performance dealers. Externally the car is recognised by the distinctive Mexico side-flashes—strictly optional!—and otherwise by the unobtrusive 1600 GT badges and 5½ in steel wheels.

To introduce the car to the press, FAVO brought along two versions of the Mexico to their Boreham test track in Essex, with a standard RS1600 and a Brian Hart-modified RS1600 to compare them with. The former Grand Prix-status track had just been resurfaced, and so, although no performance figures were able to be taken, AUTOSPORT put the new models through their paces to get some idea of their capabilities. The standard Mexico is an outstanding machine in many ways, notable for its lack of noise combined with superb flexibility and good performance. The car should prove not the slightest bit temperamental in traffic, and yet at the same time it reaches 60 mph in under 11 secs and will top over 100 mph with the standard 3:77.1 final drive. The gearbox, the same as used in the Corsair 2000E, also proved quite up to the task in hand, as did the brakes (9.625 in discs at the front and 9 in drums at the rear) which were light in application with the servo assistance.

FAVO intend to offer kits to uprate the Mexico to near RS1600 performance; in the extreme the Mexicos should have nearly 120 bhp and cost slightly less than the BDA-engined RS. The first of these tweaked Mexicos was present for the test day. The 1600 engine was fitted with a special Broad-

speed cylinder head, two twin-choke Webers and had undergone the usual polishing and balancing and was giving around 112 bhp. It was slightly noisier than the normal model, but appreciably quicker with the same degree of tractability and ease of driving. This car also had several performance options, notably a proper bucket driving seat, which made for a greatly improved driving position, and Minilite wheels.

In comparison the standard RS1600 was a great deal noisier than either Mexico, and considerably more demanding to drive as the revs were apt to drop away remarkably swiftly if one lifted off for a corner. The sensational Brian Hart RS1600, with some 135 bhp on tap, was remarkable in that its amazing speed and acceleration were achieved in much greater silence than in the standard RS1600.

To sum up, in the Mexico, the clubman has the ideal compromise for a family/town/motorway/competition car at a price which is within the range of many, and the car should sell well among this group.

JUSTIN HALER

SPECIFICATION AND PERFORMANCE DATA

Car Tried: Ford Escort Mexico saloon, price £1150 including PT.

Engine: Four cylinders, 80.98 mm x 77.62 mm (1600 cc). Overhead valves. Compression ratio 9:1; 98 bhp at 6000 rpm, 92 ft/lbs torque at 4000 rpm. Weber carburetter.

Transmission: Single plate hydraulic 7.5 ins diaphragm clutch; four-speed fully synchronised gearbox with short central remote control gearlever, ratios 2.972 (1st), 2.010 (2nd), 1.397 (3rd), 1.0 (4th).

Chassis: Steel integral construction. Independent front suspension by coil springs, Macpherson struts with integral dampers and anti-roll bar. Rear suspension by live axle with semi-elliptic leaf springs and radius arms and telescopic shock absorbers. Rack and pinion steering. Disc front brakes (9.625 ins), drum rear brakes (9 ins) with servo assistance. Pressed steel wheels with 13 ins 165 x 13 radial tubeless tyres.

Equipment: 12-volt lighting and starting. Speedometer/odometer, rev counter, fuel gauge, temperature gauge, oil pressure gauge and battery condition indicator. Heating, demisting and ventilating system. Windscreen wipers and washers. Flashing direction indicators.

Performance: 0-60 mph 10.5 secs. Top speed: 100 mph plus. (Manufacturer's figures).

AUTOTEST

Ford Escort 1600 RS (1,601 c.c.)

AT-A-GLANCE: Special version of Escort Twin-cam with detuned racing Cosworth engine. Startling performance, fair fuel consumption, harsh ride, good brakes and positive handling. Expensive, but a car with much potential.

MANUFACTURER Ford Motor Company Ltd., Warley, Essex.

PRICES
Not yet fixed.

PERFORMANCE SUMMARY

Mean maximum speed	113 mph
Standing start ¼-mile	16.7 sec
0–60 mph	8.9 sec
30-70 mph through gears	8.0 sec
Typical fuel consumption	22 mpg
Miles per tankful	200

Above: Circular headlamps are now used on the Twin Cam instead of rectangular ones. The BDA engine is slightly narrower than the Lotus twin-cam, which helps accessibility. Below: Interior trim is all black

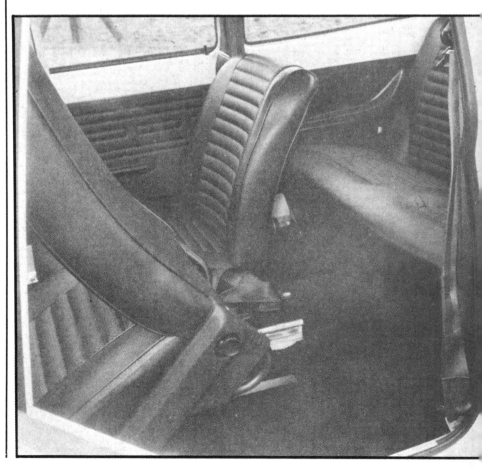

BEFORE even explaining what the 1600 RS, twin-cam BDA or 16-valve Escort (call it what you will) is mechanically, we would like to point out that it is much more a sports car than many a two-seater convertible. Any sort of a car with a top speed of 113 mph, a 0 to 60 mph acceleration time of under 9sec and a quarter-mile elapsed time of under 17sec is bound to be exciting. The 1600 RS is the kind of car we fight over in the office.

Essentially the 1600 RS is a very special addition to the Ford Escort range. It is identical with the other Escort Twin-Cam in all aspects except the engine. The RS (which stands for Rally Sport) is available through selected Ford dealers from the newly formed Advanced Vehicles Operation, and it is powered by a Cosworth BDA (belt drive assembly) unit with four valves per cylinder. It develops about 10 bhp more than the Twin-Cam with the Lotus engine, but can be further worked on to produce up to 200 bhp. At the moment the price for the complete car is not yet fixed, but it is expected to be around £1,400.

The obvious reason why Ford want to sell this car is so that the model can be homologated for international motor sport events. It is expensive as it stands for use on the road, but has a lot of potential and the kind of performance which gives ultimate satisfaction and leaves a lot of surprised drivers behind you.

Comparisons with the other Escort Twin-Cam do not seem to justify the extra price unless the buyer is someone who wants to compete seriously and is prepared to spend a good deal more money still. The extra power is entirely at the top end of the rev range, and we were hard put to match the bottom end performance of the Lotus Twin-Cam Escort we tested on 13 June 1968. This one revs higher though and we reached 6,700 rpm in each gear before the ignition cut-out began to operate. There is a red sector on the rev counter from 6,500 to 8,000 rpm and peak power is claimed to be at 6,500 rpm.

This extra bit at the top end was enough to cut the 0 to 60 mph time by a whole second and the 0 to 100 mph time by 1.3sec. Unfortunately a steady 10 mph breeze affected the top end acceleration noticeably on the MIRA horizontal timing straight and we feel the RS could reach 100 mph in under 30 sec on a still day.

Provided one obeys the handbook instructions to the letter there are no problems in starting the BDA engine from cold. One dab on the accelerator and then full choke brings the unit to life as soon as the key is turned. The choke should then be pushed back immediately, whereupon the engine runs smoothly and without hesitation. Full power is available as soon as one drives off, although it is best to wait until the oil has had a chance to warm through before indulging in high revs.

The belt which drives the two camshafts emits a high-pitched whine which is pleasant and apparently characteristic (we tried two other cars to make sure). It is not a loud noise and gets completely drowned out by the induction roar at full throttle.

First is quite a high gear, so it takes a few revs to move off smoothly. We could not break traction to cause wheelspin at MIRA, so were forced to ride the clutch all the way to about 25 mph from rest in order to keep the engine well up its torque curve (peak at 4,000 rpm). It then rocketed on to 40 mph in bottom, 60 mph in second and 86 mph in third. In top we could not pull more than 6,300 rpm, equal to 113 mph, which is the same as with the Lotus engine.

On the road the BDA is a fairly tractable unit for town driving. It likes to be kept revving and at 30 mph in top, for example, there is quite a bit of unpleasant snatch. One expects to have to use the gearbox a lot with this kind of a car and it is part of the fun of driving it.

This Ford gearbox is the close-ratio one used elsewhere in the range, although it is not the latest single-rail type. We found its operation perfect except that the lever was too far forward for most of our drivers. A simple change to the Cortina-type of lever, which is longer and cranked back, improved the gearchange tremendously. For serious competition there is an even closer set of ratios available, known as the "bullet" cluster on account of the acceleration they produce.

All the running gear and suspension of the Escort Twin Cam is the same as that of the Cortina Twin-Cam including 13in. wheels instead of normal Escort 12in. ones. The gearing with a 3.77 back axle is therefore high and the RS cruises happily at a motorway 70 mph with less than 4,000 rpm showing.

Where the Twin Cam differs from all other Escorts is in having radius rods to locate the rear axle and these effectively prevent tramp, except in reverse (driving test entrants take note). The ride is firm to the point of harshness, although there is a lot of front end dive during heavy braking. On fast corners there is virtually no roll and on rough roads the RS bucks much more than it pitches.

Above: There is a heavy-duty battery in the boot and the spare wheel is bolted to the floor with jack and wheelbrace held down by a rubber strap

Below: The deeply dished, small-diameter steering wheel has a soft plastic rim. Seat backs do not recline

ACCELERATION

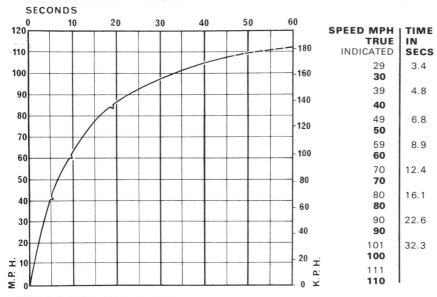

SECONDS

SPEED MPH TRUE INDICATED	TIME IN SECS
29	3.4
30	
39	4.8
40	
49	6.8
50	
59	8.9
60	
70	12.4
70	
80	16.1
80	
90	22.6
90	
101	32.3
100	
111	
110	

SPEED RANGE, GEAR RATIOS AND TIME IN SECONDS

mph	Top (3.77)	3rd (5.27)	2nd (7.59)	1st (11.22)
10–30	—	—	5.2	3.4
20–40	—	6.7	3.8	2.9
30–50	10.1	5.9	3.9	—
40–60	9.2	5.5	4.0	—
50–70	9.5	6.2	—	—
60–80	10.3	7.2	—	—
70–90	12.5	—	—	—
80–100	16.9	—	—	—

Standing ¼-mile
16.7 sec 81 mph
Standing kilometre
31.2 sec 99 mph
Test distance
1.315 miles
Mileage recorder
3 per cent
over-reading

PERFORMANCE

MAXIMUM SPEEDS

Gear	mph	kph	rpm
Top (mean)	113	182	6.300
(best)	113	182	6.300
3rd	85	137	6,700
2nd	60	97	6,800
1st	40	65	6,800

BRAKES

Retardation measurements made with Bowmonk decelerometer

(from 70 mph in neutral)
Pedal load for 0.5g stops in lb

1	26	6	30-34
2	26	7	34-38
3	26	8	34-38
4	26-28	9	36-40
5	28-30	10	38-42

RESPONSE (from 30 mph in neutral)

Load	g	Distance
20lb	0.31	97ft
40lb	0.68	44ft
60lb	0.95	32ft
80lb	1.06	28.5ft
Handbrake	0.34	89ft
Max. Gradient 1 in 3		

CLUTCH

Pedal 35lb and 5in.

MOTORWAY CRUISING

Indicated speed at 70 mph	70 mph
Engine (rpm at 70 mph)	3.960 rpm
(mean piston speed)	1.980 ft/min.
Fuel (mpg at 70 mph)	26.1 mpg
Passing (50-70 mph)	5.6 sec

COMPARISONS

MAXIMUM SPEED MPH

Lotus Elan + 2S	(£2,476)	118
Alfa Romeo 1750 GTV	(£2,431)	116
Ford Escort 1600 RS	(£)	**113**
Sunbeam Rapier H120	(£1,504)	105
Triumph Vitesse 2-litre	(£1,001)	101

0–60 MPH, SEC

Ford Escort 1600 RS	**8.9**
Lotus Elan + 2S	8.9
Sunbeam Rapier H120	11.1
Alfa Romeo 1750 GTV	11.2
Triumph Vitesse 2-litre	11.9

STANDING ¼-MILE, SEC

Lotus Elan +2S	16.6
Ford Escort 1600 RS	**16.7**
Sunbeam Rapier H120	17.7
Alfa Romeo 1750 GTV	18.0
Triumph Vitesse 2-litre	18.4

OVERALL MPG

Lotus Elan +2S	27.1
Alfa Romeo 1750 GTV	23.9
Triumph Vitesse 2-litre	23.5
Sunbeam Rapier H120	21.9
Ford Escort 1600 RS	**21.5**

GEARING (with 165-13in. tyres)

Top	17.7 mph per 1,000 rpm
3rd	12.6 mph per 1,000 rpm
2nd	8.8 mph per 1,000 rpm
1st	5.9 mph per 1,000 rpm

TEST CONDITIONS:
Weather: Fine and Sunny. Wind: 10 mph. Temperature: 10 deg. C. (50 deg. F.). Barometer 29.65 in. Hg. Humidity: 35 per cent. Surfaces: Dry concrete and asphalt.

WEIGHT:
Kerb weight 17.1 cwt (1,920lb—870kg) (with oil, water and half full fuel tank). Distribution, per cent F, 51; 49 R. Laden as tested: 21.1 cwt 2,364lb-1,070kg).

TURNING CIRCLES:
Between kerbs L, 30 ft 8 in.; R. 31 ft 3 in. Between Walls L. 32 ft 3 in.; R. 32 ft 10 in. steering wheel turns, lock to lock 3.5.

Figures taken at 4,100 miles by our own staff at the Motor Industry Research Association proving ground at Nuneaton.

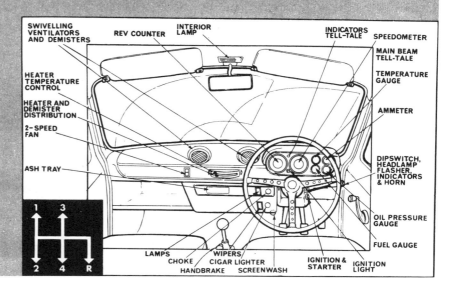

CONSUMPTION

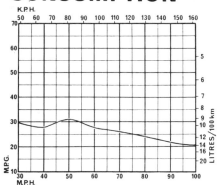

FUEL
(At constant speeds—mpg)

30 mph	. . . .	29.9
40 mph	. . . .	28.2
50 mph	. . . .	31.0
60 mph	. . . .	27.6
70 mph	. . . .	26.1
80 mph	. . . .	24.0
90 mph	. . . .	21.4
100 mph	. . . .	20.2

Typical mpg . . . . 22 (12.8 litres/100 km)
Calculated (DIN) mpg 23.7 (11.9 litres/100km)
Overall mpg . . . 21.5 (13.1 litres/100km)
Grade of fuel mixture . . . 3-star (min. 94 RM)

OIL
Miles per pint (SAE 20W/50) 300

SPECIFICATION
FRONT ENGINE, REAR-WHEEL DRIVE

ENGINE
Cylinders	. . 4, in line
Main bearings	. 5
Cooling system ·	Water, pump, fan and thermostat
Bore	. . . 80.97mm (3.19in.)
Stroke	. . . 77.6mm (3.06in.)
Displacement	. 1,601 cc (97.7 cu.in.)
Valve gear	. Twin overhead camshafts, belt driven, four valves per cylinder
Compression ratio	10 to 1. Min. octane rating: 94
Carburettors	. Two Weber 40 DCOE 48
Fuel pump	. AC Mechanical
Oil filter	. . Full-flow, renewable element
Max. power	. 120 bhp (DIN) at 6,500 rpm
Max. torque	. 112 lb.ft (DIN) at 4,000 rpm
Max. bmep	. 172 psi at 4,000 rpm

TRANSMISSION
Clutch	. . . Borg and Beck, diaphragm spring, 8.5 in. dia.
Gearbox	. . . 4-speed, all-synchromesh
Gear ratios	. Top 1.0
	Third 1.40
	Second 2.01
	First 2.97
	Reverse 3.32
Final drive	. . Hypoid 3.77 to 1

CHASSIS and BODY
Construction	. . Integral steel body and chassis

SUSPENSION
Front	. . . . . Independent, MacPherson struts, coil springs, anti-roll bar
Rear	. . . . . Live axle, half elliptic leaf springs, radius rods, telescopic dampers

STEERING
Type	. . . . . Rack and pinion
Wheel dia.	. . 14 in.

BRAKES
Make and type	. Girling disc front, drum rear
Servo	. . . . . Girling vacuum
Dimensions	. F 9.63 in.dia.
	R 9.0in. dia. 1.75in. wide shoes
Swept area	. F 190 sq.in., R 96 sq.in.
	Total 286 sq.in. (270 sq.in./ton laden)

WHEELS
Type	. . . . . Pressed steel, four studs 5.5 in. wide rim.
Tyres—make	. . Various, India on test car
—type	. . Autoband, radial ply, tubeless
—size	. . 165-13in.

EQUIPMENT
Battery	. . . . 12 volt 38 Ah
Alternator	. . . Lucas 17ACR 35 amp a.c.
Headlamps	. . . Lucas sealed beam 120/150 watt (total)
Reversing lamp	. Extra
Electric fuses	. . 6
Screen wipers	. 2-speed
Screen washer	. Standard, pedal operated
Interior heater	. Standard
Heated backlight	Not available
Safety belts	. . Extra
Interior trim	. Vinyl seats: Black pvc headlining
Floor covering	. Carpet
Jack	. . . . . Screw pillar
Jacking points	. One each side
Windscreen	. . Laminated
Underbody	. . None after painting

MAINTENANCE
Fuel tank	. . . 9 Imp. gallons (no reserve) (40.9 litres)
Cooling system	. 12.5 pints (including heater)
Engine sump	. . 8 pints (3.6 litres) SAE 20W/50. Change oil every 3,000 miles. Chage filter element every 3,000 miles.
Gearbox	. . . . 1.75 pints SAE 80EP. No change needed
Final drive	. . 2 pints SAE 90 Hypoid. No change needed
Grease	. . . . No points
Tyre pressures	. F 24; R 26 psi (normal driving) F 28; R 28 psi (fast driving and full load)
Max. payload	. 912 lb 415 kg)

PERFORMANCE DATA
Top gear mph per 1,000 rpm	. . . . 17.7
Mean piston speed at max. power	. . . . . 3,300 ft/min
Bhp (DIN) per ton laden	 113

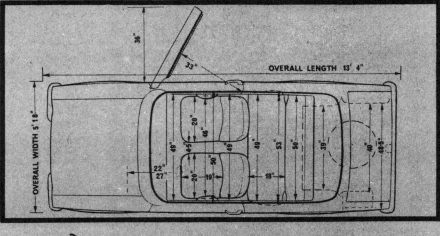

STANDARD GARAGE 16ft x 8ft 6in.

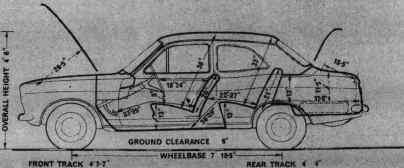

SCALE 0.3in. to 1ft.
Cushions uncompressed

AUTOTEST

FORD/1600 BDA . . .

With 3¼ turns between 31ft turning circles, the steering does not sound high geared, yet it reacts exceedingly quickly, making this an easy car in which to flick through a roundabout or dart through a line of traffic. With such a beefy shove of acceleration available in any gear the RS is tremendous fun through twisty lanes, when it really comes into its own.

The cornering characteristics are neutral all the way up to the point where the rear wheels lose adhesion. At MIRA we found it hard to do anything dramatic except take the bends extremely fast, dead on line. In the ultimate condition the tail can be held out and the steering played against the throttle, with absolute confidence. In the wet it is much easier to flick the tail out by excessive use of the throttle, but the driver feels everything is just as much under control as on a dry road, even though he must reduce speed.

The Twin Cam is one model which seems to have escaped Ford's much vaunted Noise, Vibration and Harshness department and this is particularly true of the RS. There are resonances and vibrations which come and go through the rev range, exciting various bits of the body and trim which "tizz" in sympathy. One feels them through the seat and steering wheel too, but they are mostly of a minor nature and somehow seem excusable in a car of this nature.

Brakes are discs at the front with a vacuum servo to relieve the effort needed with hard pads. On India Autoband tyres we exceeded 1g comfortably on our new Bowmonk decelerometer with only 80lb on the pedal and all four tyres marking the tarmac evenly. In the wet we noticed a tendency for the fronts to lock up early, but only under very heavy braking. During fade tests the effort rose slightly, but not enough to worry the driver nor even be noticed under normal hard use. The handbrake held securely on the 1-in-3 test hill and recorded 0.34g on its own from 30 mph.

Despite slightly heavier consumption at low speed, the RS returned exactly the same overall figure as the Lotus Twin Cam, 21.5 mpg. Where the BDA engine has the advantage is in requiring only 94-octane fuel instead of 100-octane super premium. We even tried a tankful of regular two-star (92-octane) without any signs of pinking or running on, which is a really remarkable achievement for a high-performance engine with a compression ratio of 10 to 1.

The rest of the car is fairly normal Escort GT and much of our previous criticism of the switches and supplementary gauge positions applies equally to the RS. The heater works well in typical Ford fashion and there are two-speed wipers. The floor button for screen washers is difficult to reach.

Twin Cams now have proper circular headlamps instead of rectangular ones and they are much better for the change. The battery is a heavy-duty one and located in the boot. It has no cover, so loose metal objects being carried must be lashed down away from the exposed terminals. The spare wheel lies flat on the boot floor, taking up a good proportion of the available luggage capacity.

It is hard to think of a sporty driver who would not be completely delighted with a 1600 RS, yet in the same breath it is equally hard to think of someone who would pay this much money for a road car looking like every other Escort. Yet the RS certainly appeals so much to us as the right kind of high-speed package that we have arranged to keep the test car for a long-term assessment over 10,000 miles. It is not really an easy car to drive smoothly around town, but away from speed limits it streaks along with a rare dash of vigour and all the right sounds to thrill the enthusiast. □

Below: The Cosworth BDA engine is compact with a sturdy and simple appearance. The cogged belt camshaft drive is protected under a cover

Below: Standard rim width is 5½in. and radial-ply tyres are fitted. Later cars will have 1600 RS badges

ESCORT MEXICO

Ford introduce a less expensive alternative to the Twin Cam and RS 1600

FROM the moment it appeared (in January 1968), it was abundantly clear that the Escort had considerable sporting potential. Competition drivers and wealthy enthusiasts were catered for amply by the Escort Twin Cam, but there was still room for an improved-performance version of the Escort GT for use in club events and on the road. An obvious way of achieving this was to use a larger power unit, and it wasn't long before many of the tuning specialists were offering 1600 GT versions. As can be imagined, these have a distinctly lively performance and have since become deservedly popular.

Many people, ourselves included, have wondered whether Ford would fill this obvious gap in their own Escort range. With their customary caution, they couldn't settle for the mere substitution of a larger engine and higher gearing in an otherwise standard car. A properly engineered vehicle would inevitably complicate an already difficult production situation. Not until the formation of Advanced Vehicle Operations did the production of such a car become feasible. Based at Aveley in Essex, AVO has the capacity to produce around 100 Mexicos a week. After sampling the car, we shall not be at all surprised if demand soon outstrips supply.

Together with the Escort RS 1600 (also an AVO product), the Mexico is to be retailed exclusively through Ford Rallye Sport dealers, of which there are 66 in the UK. The Lotus-powered Twin Cam, on the other hand, continues to be handled by all Ford dealers.

Specification

Far from being a pepped-up Escort GT, the Mexico is based on the Twin Cam and RS 1600 models. It utilizes the same heavy-duty body shell and, except for engine and clutch, the same running gear. Equipment is also much the same, differences being confined to headlamps (Lucas 75/50 watt, instead of Carello quartz-halogen), alternator (Lucas 15 ACR 28 watt, in place of 17 ACR 35 watt), oil cooler (deleted on Mexico), seats (Deluxe, not GT) and floor covering (rubber mats, instead of carpet). There are

Other than the "rally" flashes and Mexico emblems (both delete options), only the 1600 GT badges distinguish the Mexico from its twin-cam stablemates. The Cibié Oscar lamps are extra (£7 15s each), as are the Minilite wheels (see text)

ESCORT MEXICO...

three colours—white, maize (yellow) and sunset (red), all with black interiors. It comes complete with "rally" flashes and "Mexico" door emblems, but these are a delete option. Including delivery, it sells for £1,150 4s.

Performance

Having covered little more than 1,400 miles when put through its paces at MIRA, the Mexico was still too tight to give of its best. Weather conditions, too, were far from ideal. Adding to the difficulties was a grossly inaccurate tachometer. This over-read to the tune of 500 rpm at the top end, a fact only discovered on our return to base. Nevertheless, the results are impressive. MIRA's banked circuit was lapped in torrential rain at 99 mph with 103 mph coming up on the fastest straight. Cruising at around 85 mph is surprisingly fuss-free. Wind noise, too, is pleasantly low. In fact the Mexico feels substantially more refined than its twin-cam stablemates, being more akin to the Escort GT in this. There is rather more bump-thumping on rough roads and the engine is considerably harsher above 5,500 rpm. In all other respects, however, it compares very favourably.

Despite appallingly wet conditions, the Mexico returned a 0-60 mph time of 10.7 sec, placing it roughly mid-way between the Escort RS1600 and the Capri 1600 GT (the latter tested with 4 bhp DIN less than in current form). Traction proved surprisingly good and we doubt whether the step-off would be

Unlike twin-cam models, the Mexico has rubber mats. Excellent cloth-upholstered Contour seats are extra (see text)

SPECIFICATION FRONT ENGINE, REAR WHEEL DRIVE

ENGINE

Cylinders . . . 4, in line
Main bearings . 5
Cooling system . Water; pump fan and thermostat
Bore 80.97mm (3.19in.)
Stroke . . . 77.62mm (3.06in.)
Displacement. . 1,599 c.c. (97.6 cu.in.)
Valve gear . . Overhead; pushrods and rockers
Compression ratio 9-to-1. Min. octane rating: 97
Carburettor. . . One Weber 32 DFM compound twin-choke
Fuel pump . . . AC mechanical
Oil filter . . . . Full flow, renewable element
Max. power . . 86 bhp (DIN) at 5,500 rpm
Max. torque . . 92 lb.ft (DIN) at 4,000 rpm

TRANSMISSION

Clutch . . . . Borg and Beck, diaphragm spring, 7.5in. dia.
Gearbox. . . . 4-speed, all synchromesh
Gear ratios . . . Top 1.0
　　　　　　　　 Third 1.40
　　　　　　　　 Second 2.01
　　　　　　　　 First 2.97
　　　　　　　　 Reverse 3.32
Final drive . . . Hypoid, 3.78-to-1

CHASSIS and BODY

Construction . . Integral steel chassis and body

SUSPENSION

Front . . . . . Independent, MacPherson struts, coil springs, anti-roll bar
Rear . . . . . Live axle, half-elliptic springs, radius rods, telescopic dampers

STEERING

Type . . . . . Rack and pinion
Wheel dia. . . . 14in.

BRAKES

Make and type . Girling disc front, drum rear
Servo . . . . . Girling vacuum
Dimensions. . . F 9.63in. dia. R 9.0in. dia. 1.75in. wide shoes
Swept area. . . F 190 sq.in. R 96 sq.in. Total 286 sq.in. (279 sq.in./ton laden)

WHEELS

Type . . . . . Pressed steel, four-stud fixing, 5.5in. wide rim (6in. wide Minilite on test car)
Tyres—make . . Various; Goodyear on test car
　　　—type . . G800 radial ply tubeless
　　　—size . . 165-13in.

EQUIPMENT

Battery . . . . 12 Volt 38 AH (53 AH on test car)
Alternator . . . Lucas 15 ACR 28 amp a.c.
Headlamps. . . Lucas sealed beam, 150/100 watt (total)
Reversing lamp . Standard (2)
Electric fuses . . 6
Screen wipers . 2-speed, self-parking
Screen washer . Standard, pedal operated
Interior heater . Standard, air-blending
Heated backlight Not available
Safety belts . . Extra
Interior trim . . Vinyl seats, pvc headlining
Floor covering . Rubber mats
Jack . . . . . Screw pillar
Jacking points . One each side
Windscreen . . Laminated
Underbody
　protection . . None after painting

MAINTENANCE

Fuel tank . . . 9 Imp. gallons (40.9 litres) (no reserve)
Cooling system . 11.5 pints (including heater)
Engine sump . . 8 pints (3.6 litres) SAE 10W/30. Change oil every 6,000 miles. Change filter element every 6,000 miles.
Gearbox. . . . 1.75 pints SAE 80EP. No change needed
Final drive . . 2 pints SAE 90EP. No provision for changing
Grease . . . . No points
Tyre pressures . F 24; R 26 psi (normal driving) F 28; R 28 psi (fast driving and full load)
Max. payload . . 934 lb (424 kg)

PERFORMANCE DATA

Top gear mph per 1,000 rpm 17.6
Mean piston speed at max. power . . . 3,360 ft/min.
Bhp (DIN) per ton laden 84

much improved in dry conditions. Gear-changes were made at 6,500 rpm indicated, later found to represent a shade under 6,000 rpm actual. A look at the acceleration times in each gear suggests that it would have been advantageous to delay the changes slightly, but we feel that few owners are likely to do this. Capri models using the same engine, in fact, have tachometers red-lined at this speed.

Comparatively high gearing (17.6 mph per 1,000 rpm) means that it pays to use the gearbox. This is the close-ratio, three-rail unit employed in the twin-cam cars. Ratios are just right, and the change-quality amongst the best in the business. The absence of fuss can easily trick one into thinking that top-gear performance is a little lacking, but a look at the figures soon dispels such notions. It beats even the RS 1600 below 70 mph (top gear), and is substantially brisker than the Capri 1600 GT and the much lower-geared Escort GT.

Petrol consumption for the whole of the test period averaged 27.5 mpg. This included performance testing at MIRA (averaging 22.6 mpg) and a trip to Cornwall (returning an impressive 31.9 mpg). Oil consumption is negligible.

Bearing in mind that the suspension and steering are identical with those employed on the twin-cam models, it is no surprise to find that the Mexico has ample reserves in both departments. The ride is firm, but by no means harsh. Radius rods do a good job of locating the live rear axle, but there is sometimes a trace of bump-skidding on uneven corners. Although fairly quick, the steering is still reasonably light. It also feels more efficient mechanically than on some earlier Escorts. While this results in a little kickback on rough roads, there is never enough to cause concern.

The Mexico is primarily an understeering car. In most circumstances, there is ample power to achieve an ideal balance. Our test car was equipped with 6 in.-wide Minilite wheels (representing a total outlay of £108 18s, including the spare), shod with Goodyear G800 radials. This set-up results in excellent wet-road adhesion; unlike our long-term RS1600, the Mexico rarely spun its wheels during normal driving.

When surfaces are particularly greasy, the car's basic understeering qualities become much more apparent. In extreme cases, this can result in front-end breakaway. On the tighter bends, breaking traction at the rear soon has the car pointing the right way. Unless one can be sure of achieving this, however, a better solution is to lift off. This results in a definite decrease in understeer, the car tightening its line quite markedly. Overall, we found the handling very much to our liking.

The brakes are really superb. Pedal efforts are moderate and there is never a trace of fade during road use.

Amongst the extras on the test car were a pair of cloth-upholstered Contour seats, that on the passenger's side being of the fully reclining pattern. Although expensive (£18 10s for the driver's, £32 7s 6d for the passenger's), these are supremely comfortable. In fact, we would class them as among the best we have ever sampled.

Most people thought the driving position good, but one or two felt that a less-dished steering wheel would be an improvement. Although the lighting and wiper switches were in the old location, production models will have the much-improved 1971 layout.

The Mexico is one of the most logical cars to appear in recent months. For the price, it offers outstanding performance and roadworthiness, plus considerable scope for further development. It deserves to succeed, as it undoubtedly will. □

PERFORMANCE CHECK

Maximum speeds

Gear	mph		kph		rpm	
		Capri		Capri		Capri
	Mexico	1600 GT	Mexico	1600 GT	Mexico	1600 GT
Top (mean	99	96	159	155	5,620	5,400
(best)	103	98	166	158	5,850	5,500
3rd	82	77	132	124	6,500	6,000
2nd	57	53	92	85	6,500	6,000
1st	38	36	61	58	6,500	6,000

Standing ¼-mile,
  Mexico: 18.0 sec 77 mph
  Capri 1600 GT: 18.8 sec 72 mph
Standing **Mexico:** 34.0 sec 92 mph
kilometre **Capri 1600 GT:** 35.1 sec 85 mph

Acceleration, **Mexico:**	3.9	5.8	7.9	10.7	14.5	20.2	30.8	
Capri 1600 GT:	4.2	6.4	9.4	13.4	18.4	27.5	44.7	
Time in seconds	0							
True speed mph	30	40	50	60	70	80	90	100
Indicated speed MPH,								
Mexico:	30	40	50	60	70	82	94	105
Indicated speed MPH,								
Capri 1600 GT:	32	42	52	62	72	82	92	—

Speed range, Gear Ratios and Time in seconds

Mph	Top		3rd		2nd		1st	
		Capri		Capri		Capri		Capri
	Mexico	1600 GT	Mexico	1600 GT	Mexico	1600 GT	Mexico	1600 GT
10-30	—	12.0	6.9	8.0	4.5	5.2	3.1	3.3
20-40	9.5	11.0	5.9	7.0	4.0	4.6	—	—
30-50	8.6	10.0	5.6	6.8	4.3	5.2	—	—
40-60	8.7	10.6	6.2	6.3	—	—	—	—
50-70	9.4	11.9	7.4	9.5	—	—	—	—
60-80	11.3	14.7	—	—	—	—	—	—
70-90	16.5	25.8	—	—	—	—	—	—

Fuel Consumption

Overall mpg. **Mexico:** 27.5 mpg (10.3 litres/100km) **Capri 1600 GT:** 24.8 mpg (11.4 litres/100km)

NOTE: Since the Capri 1600 GT was tested (*Autocar*, 13 February 1969), power output has been increased from 82 bhp (DIN) to 86 bhp (DIN)

Above: *Under-bonnet layout is neat, and accessibility good.*
Right: *Battery lives in what is spare-wheel well of standard models; it has no protective cover. Spare considerably reduces luggage space*

Below: *Lighting and wiper rocker-switches are more conveniently located on production models (test car based on 1970 body-shell). Steering wheel is much better finished than on earlier twin-cams*

'DID YOU go to Mexico, then?' asked the M1 petrol pump squirter, looking at the World Cup Rally's destination plastered on the doors of the Escort we were driving.

Answer was negative for car and driver alike, but at least the said Escort had a lot to thank The Longest Rally for. Not content with cashing in solely on the immediate publicity which winning the Rally gave them, Ford had the great idea of a more permanent way of recording their magnificent achievement. Hence the Escort Mexico, Ford's new 'clubman's Rally car', which follows the same lines as the World Cup cars by using a push-rod 1600GT mill in an RS 1600 body.

What the Mexico is meant to be is a take-over bid for the ordinary clubman's market, dominated by the ageing Mini-Coopers for the last nine years. At £1150 a cheaper alternative for those who can't afford to buy or prepare a Twin-Cam or an RS 1600 (at £300 more). Even as a quick road car it's an attractive proposition at the price and without spending too much on it, performance can be brought almost to a par with the RS 1600, yet still keeping the cost well below.

True, this has all been done before by people such as Lumo with their Pirana, a 1300GT shell with a 1600 engine dropped in. But the pukka Ford version has the advantage of the Twin-Cam/RS 1600 shell and running gear, a stronger gearbox (2000E) and full Ford backing through the Ford Rallye Sport dealer network. No ordinary production line job either, for Ford AVO are doing the assembly and marketing from Aveley, and they're working on a whole range of tuning equipment to suit.

Having the heavy-duty RS 1600 shell, for your money you get the up-rated, stronger front struts giving marked negative camber, $5\frac{1}{2}$J x 13 in steel wheels shod with 165 radials with the arches flared to suit, twin upper radius arms at the back, and to make sure it stops effectively brakes are servo-assisted 9.6 in diameter discs front and 9 in drums rear.

Then you get an alternator thrown in, 75/50 watt round headlamps (not those hopeless square things, thankfully), twin reversing lights and full GT instrumentation, with speedo, rev counter, fuel, oil pressure and water temperature gauges and a battery condition indicator.

Ford have thoughtfully tweaked the 1600 cross-flow, bowl in piston, 9:1 CR, 5 main bearing engine for '71 so that it now turns out a handy 98 bhp gross at 6000 rpm, fair-enough power for the weight of an Escort. Max torque is 92 lb/ft at 4000.

Well, we got our hands on a 'standard' Mexico and gave it a real good

From win to showroom — we test Ford's new clubman's Escort

MEXICO

pasting to see whether it really lived up to that 'clubman's Rally car' tag. Standard it was supposed to be, but the one that turned up looked more like a genuine World Cup car, with $5\frac{1}{2}$J Minilite wheels, Tech-Del sumpguard, full set of Cibiés and those beautiful cloth-covered seats — bucket for the driver and reclining with head-rest for the navigator, wife, girlfriend or whatever you happen to be using the car for. Fortunately the modded looks were only skin-deep, engine, suspension, transmission being normal production, so at least we can give you driving impressions of the standard job.

And believe us, we've never found a car so chuckable, safe and sheer bloody fun since our days with modified dry-suspension Cooper Ss.

With suspension pinched from the 'quick' Escorts, but a lighter engine lump, balance was superb, so that nearly all conditions, just a shade of understeer stabilising the job. The harder you pushed it the more it seemed to glue itself down, and only at top-of-the-scale speeds did the back end start to drift out gradually. Unexpectedly tightening bends couldn't catch it out; just put on more lock and round it went. Or if the bend became a bit dramatic, tweaking the

16

wheel and booting the throttle brought the tail out sufficiently to point it in the right line.

We know a lot of supposedly good roadholding cars that turn out frightening on slimy, sodden roads, but not the Mexico. More fun than ever, in fact and without gentling the throttle foot. Adhesion remained tremendous and all that happened was that the tail came round a bit more to make wheel twiddling more enjoyable. We've never reckoned much to Goodyear G800s in the wet till experiencing them on this Escort. They were great.

If your style of driving's completely

Above: Pampered with luxury we were, with cosy works seats. But a bit spartan otherwise — no carpets even. Left: Ready for the forests, bedecked with Cibies. Right: Doesn't look special, but plenty of poke. Below: Boy-racer stripes are a no-cost option.

sideways on the loose or slippery tarmac, that was on too, though a matter of the brutals with the wheel and throttle to twitch it broadside — the tail wouldn't come right round of its own accord. Correction was simple.

Twisting, winding lanes with a bit of damp and farming muck found the Mexico in its element and few things if any would manage to keep up with it in those conditions. And all without giving us the frighteners.

Handling and roadholding terrific maybe, but we did feel the need for stiffer damping, particularly on rebound, And some not-so-rough tarmac even brought on axle patter. A fair amount of roll, too, so would obviously need stiffening for serious comp work.

Using brakes built to cope with a lot more power than the Mexico turns out we expected them to be good and weren't disappointed. Reasonably light but firm and sensitive. Only problem was a tendency for the fronts to lock under very heavy braking and on suspension rebound — this last being more a result of damping inadequacies, though. A lot of nose-dive, too.

Real beauty of this device was the rack and pinion steering. So precise and responsive that it almost reads your thoughts and looks after itself. And that deep-dished leather-rimmed wheel was just right.

Then there was the gearchange. Ford are the masters in this line and they've showed it once again with the Mexico. Sweet, precise and as fast as the hand can move.

We were a bit spoilt in impressions of this car by that fabulous bucket seat; superbly comfortable and form-hugging so that this as much as the general feel of the handling made us part of the car. Perhaps with the standard seat we wouldn't have felt so impressed. Why oh why can't AVO put

these seats in as standard for the price? We reckon they make 25 per cent difference to driving appeal. Available through Rallye Sport dealers at £18.50, Part No. CD1000/15A. That equally good reclining passenger seat with so many uses comes for £32.37½, under Part No. CD1000/16A.

With the seat and wheel comes an ideal driving position, though again, not so good with the standard seat. At first the wheel seemed too close, yet after a few rapid miles it was obvious that this arrangement suited the car's characteristics.

Hidden down under the bottom facia contour the light and wiper switches were damned near impossible to find by feel and at night we confused the switches more than once, which could have had embarrassing consequences. As for the heater switch consequences. As for the heater switch, it may have been convenient for the passenger, but certainly not the driver. With fixed belts instead of the inertia ones fitted, we'd have cursed even more.

Sound level was fairly low for a sporting car — in fact engine noise was disappointingly flat for a car with such pretensions. But at least it kept the law at bay.

Buy a Mexico Escort and you don't need a vibra-massage machine to keep you slim. Ours had one long vibration period from starting to stopping, but particularly pronounced at

45-50 mph in top.

Perhaps because of the flat engine note performance didn't feel as quick as it actually was. Even then it wasn't exactly the quickest road burner in the business, though with its handling there could be few things to beat it from A to B. If anything it felt a bit high-geared on the 3.77:1 final drive, though it would still whip up to 6500 (the red line) in the three usefully close lower gears. And we even managed 6000 in top, which at 17.8 mph per 1000 works out at over 107 mph. More normal top gear max was about 5800.

Normal max cruising gait was about 95 without straining things.

Being a largish cooking engine in a small body, tractability wasn't lacking and top gear could be pulled from below 20 mph. Lifting off below about 50 in top and then re-applying power occasionally found a flat spot. Probably something to do with choke progression in the Weber.

Axle wind up interfered with standing-starts and at the same time there was a noise as though the nearside rear tyre was catching on the wheel arch, noticeable on sharp right handers with the power on, too.

The Mexico may have its faults, but they're all of a minor nature and mostly common to the Twin-Cam. And nobody can say that that hasn't proved successful! It's real beauty is that it comes as a cheap package adequate for ordinary club work, can have its shell and running gear modded on the same basis as competition Twin-Cams for more serious work, but has an engine which isn't expensive to modify. Tweak a BDA fully and run it for a season and the bill will run into four figures, something the ordinary clubman can't afford. A cross-flow 1600 could be modded to the ultimate and kept running for a few hundred.

As a road car in its basic form we loved it and can't wait to get our hands on a modified version.

AVO intend to offer three stages of tune for the Mexico's engine, but as we write, details aren't finalised. **CR**

Performance:
0-30: 3.2 sec; 0-50: 7.9 sec; 0-60: 10.4 sec.
Maximum speed: 103 mph.

When the Escort Mexico first came out, it was quite literally in a class of its own. Since the demise of the Lotus Cortina or Cortina Lotus or whatever it was called, there's been just nothing else offering that sort of performance at that sort of price in that particular class of car, namely small four seater saloons. With the advent of Chrysler's Avenger, though, heads turned to the renowned Hillman tuners to produce a version with a little more in the way of power from what was recognised as an eminently tuneable basic lump.

Narrowly beating the factory GT version on to the street were Davenport Vernon with the Master Avenger. We tested it, and it seemed to be pretty good value for money, but then it wasn't a very expensive conversion and so the increase in performance was obviously nowhere near the ultimate available. Jan Odor of Janspeed reputedly has a very powerful version about his Salisbury works, but we haven't got around to seeing it yet. One we have just tested is the Hartwell Avenger.

Team Hartwell, as you probably know, have been the people to buy added power for Rootes motors from for a long time, and have recently won acclaim for their various performance options for Imp engines. (You wanna know more about that? Keep reading CC.) So we were very pleased to fix up a road test of their new car when invited to do so.

Barry Green is Hartwell's Man In Charge Of Extra Power, and before we took to the road in his idea of what an Avenger should be, we discovered from him exactly what had been done to it. Costliest items were the head and carburettor kit, at £40 and £45 respectively. The head is quite extensively modified, with the ports jig-bored to give straighter induction and exhaust, enlarged throats and polished and balanced combustion chambers. Compression ratio is upped to 10:1, and double valve springs are included in the price. Can't be bad. The carb kit is fairly drastic too. Twin Stromberg CD 150 carbs sit atop an alloy manifold, and are operated by a Hartwell control linkage that has a bit less slop in it than the standard one.

The exhaust system, featuring four branch extractor manifold, all pipes and a high efficiency box, works out at £28. Sports camshaft was a very reasonable £5.50, a set of 5½J steel wheels came to £27.50, and uprated front and rear springs to Hartwell's own specification hit the chequebook to the tune of £18. If you add that little lot up and then add the fitting charges, it comes to £208, which gives a new price for a converted Avenger 1500 GL of £1263, which — click click — works out at £113 more than a Mexico. There are, of course, other bits and pieces available from Team Hartwell, such as oil coolers, brake servos, rev counters, and oil pressure/water temperature kits, all of which could be Good Things To Have on a conversion like this.

Having had a closish look at what Hartwell give you for your money, let's have yet another look at the Mexico specs. For a kickoff, we all know about the strong, rugged and reliable 1600GT unit that churns out a tidy 98bhp. But really, there's quite a lot more to it than that. The bodyshell is the

strengthened one that first featured in the Twin Cam and RS 1600 versions, and the drive train is from the same source. Marvellous gearbox from the 2000E was, as all Escort boxes we've used, just about foolproof. Suspension is predictably uprated, main difference being strengthened front struts. For the £1150 asking price the Minilites are unfortunately not included; standard wheels are steel 5½ x 13. The brakes (disc front, drum rear), also confidence-promoting, are servo assisted, and really haul the car down to a dead stop in a very short space of time. All the Mexicos on the Press test fleet were equipped with Contour seats; very expensive and very, very good. Again, they're an optional extra, and if my memory serves me right they work out at about £50 a pair. Very necessary for intending rallyists. Rallyers? Rallymen? Lunatics? Also thrown in for the basic price are reversing lights, alternator, and a complete set of gauges.

So there we have the contenders. A 100cc difference in capacity, but a lot of work put in on the smaller engined model. Side bets were laid, timing devices loaded into boots, and we set off to the test track.

Well, to cut a long story short, the Escort was faster all round, which is the way things should have been. But the interesting thing is how close the Avenger was in every respect. Look at the times we obtained.

	AVENGER	MEXICO
0-30	3.4 secs	3.4 secs
0-40	5.6 secs	5.2 secs
0-50	8.0 secs	7.4 secs
0-60	10.6 secs	10.2 secs
SS ¼ mile	18.8 secs	18.0 secs

Both cars run out of everything at a little over the ton.

On the track, too, the Mexico's purpose designed suspension setup showed up slightly better. But again, only slightly. The Hartwell modded suspension on the Avenger consisted of shorter, stiffer coil springs, giving a rather lower ride height. Interesting point here in that on our test, the Mexico was shod with G800s, while the Avenger had SP68s. Now without driving both cars with both sets of wheels it's obviously impossible to state categorically that one tyre is basically better than the other. I've always preferred the G800 personally, but have since found that I'm almost alone in this, disagreeing with Barry Green of Team Hartwell who really rates the SP68 as the tyre to be on for this particular class of car.

On the handling course, the Mexico seemed to go round just that little bit flatter and faster and hang on just a tiny bit longer than the Avenger, and it felt to me as if the Avenger started to drift just a little bit earlier. The Avenger, naturally enough, was endowed with a fair bit more in the way of body lean despite its stiffer springs, but then again, it does give a considerably less solid ride. The Escort really feels as if it was designed for the track, whereas the Avenger's family origins betray it to a small degree.

But not all of us drive on test tracks all the time (profound statement of the month) and there's no doubt that for a long journey the Hillman would be the car to take. It's far quieter, a lot smoother, and pulls from a considerably lower speed in top, and as such it's ideal for touring and high speed commuting (although it lacks the high speed swervability of the Ford), but in truth it's very much at home in the High Street as well. For the family type who needs four doors, lets his wife use the car for shopping but likes a bit of fun when she's not with him (space for girlish giggles), and even has an occasional motorised holiday, there's little to beat Hartwell's Avenger. This is where it begins to seem that despite the similarity of the two cars in some respects, they really were designed to fulfil different roles in life.

In smoothness, it must immediately be

TWIN TUNE~TEST MEXICO VS HARTWELL AVENGER

MEXICO VS HARTWELL AVENGER

said that the Ford loses out. There's quite a lot of boom through the panels, and enough vibration from the engine to make journeys of over 100 mile duration something of a headache. In compensation for this, though, the driving position is perfect, and really tailored for relaxed driving, whereas the Avenger's seating arrangement obviously has to be something of a compromise. Tell you something though. Remember those switches for the screen wiper and lights? Way down by the driver's left shin? Good news, ergonomics fans, good good news. They're to be higher and more to the left on production Mexicos, and I could actually reach the ones on the test car while I was belted in. I'm really sorry to have gone on so long about the location of these switches in previous articles about the Mexico, but they were really impossible in their previous positions.

So. Given the choice, the out and out rally enthusiast would probably make for the Escort. Advantages are a slightly lower price than a Hartwell converted Avenger, with slightly more performance and a better possibility of obtaining extra tuning parts from local (AVO) dealers. Also better basic instrumentation. The Avenger scores in the sophistication department. As previously mentioned, it's a considerably smoother car than the Ford; much quieter and more relaxing to drive. It also has four doors, frequently a distinct asset. The performance is only marginally poorer than that of the Ford, and the handling leaves little to be desired. Though naturally enough Hartwell prefer to work on a new car, one of the important things about their conversion is that it can be fitted to cars of any age. The test car, in fact, had spent the first few years of its life as a self-drive hire hack, and apart from a few minor blemishes on the bodywork it didn't seem to be any the worse for its rude upbringing. So for £208 odd, those who bought early Avengers can now turn them into smooth GT eaters, and give the hot Escort types a very good run for their money.

We gather from another magazine that deals with things automotive (None of you lot read other magazines, do you? Good.) that the Janspeed Avenger can be persuaded to reach 60mph in 9.6 seconds. That's very, very quick. Is it to be the ultimate available for hot Avengers? I rather think Barry Green and Ray Payne down at Hartwell will someday have something to say about that. As for the Mexico, well, it's pretty damned good as it comes to you straight from AVO. But should you feel the need. . . . AVO are always there to sell you a little something extra. **AA**

GOODBYE BOMB

Second 10,000 miles in the Escort RS1600

By J. R. Daniels, BSc

Troubles started to show up in the second half of our Escort RS1600's time with us, but nothing managed to bring the car to a halt—or dim our admiration for its sporting behaviour

RATHER less than a year ago, I ended my report on the first 10,000 miles of the staff Escort RS1600 by emphasizing how reliable it had been. As is sometimes the way, the report had hardly been sent to press when something went wrong. Not only did it go wrong; it was, as it turned out, a harbinger of worse to come.

Suddenly, without any preliminary warning, the Escort went on to three cylinders as it was being toddled gently through inner London. A quick blast, that almost infallible remedy for an oiled plug, failed to have any effect. It was at this point that I learned how difficult it is to remove the sparking plugs from the BDA engine without the appropriate long-reach plug spanner. Eventually I managed by nesting two box spanners together and fishing for the loosened plugs, but my temper was not improved when it turned out that there was

GNO 425H

20

nothing obviously wrong with any of them.

By then it was too late in the evening to do anything else (the plugs are Autolite Racing AG15s, not easy to come by), so I determined to call in on the Ford press fleet garage at Brentford on my way to the Farnborough Air Show the following day, to see if they could find what was wrong.

I was within a couple of miles of Brentford when the car suddenly went back on to four cylinders. Being on three in the RS1600 is not unduly embarrassing, it just leaves you with a rough engine, terrible fuel consumption and about the same performance as an Escort GT in standard trim. Still, it was nice to feel that the punch of the remarkable little engine had suddenly returned. It stayed like that all day, but the moment it saw a 30 limit sign on the way back into London, the fourth cylinder went out again.

Next day, all four plugs were duly replaced. There was still nothing wrong with any of them as far as one could see, but the new set restored the performance of GNO 425H to its former glory, and the car continued to back up my opinion that, whatever its drawbacks for long journeys, it is one of the greatest commuting cars ever built. This was not just my opinion, but that of every member of staff, most of whom took a great delight in driving the car as it was meant to be driven.

The next spot of trouble cropped up at 12,000 miles. After the car had been in other hands for a week, I had to take it on a short journey to north London. When I tried to start it, it fired up dismally on two, and wouldn't (not surprisingly) idle. This was bad, for losing half the engine brought down the performance to Escort 1100 standards, if not worse; although it is worth noting that the car was still drivable.

Since I was late for an important appointment, I duly drove it, and was rewarded with action from the third cylinder after three or four miles. After a similar interval, the whole engine was restored to health.

Nobody has ever admitted to it, but I suspect that this episode was due to someone's over-enthusiastic use of the choke. Never in the whole life of GNO 425H did I use the choke at all, since a few hefty shoves on the accelerator invariably primed the Webers sufficiently for a first-time start. Given one clumsy cold start by somebody who didn't realize this, perhaps just to move the car around our crowded car park, and then perhaps another, similar attempt soon afterwards, and the engine might well be flooded beyond redemption.

Left: After cleaning, the oil- and travel-stained engine compartment still looks presentable, although most of the original blue paint has long since peeled off the cam covers, between which the sparking plugs are well and truly recessed. Above: No instrument troubles have been experienced in the 20,000 miles, which speaks well for the Escort GT panel. The minor instruments are not too easy to read, however. Below: Although the back seat is relatively stark and simple, plenty of people have travelled in it without too much complaint. Ride is worse in the back, but noise is worse for those in front

Below: Three successive roundings of the same corner produced these three pictures, illustrating just how far the tail can be swung out of line with safety. Although there is a feeling that the car will roll rather than spin, and it tends to look that way from outside, little untoward ever actually happens, even when (as in the first picture) the road changes surface and the inside front wheel lifts. Stronger nerves are needed by photographer (Peter Cramer in this instance) than driver

LONG TERM TEST
FORD ESCORT
RS 1600 . . .

Late service

Such is the pressure under which we work from Motor Show time until the end of the year that the Escort's scheduled 10,000 mile service was finally carried out at 12,500 miles. Because of the apparent difficulty of getting work done on the car through normal channels (the RS1600 is handled only by Fordsport dealers, who are still comparatively rare birds) and for the sake of speed, the job was done by Alf Belson's competent team at Brentford.

Apart from all the usual items, they replaced the camshaft drive belt as a precautionary measure, and also advised the replacement of three of the tyres. They also pointed out (to my shame) that the spare wheel, which I had never used, was flat because of a porous rim. The front brake pads, naturally, needed replacing, but otherwise it seemed that the car was still in rude mechanical health.

The only thing which suggested otherwise was the oil consumption. This had always been poor, but by now it was down to a pint every 120 miles or so, and distressingly often I found the oil a couple of pints down because some drivers failed to appreciate what even a fairly short run could do to the level. The car was still giving its characteristic puff of oil smoke when power was applied after a period on the overrun, but otherwise there was no sign of where the oil might be going to. I wasn't unduly worried at this stage. Indeed, in some ways I would rather have an engine which is using a lot of oil than one which is using none at all; I often wonder what is lubricating some of the oiltight marvels which are claimed never to lose a drop between changes.

One related problem did show up, however, and that was when an unwary driver failed to turn the oil filler cap fully home. For the second time in its life the car came home with the whole engine compartment dripping oil (I had fallen into the same trap myself very early on). When it happened again a couple of weeks later with yet another driver in charge, I began to think about sticking a Dymo-tape notice by the oil filler. . . .

By the time 15,000 miles was on the clock, GNO 425H would not tolerate anything but five-star petrol. In my first long-term report I described how the octane requirement had crept up from its original two-star rating, and how the scientists at the Esso Research Centre had warned me that in theory I needed five-star to avoid pinking at all times. At that point the problem area was very limited, and I could always avoid it by either opening or closing the throttles, whichever happened to be more convenient. Gradually, however, the problem spread and eventually a constant diet of five-star was the only answer.

Transmission troubles

In the original report, I expressed surprise that the transmission had stood up so well to the pounding it was taking, not only in the hands of commuting staff members but also in the course of several trips to the MIRA track.

Finally, trouble did start to manifest itself in the form of clutch slip. I had always thought that if anything went, it would be the clutch, so I was right at least as far as that went. There was only a suggestion of slip at first, when the engine was pulling hard in a high gear.

Gradually things got worse, but somehow the car had to limp along for three hundred miles until one day the driver of the moment announced that things had got a lot worse. Brentford then replaced the centre plate, and the car felt as good as new once more.

One more trip to MIRA was in store for the Escort, to see how the performance had been affected by the extra months of toil. The results astonished me. Except in top gear, where it seemed to have lost just a little of its top-end punch, the car was quicker than it had been in the original road test. The standing start figures were similarly improved. Confidence in the new clutch, complete familiarity with the car, and third-worn tyres made it possible to keep the wheels spinning all the way from rest, dropping in the clutch abruptly at 6,000 rpm. In this way nearly half a second was carved off the time to 60 mph. At the top end, though, the maximum speed had definitely suffered and she would pull "only" 111 mph.

Plugs again

Quite soon after this final figuring session, at 18,500 miles, Mike Scarlett reported that the Escort was back on three cylinders. Since he knew all about the required starting procedure and is not the sort of bloke who goes about flooding engines, it looked like a repetition of the previous trouble.

This time, however, the number four plug was sooty, black and horrible when it was taken out. We cleaned it carefully, regapped it and put it back, but it made no difference. It seems that once these rather special plugs have been run oiled-up for any distance, there is no prospect of reclaiming them. A new plug solved the problem once more.

Thereafter, my time with the car drew to its end, and at 19,500 miles it came as close as it ever did to letting me down completely. Starting up one morning to drive to work, I found that the ignition warning light stayed on. Sure enough, the fan belt had come off, and its

Comprehensive valeting by the staff (from left to right, Martin Lewis, Geoff Howard and Ray Hutton) succeeded in making the car look ten times better, but couldn't restore it to showroom condition. RS1600s come any colour you like as long as it's white, and this eventually gathers a permanent and uneven stain. The dribble mark from the petrol filler cap is virtually indelible. Left: the spare wheel and battery take up quite a lot of room in the unlined boot. Right: bringing the interior back to a decent standard. As one of the office's few smokers, Martin Lewis felt obliged to do something about the car's interior

remains were twisted round several under-bonnet components.

I elected to limp into the office, diving down a side street and parking each time the temperature gauge needle went into the red, and waiting a few minutes for the heat to subside. It only took me twice as long as normal to reach the office, and I gratefully handed the car over to our own garage to have a new belt fitted.

Later that day, they called me down to have a look. Apart from the fact that nobody in London seemed to have the listed belt in stock, they were slightly put out by the extent of the job. To get the new belt on, you first have to take off the camshaft drive belt cover (but not, mercifully, the belt itself). But to get off the cover, you have first to take off the fan; and while the fan *can* be taken off with the radiator *in situ*, it is really much easier in the long run to take the radiator out altogether!

For its final fling, the car went on to three cylinders once more. This time I went straight to the number four plug, and sure enough it was dreadfully sooted up. Despite the fact that I had been much quicker about it this time, I was still too late to save the plug, and it began to look very much as though there was ring trouble in that cylinder, leading to the throwing up of a lot of oil into the combustion chamber. By this time, however, the car had clocked up 19,970 miles, and two days' pottering brought it to the target figure.

Looking back

While I couldn't possibly claim that the second 10,000 miles made as good an impression as the first, it is worth emphasizing once more the car's background of unremittingly hard driving. It never left Britain, and perhaps one-third of all its mileage was done in the Greater London area. Only twice (with the clutch and with the fan belt) did it really let us down, and it never left anyone completely immobilized. Overall fuel consumption for the second period was worse than for the first, reaching 22.9 mpg. I see that most of the staff managed to get handsomely below 20 mpg at some time or other, but I never had the chance to achieve my great ambition of bettering 30 mpg, brim-to-brim, on the road.

What really endeared the car to us was its superb handling and the response of its engine, which put it almost in a class of its own for A-to-B traffic work. At the other extreme, I have awful memories of its rock-hard ride, high noise level and poor sidewind stability on long trips. I suspect that side of it will be forgotten soonest, however, and the overall impression of a car which was *fun* will remain. The Cortina 2000 which is coming to replace it will inevitably cosset my ageing frame in a way the Escort never did, but it will have to do well to gain the same feeling of affection. The Escort may look like a chunky little saloon, but under the skin it is a sports car *par excellence*. □

PERFORMANCE CHECK

Maximum speeds

Gear	mph		kph		rpm	
	R/T	Staff	R/T	Staff	R/T	Staff
Top (mean)	113	111	182	179	6,300	6,200
(best)	113	115	182	185	6,300	6,400
3rd	85	85	137	137	6,700	6,700
2nd	60	60	97	97	6,800	6,800
1st	40	40	65	65	6,800	6,800

Standing ¼-mile	R/T:	16.7 sec	81 mph
	Staff:	16.4 sec	84 mph
Standing	R/T:	31.2 sec	99 mph
kilometre	Staff:	30.6 sec	99 mph

Acceleration:								
R/T:	3.4	4.8	6.8	8.9	12.4	16.1	22.6	32.3
Staff:	3.1	4.6	6.2	8.5	11.6	15.1	21.2	31.2

Time in seconds								
True speed mph	30	40	50	60	70	80	90	100
Indicated speed mph R/T:	29	39	49	59	70	80	90	101
Indicated speed mph Staff:	30	40	50	60	71	82	93	104

Speed range, Gear Ratios and Time in seconds

Mph	Top		3rd		2nd		1st	
	R/T	Staff	R/T	Staff	R/T	Staff	R/T	Staff
10-30	—	—	—	7.0	5.2	4.5	3.4	2.8
20-40	—	10.2	6.7	6.0	3.8	3.5	2.9	2.6
30-50	10.1	9.7	5.9	5.6	3.9	3.7	—	—
40-60	9.2	9.9	5.5	5.5	4.0	3.9	—	—
50-70	9.5	10.3	6.2	6.0	—	—	—	—
60-80	10.3	11.2	7.2	7.1	—	—	—	—
70-90	12.5	13.2	—	—	—	—	—	—
80-100	16.9	17.4	—	—	—	—	—	—

Fuel Consumption

Overall mpg	R/T:	21.5 mpg (13.1 litres/100km)
	Staff:	22.9 mpg (14.0 litres/100km)

NOTE: "R/T" denotes performance figures for Escort RS1600 tested in *Autocar* of 30 April 1970

COST and LIFE of EXPENDABLE ITEMS

Item	Life in Miles	Cost per 10,000 Miles
One gallon of 5-star fuel, average cost today 35p	22.9	£153.00
One pint of top-up oil, average cost today 18p	180	£10.00
Front disc brake pads (set of 4)	14,000	£2.95
Rear brake linings (set of 4)	30,000	£1.75
Tyres (front pair)	14,000	£12.20
Tyres (rear pair)	18,000	£9.50
Service (main interval and actual costs incurred)	3,000	£20.00 (1)
Total		**£209.40**
Approx. standing charges per year		
Depreciation		£100.00 (2)
Insurance		£41.55 (3)
Tax		£25.00
Total		£375.95

Approx. cost per mile = 3.76p (for second 10,000 miles)

NOTES: (1) Estimated cost based on three services including oil changes
(2) Depreciation based on trade-in value £950 at 10,000 miles, £850 now. **Overall** cost per mile for entire 20,000-mile period is 5.65p/mile, since cost is affected greatly by depreciation figure
(3) Cost with 65 per cent no claims discount, car garaged in London, £25 compulsory excess and driving restricted to named drivers over 30

MEXICO MATTERS

The Fast Ford Escort
in
Ordinary Usage

THE REAL MEXICO!—The Ford Escort in which Mikkola and Palm won last year's World Cup Rally.

AS I WRITE, there is trouble at opposite ends of the motoring spectrum. Rolls-Royce have run out of money. Ford has run out of workers. One cannot believe that these famous makers will just fade away, and one hopes that both companies will soon be in full productive capacity again.

Meanwhile, I have been making use of an untuned Ford Mexico, fitting in some motoring in this lively Escort between other road-tests. Last year I got to know the Ford RS1600 pretty intimately and, having forgiven it for not being able to digest its timing belt, was sorry when the time came to return it to Ford's Press Department. Now, I am glad to say, it has been replaced by an Escort Mexico. This particular Mexico is in eye-catching maize-yellow paintwork, but there is not much embarrassment to this nowadays, when all manner of cars come in bright and cheerful hues and you see the Uncles and Aunts commuting unconcernedly in Minis and Dafs the colour of over-ripe oranges. The "Mexico" badges and speed stripes are not fitted, so this Escort has a touch of Q-car about it, being labelled an Escort GT. But shove the throttle open and its rally ancestry is soon apparent. It is shod with those grippy Goodyear G800s on Minilite wheels and has Contour competition-type front seats, the latter as grippy as the tyres and comfortable except that, sitting fairly close to the steering wheel, the driving throne slid along its runners like a rocket-launched sled when I had to crash-brake! It locks one notch further back than I really care about—I suppose I should grow longer legs.

I took the car over with 5,117 miles on its decimal odometer (no trip) and promptly set off on a long non-stop journey. Why not? Had not the excellent Alf Belson, who handed over this eye-catching Escort, said that it had been serviced and shouldn't require any attention for 10,000 miles?

Having read all the praise bestowed on the Escort Mexico by a colleague in the December, 1970 and January, 1971 issues of MOTOR SPORT, I felt that I was about to enjoy myself, although I had hoped "my" Mexico might have had those Cibie Oscar auxiliary lamps which are listed as an extra (however, pen-pushers cannot be choosers, and the Lucas headlamps light the way quite effectively).

The Ford Escort Mexico which you can buy, a road-going rally-proved saloon, for £1,150.

Initial impressions? Not having driven the RS1600 for some time, the heavy clutch and servo disc/drum brakes that don't do anything much until the pedal goes well down (O.K. thereafter) couldn't be ignored, until I had become accustomed to Mexico motoring, and I missed the background "cammy" noise from under the bonnet, which in the RS1600 had sometimes had pedestrians spinning round and mouthing "BDA" as one accelerated away from traffic tangles.

The push-rod power unit of the Mexico is far more civilised, a prompt cold-commencer like all Fords, but provides very adequate acceleration—and that could be regarded as the understatement of the month by owners of more staid machinery. Only when in a genuine hurry or truly in a mood to "play bears" is the difference in step-off between twin o.h.c. and 16 valves and knitting needles and eight valves noticeable, without recourse to a stopwatch. (Would Georges Roesch have faintly approved?) One thing which was immediately appreciated was Ford's repositioning of the Escort's previously exasperating switch-gear. The two under-facia switches operated by the left hand work heater-fan (two-speed) and wipers, the lamps-switch now being similarly placed but for right-thumb actuation. This still involves a fair stretch, but is far better than the original fumbly arrangement, which could plunge even drivers experienced in Escorts in sudden darkness when they jabbed for the wipers. The Mexico also had a useful foot-operated wash/wiper.

There is little need for me to enlarge on the characteristics of this Escort Mexico—the impressive road-holding, the instant-response to the accelerator, the manner in which this two-door family-size box clings on round acute bends, or what can be done by a flick of the light, so responsive rack-and-pinion steering and the right foot! On open roads or for traffic work the Mexico is fun, and very reassuring. Its dished, thick-rimmed leather-grip steering wheel tends to blank some of the small dials (fuel, oil, heat and battery), the lamps-dip stalk feels a bit brittle, and the ride can be lively, making the body rattle, the power roar intrudes as one opens it full out. But what FUN!

The gear change is extremely good; a real treat, in fact after a terrible week driving an XJ6 Jaguar with a clutch apparently specially contrived as a leg-muscle-developer and a quite horrid gearbox—all credit to Ford for endowing inexpensive cars with enjoyable gearboxes, especially as some luxury-car manufacturers cannot manage this and have to turn to automatic fool's transmissions to hide their incompetence . . . The rally-tough bodyshell which the Mexico shares with the RS1600 may not be strictly necessary for ordinary motoring but it is nice to have, even when your "yumps" are minimal compared to Mikkola's.

There is not much more to say, at this stage. The Mexico ran 282 miles on its first brimful tank of fuel (approximately 31 m.p.g.), compared to the 274 miles I got from a tanked-up RS1600. So far the little yellow horror has done 2,000 miles in my care, at roughly 1,700 m.p.p. of Castrol GTX and without trouble, apart from vibration severing the air-cleaner snout from the drum; so that it was promptly run over. The engine doesn't apear to miss it, however. More later, about this fascinating Ford.—W. B.

BDA+£263=150 bhp

THE ESCORT RS 1600 is so quick in its standard form that one could be forgiven for wondering why anybody should consider tuning one for road use. After all, at £1517 this is a very expensive Escort, with no more luxuries than the under £1000 versions, and to spend good money on tuning its BDA engine would seem to be pricing it out of sensible expenditure.

The lie to this argument was given to us when we sampled the 150 bhp Stage 1 tuned BDA offered by Ian Walker Racing at 236 Woodhouse Road, London N12 (01-368 6281/3), who have successfully proved that tuning the 16-valve, 120 bhp, Formula 2 derived engine can create a power unit hard to beat in flexibility and docility by any other four-cylinder engine. Yet unleashed it is capable of turning out acceleration figures which few cars other than monster V8s could achieve with the same lack of fussiness.

A 0-60 time of 7.4 sec, knocking almost a second off the standard figure, partly because of the test car's 4:1 instead of 3.77:1 diff, admittedly, would do credit to most quick exotica.

Such a Walker conversion means an engine removal and strip, which couldn't be expected to be cheap. With the unit in pieces attention is focussed first on the bottom end: Ian Walker considers that though the standard bottom end might well prove adequate for the extra power, it's better to be safe than sorry, so steel mains caps and competition shells are fitted, clutch, flywheel, crank, pistons and rods are dynamically balanced and the block is line bored.

The extra bhp comes from gas flowing the head, increasing the compression ratio to 10.5:1 and improving valve timing and lift with IWR RS 1 cams, the result of experiments with numerous profiles. Having seen the diabolically uneven, rough porting and throat areas on production BDA heads, we're sure that the headwork alone must have been worth a considerable amount of horsepower.

Finishing touches come from rejetting and rechoking the Webers and setting up the ignition to suit the mods.

Cost of all this work is £263 including labour and parts.

On turning the key for the first time we were instantly amazed at the lack of noise; the exhaust note remained a gentle burble, without harshness or bite even when taken up to max revs, only the whine of the cam drive intruding. Not at all what one would expect from such a high efficiency engine — 150 bhp is a lot of horsepower from 1600 ccs.

Instant throttle response, a superb ability to rev and a typically Escort-speed gearchange made for pleasurable through-the-gears work. The lower gears had only to be held momentarily going upwards because of the low diff and once in top the gearing urged it up to its maximum speed of 114 mph on any short straight.

Trickling through traffic in top gear with a light throttle found the engine equally as happy as when revving its head off in intended fashion. There was simply no sign of this being such a highly tuned machine in heavy town work. No fluffing, no refusal to tick over except on one occasion when we were stuck in a solid traffic jam moving at about one foot per minute, when one plug sooted up briefly.

Gilding the 16-valve lily seems stupid for road use — until you see the result. Clive clued up on Ian Walker's expensive but effective Escort.
PS: Didn't fancy the roll bar below, thank you very much).

PHOTOS: JASPER SPENCER SMITH

Starting from cold was simply a matter of a few pumps and away, with equal lack of temperament when hot.

Power per cc, this was the most docile engine we can remember.

Figures taken on a rolling road showed a staggering increase in power at the wheels in top gear throughout the range over figures for the standard car — 2 bhp up at 30 mph progressing to 26 bhp increase at 100 mph!

The removal of the standard engine's 6500 rpm cut-out meant that the 7500 rpm maximum could be used if required, though we found that it was unnecessary to go much above 7000.

Our only regret about the test car was that the handling hadn't been sorted to suit the power. In fact it was worse than normal, an extra front roll bar strapped to the existing one having cut down roll as intended, but with the penalty of making this the most understeering Escort we've sampled. It would

have been more enlightening to have tried the beautiful engine in an effective chassis installation.

Though in the application tried the Walker BDA proved an inspiring road engine, it impressed us as a unit crying out for Rally use, its flexibility and torque being so superior to a normal twin cam of similar output. It would surely provide adequate power for most Escorteers, yet because it isn't asking a lot from the engine with so much more potential to be had, it ought to be highly reliable.

Walkers will also do a Stage 2 RS conversion, adding IWR RS 2 cams and special forged pistons to the Stage 1 spec, at an all in price of £340.
Performance from the IWR RS 1600:
0-30 mph 2.9 sec; 0-40 4.1; 0-50 5.7, 0-60 7.4; 0-70 9.4; 0-80 12.3; 0-90 15.9; 0-100 22.8. Maximum speed 114 mph, limited by gearing. **CR**

RS 1600

YOU MAY NOT HAVE HEARD, BUT the Ford Motor Company are producing just about the best little sports car that not very much money will buy these days. And being basically a pure enthusiast's car it is not to be recommended to graduates of the all - refinement - and - no - work school of motoring. The fact that the £1517 Escort RS1600 happens to have four seats and a tin roof are really incidental to its character; after all, getting your hair blown does not necessarily make you a sports car driver.

And sports car driver you have to be if you spend your day-to-day motoring at the wheel of an RS, which must rank as just about the most uncompromising product ever to be offered to the public through your friendly Ford dealer. It is genuinely a beast—and all the better for it!

The way Ford's cheery brochure tells it, the RS1600 is designed for the family man who wants to put zing into his motoring and who has no special desire to own a 1300GT. In fact, Fords make another car ideally suited for such a person—it's called the Mexico which has the crossflow, pushrod 1600 under the bonnet and is not nearly as pure mechanically as the RS1600. Until recently the obvious alternative was to have the Escort Twin-Cam, but that has become an extinct species, its role having been taken largely by the Mexico.

There are two ways of looking at the RS1600, though. One is to regard it as a pure enthusiast machine for road use and the other is to race, rally or whatever hot blood demands. As it stands, the RS is not desperately satisfactory in either application; for competition work quite a lot of fiddling is needed to keep it in with the pack, whereas on the road the driver must make a pig of himself to keep the 120 horses alive and kicking with reasonable vigour. And that, surely, is symptomatically traditional in proper sports cars. Be warned, though. If you see yourself as a RS driver, beware of the intractability in stop-start traffic,

which can be a real bind a lot of the time, but if you are prepared to put up with that you are half-way home to having a mistress. Mind you, we may be over-emphasising the problem; the car we had was a difficult bit of work, whereas another we drove briefly later was much smoother around town, but lacked the first car's upper end wham.

A few days after we got the RS from Fords we had to send it back because it really was running badly. They did some work on it and got it to run considerably better in traffic, although it was by no means pleasant trying to keep the plugs from fuelling up at every dawdle, or trying to get a smooth, fast start in the high ratio first gear without slipping the clutch excessively. It was, in fact, best to stick to first gear in traffic and keep the engine up on the cams where it would breathe best. Also, the 37mph first proved to be a useable cog for streaking past slow moving lorries grinding up long hills (it's the old trouble of British commercial vehicles having such diabolical power/weight ratios that they cannot get out of their own way when they are laden), whereas third, with its maximum of 85mph, was the logical choice for most other kinds of storming. From 80 onwards, top really came into its own and would let the engine spin to around 6500rpm, which is a road speed of just on 116mph—more than most people would ever want to use in restriction-ridden England. The idea of keeping the overall gearing fairly low (3.77 to one) pays off in terms of sheer performance, even if the price is fairly high noise and vibration frequencies. At 70mph the RS cruises on a light throttle with not much noise of any kind, but beyond that one becomes well aware of the hardware beating away under the bonnet. As with 30mph, the RS is hard to keep at 70 because it is not breathing efficiently, so 85-90mph become more logical figures—but don't tell the magistrate we said so!

When the engine is kept up

TWIN CAMS, 16 VALVES AND TIED-DOWN SPRINGS DO A FORD SPORTS CAR MAKE Ian Fraser reports...

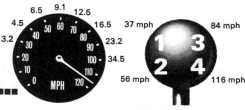

22 miles per gallon.

photography: V.L. Francis/Ian Fraser

where the horses are roaming, the RS1600 has a lot of overtaking performance which, combined with its compact dimensions, makes the car remarkably agile in the hands of the driver who is that way inclined, at the risk of offending just about everyone in sight. As we discovered, not many people like being over-taken by Escorts under any cir-cumstances, specially the likes of BMW2002s, Mercedes and the occasional XJ6 caught with its kickdown up. It is specially annoying for them because one Escort is the same as the next as far as most drivers are concerned. MGs, Triumph GT6s and TR6s are all comparatively easy meat if you disregard the fact that the TR6 has a higher top speed and cruises faster—and more noisily.

The RS engine itself is not specially highly tuned. The com-pression ratio of 10 to one demands five-star petrol and the cylinder dimensions are reason-ably close to square, with the bore at 80.98mm and stroke at 77.72mm for a displacement of 1601cc. Maximum net power of 120bhp occurs at 6500, which is also the tacho's red line and the point at which the ignition cut-out stops you going any faster. It is not a specially torquey engine, having 110lb/ft at 4500rpm and not much below it. Naturally, twin overhead camshafts are employed and they are driven by toothed rubber belts of the type also used by Fiat. The secret of the engine's deep breathing is in the fact that it has four valves per cylinder to let as much mixture as possible in from the twin Weber DCOE40 carburettors, and to dispose of the burnt gasses as rapidly as possible through the four-branch exhaust system. The wet sump has a radiator plumbed-in as standard to cool the contents of the 7.2pint sump, whereas the fuel tank capacity of nine gallons is quite inadequate for a car giving 19 to 24mpg. Crankiness in traffic is really the engine's only vice since it does not overheat, is reason-ably smooth, acceptably quiet considering the type of car it is intended to be, and very responsive on the throttle once it gets up towards the top of the torque curve. A change of camshafts could improve the low-speed performance at the cost of some upper-end punch. Even a set of hotter spark plugs would improve about-town running, but would need to be changed for the open road. The gearbox is a high, close-ratio affair with good synchromesh and a positive, light change lever whereas the clutch—heavier than in any other regular Ford—is smooth but positive in operation and quite slip free when abused. Final drive is direct to a 3.77 crown wheel and pinion in the middle of a live rear axle, located by trailing arms and suspended with semi-elliptics.

At the front, conventional Macpherson struts are employed in conjunction with coil springs and a stabiliser bar to cut down on body roll. Braking is via discs at the front and drums at the rear with power assistance that is not so sensitive as to make the stopping arrangements in any way scarey at high speeds; in fact, one has to lean quite heavily on the pedal at dead slow speeds to get the RS to stop completely. From higher up the scale the anchors are effective, but not brilliant in the manner of some of the all-disc systems. The total swept area manages 286sq in, which should be—and indeed is—virtually fade free; the handbrake is good enough not to have to worry about it while the 165-13 radials, carried on 5.5in rims, take a big grip on the road.

A big grip, that is, except on wet or damp surfaces. The cammy nature of the engine necessitates gentility with the accelerator if you want to avoid an abrupt reversal of direction, specially on round-abouts and slow corners; the RS is not quite as twitchy on long sweepers taken fast, but certainly deserves watching most of the time, particularly from inside!

Steering, by rack-and-pinion, has a strong caster action and is not specially light any of the time, but it is positive and precise enough for the car to respond instantly to any direction changes asked of it. Some of the time it changes direction without being asked, though; crosswinds make it move more than one would expect and it is very bump sensitive, even in a straight line, although not as willing to alter course when the throttle is sud-

denly closed as are the Escorts with less positively located back ends. The RS is a car in which the driver has to work hard to keep it pointing in *his* direction.

Like some of the costly GTs that inhabit this earth, the RS1600 needs to be handled almost brutally to bring out what's there. It is not a bit of good dithering around or being uncertain because the car knows it; it needs to be dumped into corners and pushed around with lots of revs and work at the helm. Then the results are rewarding enough to satisfy most drivers. There is a moderate amount of body roll, no tyre noise to speak

of, and mild initial understeer. This changes to rather definite, but controllable oversteer that can be used to advantage most of the time. Undulations and bumps can bring in the oversteer rather more rapidly than is desirable, but if you accept the RS as being that way inclined, there is nothing to worry about.

The car we had was equipped with rally seats which gave excellent lateral support but restricted the amount of rear seat leg room. People who really do take the blurb about the RS being a family car would be better to save their money and stick to the standard seats which, although

Our photographer slipped on a banana skin just as he took frontal shot (top left) of RS to show QI headlamps. Luggage boot (top right) is handicapped by intrusive Minilite spare and battery in far corner. Rally seats are RS option, well worth the expense if you don't carry people in the back (left). Instrument display is common to all upper-end Escorts (above)

not nearly as comfortable, are more in tune with the cabin dimensions. Detail equipment is quite good and includes QI 110/55watt headlamps and a six-dial instrument display, although some of the faces are obscured by the thick rim of the small diameter steering wheel. Luggage space is handicapped by the intrusive spare and battery.

The RS is a car that gives a great deal of performance for not a great deal of money and its potential for further development is seemingly boundless, finances withstanding the strain, of course. As an enthusiast's car . . . well, it's just like the good old days. ●

28

Given the works

Ford Escort

Although these shots are not in sequence, they give some idea of how happily this particular Escort will go sideways

1600S 1·8 litre

Driving Timo Makinen's 200 horsepower works RAC

Rally Embassy-sponsored Ford Escort 1600RS

In what our Rally Correspondent Peter Browning described as "a drive that made rallying history", Timo Makinen, with co-driver Henry Liddon, ran away with the early stages of last November's RAC Rally. With 12 years of international rallying and, among others, those magnificent Monte Carlo Mini exploits behind him, Makinen is still rated the world's fastest driver on difficult surfaces.

Even so, a great driver has got to have the right car and equipment under him. We drove Makinen's Embassy-sponsored 1.8-litre 1600RS Ford Escort at Ford's test track at Boreham in Essex, getting a small but delicious taste of one of the reasons behind the Finnish champion's achievement. The car, of course, is similar to the pair that Ford were preparing then for tomorrow's Monte Carlo rally.

ALTHOUGH it deigned not to snow, the weather at Boreham that day was fairly typical RAC Rally—what could reasonably be called 40mph fog. Although I have had the pleasure of driving a number of Ford rally cars lent to *Autocar* for our "Given the Works" series, this was my first visit to the famous Boreham. It made an interesting comparison with the old, latterly British Leyland, establishment at Abingdon, which is only 80 miles away as the redundant mechanic flies. No sign outside Abingdon ever said "BL Competitions Department" but it was never hard to find any notices saying "MG" once you'd got there. After Chelmsford you see signs to the village of Boreham, and the local people certainly know where to direct you thereafter. "Turn left at The Cock and it's about a mile after a turning to the gravel pits."

So off you go. Sure enough, a left turning down a narrow road is found, marked by stern warnings about the privacy of the Marconi

Angling Club's fishing on some secret mere unseen. The only other sign of the hand of man is some white rings painted on a telegraph pole, presumably by some cabbalistic telephone engineer. Not very confidently you venture up the lane. It is too insignificant to be the way to the lair of those sideways-rocketing Fords; if however they do breed them here, Heaven help you if some hairy vegetable or husky limb of a fish is hurrying back home to Scandinavia all crossed up in a 200 horsepower Escort. There isn't much room to dodge. Just as you've decided that this is simply the way into some attractive orchards after all, low buildings, a car park, a lot of wire fence and a low-rise goon box appear, likewise signs about high-speed testing and keeping out and, eventually, Ford. They obviously mean the keep-out bit, which is why the only signs painted by Ford are those mysterious white rings. The people inside are more than friendly however, like most in their line if you don't talk to them when they're up to

Ford Escort
1600S 1·8 litre

their ears in bother, and there's a far from anonymous and Puck-ishly big-eared Escort in Embassy Team colours waiting outside.

The car

Briefly it starts life as an eared Escort body shell from Ford Advanced Vehicle Operations at Aveley. Major body seams are gas-welded in addition to the normal spot-welds, and sundry areas strengthened. Crash roll-over bar protection is provided with the usual hoop braced backwards, behind the crew, plus, since Hannu Mikkola's Thousand Lakes accident—a several times end-over-ender which resulted in a frightening flattening of the front half of the cockpit and consequent damage to Mikkola from which happily he recovered—extra tubes on each side running forward over the doors. Suspension is standard in layout except for the use of twin-radius-arm location of the Taunus limited slip differential'd back axle, but the springs are heavy-duty and the dampers Bilstein, adjustable at the rear. The inevitable Minilite magnesium alloy wheels have 7in. rims as tested, though 6 and even, in bad conditions, 5in. rims are used sometimes.

One of the reasons for Makinen's star performance in the appalling weather of the RAC was some new Dunlop tyres, in which Makinen himself had no small part in developing. Unnamed at the time of writing, the new range included some "orthodox" low profile wide section radial ply sizes and a narrow 5.60-13in. cross-ply normally fitted to 5in. rims for snow. Studs are not permitted on the RAC, so in order to regain some of their grip in snow the tops of the unusually coarse tread blocks are recessed by a small amount on the snow tyre. All sizes feature the same heavy tread pattern, with the valleys in the tread much more open than usual in order to prevent clogging in heavy going.

Further chassis changes include the routing of all pipes (except the 2-1/8in. dia. exhaust) through rather than under the body (for protection from rocks), the fitting of a high-ratio steering box (giving 2.4 turns lock to lock instead of the standard car's 3.2), a twin servo braking system, a 21.9 gallon foam-filled bag tank, a rear oil tank for the engine's dry sump system, and two spare wheels. For a rally like the RAC which is held over a large number of rough roads, drum back brakes are used. Scandinavian gentlemen seen in British forests (and similarly disposed British gentlemen) in such cars and such events prefer to conduct their business crabwise for various reasons and in various ways rather than proceed straightforwardly. They say that the car can be cornered and braked better on bad surfaces, and the results of most rallies in recent years show that they are absolutely right. One of the ways of putting a car sideways is, as on Makinen's Escort, providing the car with excess rear-wheel braking by messing about with the servo ratios, so that the driver can initiate rear end breakaway with a jab at the brakes. Obviously immediate response is needed from the back brakes; drums provide that, whereas rear discs with hard pads do not, as they only respond well when hot. Drums also make the fitting of an effective handbrake easier. Drivers in some cases like to use handbrakes in the same way, so that a good one is desirable; most disc-brake handbrake arrangements are inadequate for continuous rally use—they either aren't strong enough, effective enough, or else wear out their friction materials too quickly—but on a Monte

recce car Ford were playing with an ingenious French-made Girling single piston rear disc which applies the handrake effort to the main (and only) pads. Discs all round, of course, are essential for high speed tarmac rallies or where a lot of hill work is encountered, as in Monte.

There isn't room here to deal fully with the engine changes. Cosworth are responsible for supplying a number of the parts. To gain the extra 199c.c. capacity, the bore is increased from 80.97 to 85.6mm. Different (BD3) camshafts are fitted, giving higher lift, the ports are enlarged, larger Webers (45DCOE instead of 40DCOE) are used fed by twin electric fuel pumps, ignition is provided by Lucas Opus transistorized equipment, and some attention is paid to improving little-end lubrication. The results include between 200 and 220 bhp at 7,750rpm instead of the standard 1,601c.c. BDA's 120bhp at 5,600, and between 130 and 140lb. ft. maximum torque at 5,500rpm (formerly 112 at 4,000), with a maximum allowed crankshaft speed of 8,500rpm.

This particular car was fitted with a five-speed ZF S5 18/3 gearbox and a 5.14-to-1 final drive, giving speeds on 175R-13 tyres in each gear at 8,500rpm of 49, 63, 87, 96, and 113mph. Not hopeful of being given quite detailed enough an answer, we asked if Ford could tell us the front and rear axle weights in the kerb condition. Ford's Ginger Devlin floored us with the weights on each wheel, running clockwise round the car from the left frontwheel—553, 551, 540 and 553lb.—

explaining the extra weight on the right hand rear by pointing to the oil tank which is mounted on that side of the boot. That adds up to 19.6cwt., and a front-rear weight distribution of 50.3/49.7 per cent, and that is 2½cwt heavier than the standard 1600RS. With this year's regulations outlawing Perspex windows and non-standard boot and bonnet lids, rally cars are getting heavier; this car was halfway—1972, having standard steel bonnet and boot, but plastic side and back windows.

Driving it

In the way customary with rally cars, you climb over and on to the driving seat rather than simply slide across, because of the raised sides. Buckling up the full harness takes practice, then you begin to study the controls. The most obvious difference from standard inside is the fitting of one instrument housing each side, instead of only in front of the driver, plus the neat Mada centre console with its handy document pocket. The chronometric 140mph speedometer and 10,000rpm rev counter dominate the driver's panel until he turns the ignition key, when the large half-closed eye-lidded oil pressure and charge warning lamps each side of the hand-calibrated fuel gauge come on. A combined oil pressure and water temperature gauge plus a 60-0-60 ammeter on the console are the only other gauges. The co-driver is faced by the tools of his trade, Heuer time-of-day and 12-hour stopwatches, and a single Halda Tripmaster mileometer.

Above: Power house; obvious differences from a standard 1600RS include the little toothed-belt drive for the chronometric rev counter, the bridge member stopping the MacPherson strut mounts banging their heads together, and twin servos

Left: Remarkably tidy office with non-standard dash and neat Mada centre console

Opposite, top: Boot looks roomy without two spare wheels; oil tank lives behind right wheel with twin fuel pumps. Note "cistern" for petrol gauge (necessary because of foam-filled tank). Centre: Back seat full of crash bar, VW monkey-on-a-stick jack, helmet rests, etc

Bottom: Mouthful of Lucas lumens

what look like occasional delays, one is never quite sure exactly what one is going to rev to until one has got used to the noise; I changed gear at 8,000. During the through-the-gears acceleration runs, the close ratios of the gearbox ensured that the engine never fell below its most effective speed range, especially in the higher gears. The result was short blasts of noise and fury as this incredibly lusty power unit shot up towards the forbidden but oh-so-easily entered regions of mechanical calamity beyond 8,500 in each gear. It was highly impressive, and for once required a little determination to keep one's foot down as we faithfully followed the lane lines, roaring past our abruptly looming photographer Ron Easton, Ford Competitions publicity officer Martyn Watkins and the forlornly hopeful beacon made by my staff Maxi with its headlamps on, then on into the—we hoped—lonely gloom. There was no need to worry with such performance however. In spite of tyres not suited for damp tarmac—we would undoubtedly have done better on softer compound covers—60mph came up in 7sec., 80 in 11.9, the ¼-mile in a remarkable 14.7sec. and 100 in 20.3, which is only a little over half the time a standard RS1600 takes, so that we were slowing down safely before the boards marking the end of the test straight.

It was interesting listening to the engine's voice during the acceleration runs in one gear. It would pull from about 1,500rpm, but not, as they say, so's you'd notice. Something starts to happen from about 2,000rpm onwards, a boom coming in at 2,600; it continues with moderate enthusiasm up to 3,500 where there is another boom period, and then the acceleration starts leaping from 5,000 onwards all the way to the top.

Removing the fifth wheel not a little thankfully, we went over to play on a delightful little area of middle-aged tarmac with loose gravel which has a sort of figure-of-eight shape. Here we learnt that there are indeed several ways of sliding this Escort and that it was most marvellously ready and willing to travel in that fashion without stopping or going about-face. One belted towards the corner, pointed the

front wheels as if to cross the apex by about half a car's width, then lifted off the accelerator; out swung the tail, which you then hung there by putting your foot back on the accelerator judiciously—too much so and the tail went too far, but just right and it stayed out tidily, the delightfully quick steering allowing one to catch the most horrific-seeming slides if they did go too far. If the bend went the other way on the other side, then you left the correction on, lifted off at the right moment, and round she went the other way. At first both Martin Lewis and I spent more time going slowly crabwise than a sensible person would have done going the same way without slip. But after some highly entertaining practice one became tidier, though very hot, and got round at a tolerable rate. Not that two amateurs playing silly boys on a safely open aerodrome is anything like the same as a certain Finn in the confines of a special stage walled by solid bits of scenery on and off for five days across the length and breadth of Britain, but it did serve to give us some idea.

The weather deterred us from taking up Ford's offer of some time outside Boreham on public roads, but from a brief thrash over the Boreham pavé it was clear that the ride, like that of the London-Mexico World Cup Rally winning Escort, was quite soft by rally car standards. Both brakes and clutch demanded high pedal effort which was as expected, and the steering kicked back in lively fashion over bumps. Fuel consumption could only be guessed at, around 12mpg on stages.

We both agreed that the car was probably the most easily controllable beast we had ever encountered, in spite of its high power-to-weight ratio. It was a matter of balance, and thanks to that wonderfully quick steering, handling of the very highest ease. Without a longer period of testing in various conditions, we couldn't properly evaluate pure roadholding, but despite the extraordinary ease with which one could provoke a slide, we would think that this was quite but not exceptionally good in ordinary hands. In Mr. Makinen's hands it was obviously out of the ordinary in many ways.
Michael Scarlett ☐

Turn the key, having prodded the throttle once or twice, and that noise familiar to RS1600 users begins—a quite individual sound, deep throated, husky and immediately very easily provoked by the slightest tweaks of your right foot. There is an unfamilar addition to it, a rattle which at first made me think that valve clearances were a lot wider on this engine than usual. Disengaging the clutch stopped it, showing that it came from the gearbox; if this was the first ZF gearbox you ever met, you'd find it hard to believe that this famous German company successfully supplies suitable transmissions for several very refined high performance cars, yet it is so, of course. The action of the change was very good, however, which is what matters here.

Martin Lewis and I attached our faithful fifth-wheel electric speedometer and proceeded to one of Boreham's runways which is marked out with ¼-miles and lane lines. The fog was still with us, but we were assured that no one would cross our path during the acceleration runs. It was nice to have the lanes marked, as it gave one something to keep the car lined up on in the absence of any distant point to aim at.

By now the engine was warmed up. Sitting on a starting line, revving at 5,000rpm, the clutch was released. The fat tyres spun and the car rocketed forward, slewing slightly then straightening as I tried to keep the wheelspin down; with a chronometric revcounter, an instrument which responds jerkily and with

PERFORMANCE CHECK

Maximum speeds

Gear	mph R/T	mph RAC	kph R/T	kph RAC	rpm R/T	rpm RAC
Top (mean)	113	113	182	182	6,300	8,500
(best)	113	113	182	182	6,300	8,500
4th	—	96	—	155	—	8,500
3rd	85	87	137	140	6,700	8,500
2nd	60	63	97	103	6,800	8,500
1st	40	49	65	64	6,800	8,500

Standing ¼-mile	R/T:	16.7 sec	81 mph
	RAC:	14.7 sec	89 mph

Acceleration								
R/T:	3.4	4.8	6.8	8.9	12.4	16.1	22.6	32.3
RAC:	2.9	3.9	5.5	7.0	9.0	11.9	14.9	20.3
Time in seconds	0							
True speed mph	30	40	50	60	70	80	90	100 110

Speed range, Gear Ratios and Time in seconds

Mph	Top R/T (3.77)	Top RAC (5.14)	4th R/T (—)	4th RAC (6.06)	3rd R/T (5.27)	3rd RAC (6.69)	2nd R/T (7.59)	2nd RAC (9.26)
10-30	—	—	—	—	—	—	5.2	4.8
20-40	—	—	—	7.2	6.7	5.1	3.8	2.9
30-50	10.1	7.1	—	5.4	5.9	3.9	3.9	2.5
40-60	9.2	5.7	—	4.4	4.5	3.8	4.0	3.3
50-70	9.5	5.5	—	4.3	6.2	3.0	—	—
60-80	10.3	5.0	—	4.4	7.2	—	—	—
70-90	12.5	5.2	—	5.1	—	—	—	—
80-100	16.9	7.0	—	—	—	—	—	—

NOTE: "R/T" denotes performance figures for Ford Escort 1600 RS tested in **AUTOCAR** of 30 April 1970.

By John Hartley

Marlow-Midlands Express . . .

18,000 miles in an Escort Mexico that has given lots of pleasure and some mixed experience with Ford Rallye Sport dealers

WHEN the Escort Mexico was introduced in December 1970, it filled an obvious gap existing in the Ford range for two years. In fact, several tuning firms had already shown what could be done by installing 1600 c.c. engines in Escort 1300 GTs. However, Ford's reasons for the delay were simple: the larger engine needed the 2000E gearbox and a heavy-duty axle, and these were not directly interchangeable with the standard units. In any case, the engine-gearbox assembly is such a tight fit that its installation would almost certainly have upset the production schedule in the main factory.

To overcome these difficulties, Ford decided to build the cars at their Advanced Vehicle Operations at Aveley, and to cash-in on their World Cup Rally success by calling the car the Escort Mexico. At the same time, the Mexico was intended to be the basic rally car, which it has now become.

Therefore, the Mexico shares the strengthened body, revised suspension, wheels, tyres and transmission of the RS 1600; in fact, the only significant difference is that the pushrod ohv 1600 c.c. engine is installed in place of the Ford 16-valve engines. Since the RS 1600, with its alloy engine, now costs an incredible £1,788, the Mexico is obviously a much better bet as a road car. At least, that was my reasoning, since brief experience had shown the RS 1600 engine to be rather temperamental.

I took my car over in September 1971, when it had covered 12,300 miles, mostly in the hands of the Press, so it is fair to assume that it had a pretty hard life. The car was equipped with special Contour seats, a Ford radio and Minilite 5½ in. wide wheels. The driver's seat has extra side panels giving superb lateral support, while the passenger's seat is a recliner. Both are very comfortable, and are covered in a nylon cloth, which has proved excellent in all respects. However, the seats are really too big for the car: the driver's seat is too long, and so reduces the rear leg room and will only tilt through a small angle. The passenger's seat is too wide and scrapes the side of the transmission tunnel. Since we are a three-person family this has never created any problems, and now Ford are offering slightly smaller seats.

I was relieved to find that the car did not have the Mexico boy-racer stripes, but is a plain maize — Ford's version of bright yellow-orange. I was not desperately keen on the colour at first, but it seems to improve rather than tire one with keeping.

First impressions

Inevitably, my first impression was of the excellent performance, particularly the acceleration. I was surprised to find that the noise level when cruising was low, a result of the 3.77:1 axle ratio. Equally, the clutch seemed very awkward: it required strong muscles to depress the pedal, was juddery, and seemed either in or out. At first, the effort involved seemed almost too much for my wife! Later, I did find an explanation for part of this problem, but not all of it.

Unlike most motoring writers, I maintain my car myself, and so I was quite pleased to note that attention was required at intervals of 6,000 miles, and that the owner's handbook was reasonably informative. Only Ford Rallye Sport dealers — there are 66 in the UK — handle the Mexico, so maintenance and spares availability are crucial, as I was to discover.

Since I am based outside London, the Mexico has been used for no commuting as such, and certainly well under 10 per cent of the 18,000 miles I have covered has been in city traffic. The bulk of the mileage has been absorbed in trips to the Midlands, the north of England and other outposts of the motor industry. Most of my normal routes do not involve the use of motorways, except north of Birmingham.

For this sort of use, the Mexico has lived up to first impressions. With the light body, there is plenty of acceleration for overtaking, yet the high gearing gives relaxed cruising, 4,000 rpm in top being about the legal limit. The noise level at this sort of speed is reasonably low, and is not tiring. When the engine is working hard, however, it is pretty noisy. Mexicos have a tendency to a body boom at 4,000-4,500 rpm, but mine is not too bad at all, though there is a resonance at about 2,000 rpm, seeming to come and go, which is a nuisance.

Although the car wanders quite badly in crosswinds, the high gearing makes it quite at home on motorways. However, it is at its worst on urban roads with poor surfaces. The ride of any Escort is harsh and choppy, and the Mexico is no exception. In fact, owing to the stiffened suspension, the ride is poor in most conditions, but if you are compelled to drive along an urban road at about 30 mph in top, and the surface is irregular and in need of repair, then you are seeing the Mexico at its worst.

Of course, this harshness becomes the firmness that complements the road holding at speed on twisty undulating roads. Here, the car is pure fun to drive. It has enough performance to make life interesting, and the neutral handling is excellent, with more than enough reserve cornering power for normal conditions. However, although the steering is precise, it is completely dead, giving virtually no feel. I think this stems from two reasons: too much friction in the steering rack, and Ford's notorious miserliness with castor which extends even to this car. Despite the small steering wheel, I have found the steering reasonably light.

Goodyear G800 tyres were fitted to the car, and these proved satisfactory. Their grip in the wet is adequate, but as soon as there is any sign of mud or grease, they almost seem to give up altogether.

Amazing economy

Undoubtedly, the excellent fuel consumption of the Mexico has been the most surprising feature of the car. Throughout, the consumption has averaged 32-34 mpg. At first I thought that the high insurance premium and £50 excess were cramping my style rather, but subsequent events — including more advantageous insurance terms — suggest other reasons.

Because the car is so light, it is almost always cruising on a small throttle opening, and the secondary choke on the carburettor only comes in for accelerating. Therefore, the engine requires little fuel for open road use — and that is the sort of use my Mexico gets nearly all the time.

Certainly, compared with other cars I have used, the Mexico has proved the quickest and most economical on several trips. This experience would seem to bear out the tests carried out by *Autocar* into economy — put a big engine in a small car and you get the best of both worlds.

Oil consumption has also proved to be low, being in the region of 2,000 mpp, while the radiator has been topped up perhaps twice in a year. Since the battery is mounted in the boot, it rarely needs topping up, which is just as well since it tends to be forgotten, being out of sight.

General convenience

An enormous number of factors affect the convenience of a car in daily use, and the Mexico has its share of irritants. For a start, on the bonus side, the basic controls are excellent, but although the gearshift is slick, the lever is 3-4 in. too far forwards. Then, the car is cursed with the facia of the Escort GT, so most of the minor controls are out of reach, and two of the instruments are obscured by the rim of the steering wheel. However, the speedometer and tachometer are fine, clear instruments directly in front of the driver. Another excellent feature is the foot-operated washer, which also operates the wipers as long as it is depressed.

Perhaps the most irritating feature of the car was the flimsy parcel shelf, which vibrated so much that maps and oddments kept being thrown on the floor. Eventually, I got so fed up with this that I reinforced the shelf with hardboard, and increased the depth of the rail at the front — but it is still pretty shaky.

Another potential inconvenience is the boot, with the spare wheel lying on the floor, and the battery behind one wheel arch. In fact, this has not bothered me too much, perhaps because I am used to packing things into small boots. Of course, Ford have now re-arranged the boot by moving the battery to the engine compartment, and mounting the spare wheel upright behind one wheel arch, but I am not sure that this

Above: The hard-working Mexico with Autocar Road Test fifth-wheel speedometer fitted having performance figures taken, with the author in the passenger seat observing our electronic timer. Unfortunately pressure of work denied any chance of re-taking figures in better weather; rain began falling during the test session

Right: Bits that bust: above the clutch itself, perhaps forgivably worn, the cracked clutch release lever and (on right from top) the spacer, release bearing and its cover — all at 22,050 miles. "Dry" prop-shaft cross and leaking damper showed up at 28,000 and 25,000 miles respectively

Below: Pitted Minilite

Opposite page: Got too big for its boot — the spare wheel takes up extra luggage space

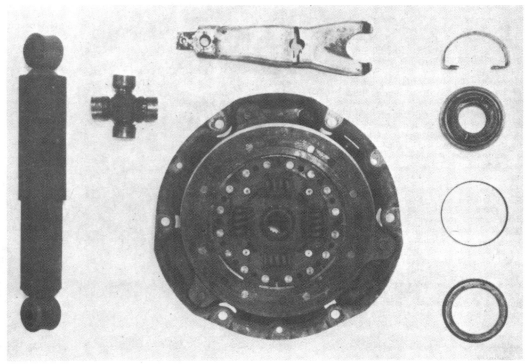

Marlow-Midlands Express . . .

is an advantage; the obvious answer is Total Mobility tyres with no spare!

Clutch failure

With two exceptions, my Mexico has been completely reliable, normally starting easily when cold, and generally doing as asked. However, at 22,050 miles, the clutch suddenly failed to disengage. It happened one Saturday morning in the summer; on my way to the golf club, it became apparent that the clutch was barely disengaging, and by the time I arrived home, it had given up altogether.

When I removed the gearbox, I found that everything aft of the clutch slave cylinder was unserviceable. The clutch release lever had caused the failure by cracking across the hole on which it pivots. The lever had bent, and eventually, the piston had come right out of the slave cylinder and jammed.

Inspection showed that the clutch driven plate was right down to the rivets, and that the pressure plate was scored in three areas. The dust shields on the release bearing were broken, as was one of the springs that secures the lever to the horse shoe spacer. The knife-edges of the spacer were worn badly, and one side of the curved portion was worn away — in other words the lot were useless, and replacement cost £16.

In view of the hard life of the car during the first 12,000 miles — when, incidentally, it evidently gave no trouble — the fact that the driven plate was worn out is reasonable enough. The scored face of the pressure plate leaves something to be desired, but this could have resulted from abuse. On the other hand, the failure of a simple component like a clutch release lever at any mileage, let alone only 22,000 miles, is quite inexcusable.

To reduce the wear on the spacer, the design of the clutch, release bearing, and spacer, have all been modified. However, for a satisfactory solution, I think the mechanism needs re-designing to eliminate the spacer.

At 25,000 miles, the tyres needed replacing, but by this time I had started scrubbing in tyres for the *Autocar* wet tyre test programme. They were scrubbed in at the rear, and this revealed that on the Ford RS wheels, some of the 185 section tyres fouled the wheel arches. These 70 Series tyres also emphasized the harshness of the Mexico suspension. When the tyre test programme was completed, I had two almost new Goodyear G800s — the spare and one new one — and am wearing in a pair of Avon 165-13 radials at the front, which so far seem to be pretty good.

At about this time, it became clear that one of the rear dampers was leaking enough to be ineffective, and so a pair of new rear dampers were fitted. This is a fairly simple job, although one of the lower mounting sleeves was rusted to the pin on the axle bracket.

A little later on, at about 28,000 miles, the Mexico reached its nadir, and for a short time became not worth living with. First, an unpleasant transmission vibration developed, and then one morning it refused to start. It was cold and damp, and the car was needed immediately, so I didn't try to tackle the problem till lunchtime; it still would not go, and it was not until I had fitted new plugs and

points, and charged the battery that I managed to overcome the dampness and get it going. It was obviously a freak set of circumstances.

The vibration stemmed from the front propeller shaft universal joint, which was replaced. The rear one seemed to be perfectly satisfactory. However, inspection of the worn front joint showed that one of the needle rollers was dry and had disintegrated, while one other was worn badly. The disintegrated bearing looked as if it could have been greased inadequately during assembly; if it had been greased correctly, then clearly universal joints do need greasing in service, perhaps at 12,000 or 18,000 miles. The absence of the grease nipple seems to be one more case of the British motor industry spoiling the product for a ha'porth o' tar.

Once the joint was renewed, the vibration disappeared of course, the engine was starting properly, and the car was a joy to drive again. Apart from a new pair of wiper blades, and a fuel filler cap, inadvertently pocketed by a filling station attendant somewhere in Hampshire, no other unscheduled replacements have been made.

Spares problems

With its straightforward design, the Mexico is ideal for the do-it-yourself mechanic. However, the spares situation is not always as simple. My first service was at 15,000 miles, and involved the replacement of three filter elements — for the air cleaner, oil filter and brake servo air intake. There are two Rallye Sport dealers near my home, Gowrings of Reading being about 12 miles away, and Norman Reeves of Slough about 10 miles away. On that occasion I went to Gowrings, who had only the oil filter element in stock. The others were ordered, and arrived within about a week; reasonable service, but the waiting and unnecessary journey were a nuisance.

When the clutch failed, it was more convenient to try Norman Reeves. The only parts in stock were the clutch release lever and

the bearing, and of the other items, only the driven plate was normally stocked. The parts were therefore ordered on the "Vehicle Off Road" (VOR) system, and thanks to the efficiency of Ford AVO, the clutch and driven plate were delivered to Norman Reeves within two days — much to the surprise of the storemen!

However, the story of the essential spring clips, parts that had to come from Daventry, was quite different. Fortunately, I found that the springs were used on the Classic and Corsair, and was lucky enough to find some at another dealer, which was just as well, as the storemen at Norman Reeves did not seem concerned that the absence of these tiny parts was keeping the car off the road.

In fact, I went back a week later to see if the springs had arrived, and the storeman rummaged about under the counter in a pile that included a Transit wing, a steering wheel, some pedals and various packages. He was unable to find the springs, which was hardly surprising.

This incident left me feeling that the system could be improved. After all, with only 66 dealers to choose from, Mexico and RS1600 owners are entitled to better than average service. Ford claim that on the VOR system parts are normally despatched within three days of being ordered, but the efficiency of the system depends on how promptly the dealer orders the parts. If my experience at Norman Reeves is typical — and, to be fair, subsequently, things seemed to run much more smoothly when I needed parts — then there are plenty of chances for things to go wrong.

One way of reducing the consequences of this problem is to find out what parts of the Mexico are used on other models, and then you can shop around at any Ford dealer. In fact, the engine is as the Capri (1969-72), and the gearbox from the Corsair 2000E. Since my Mexico has been reliable, the spares situation has been a niggle rather than a problem.

Excellent package

These criticisms apart, the Mexico is a fine car, and the faults are forgotten as soon as the open road is reached. It makes a very sensible alternative to a mass-produced sports car and is proving ideal for rallying.

Now that mine is two years old, the paint has chipped in several spots around the wheel arches, and there are a couple of bubbles. Generally, though, the finish inside and out is still good. The cloth covered front seats have proved outstanding in all conditions, and are wearing well. One of them shows no ill-effects from a dousing in turkey fat just over a year ago. After a wash in detergent, the seat looked as good as new. On the other hand, the finish of the Minilite wheels has deteriorated badly. They are pitted over a wide area, and even the chromium plated centre caps are rusty.

There is no doubt about it: the Mexico has been fun to drive, it has been reliable, and the running costs have been reasonable. Incidentally, the figures in the running costs table include the normal labour costs for the various jobs.

Despite the pleasure the Mexico has given me, I think some improvements could be made; for example, the cost and Ford AVO tag warrant a much better instrument layout with all the minor controls on the steering column, and the car could do with more feel in the steering. Personally, I would like to see less harsh suspension, a slightly bigger boot, and a bit more power — the car could certainly handle it. Nevertheless, the Mexico is a match for many sports cars, and to my mind is a much more practical road car than the RS1600. I'm keeping mine for a bit yet. □

COST of OWNERSHIP

Running Costs	Life in Miles	Cost per 10,000 miles
		£
One gallon of 4-star fuel average cost today 36½p.	32.4	112.50
One pint of top-up oil, average cost today 21p.	2,000	0.63
Front disc brake pads (set of 4)	36,000	0.97
Rear brake linings (set of 4 exchange)	30,000	1.08
Dunlop SP 68 tyres (set of 4)	25,000	15.55
Service (main interval and actual cost incurred)	6,000	35.70
Total		166.43
Running cost per mile:	1.7p.	
Approx. standing charges per year		
*Insurance		36.00
Tax		25.00

Depreciation
Price when new		1,150.00
Trade in cash value (approx.)		800.00
Typical advertised price (current)		900.00
Total cost per mile (based on cash value)	5.8p.	

*Insurance cost is for 35-year-old driver living in Buckinghamshire with 65 per cent no claims bonus

Top: Ford's delightfully compact 1600 pushrod engine fits easily into the under-bonnet space, making the work of routine servicing easy
Centre: Comfortable qnd well-locating driving seat (half seen here) with the reclining passenger seat lifted to allow someone into the back

Above: From the induction side, the air-cleaner makes accessibility appear less reasonable that it is
Opposite page: Less than ideally planned Escort GT dash looks neat at first but still has awkward switches

PERFORMANCE CHECK

Maximum speeds

Gear	mph R/T	mph JH	kph R/T	kph JH	rpm R/T	rpm JH
Top (mean)	99	102	159	164	5,600	5,800
(best)	103	103	166	166	5,850	5,850
3rd	82	82	132	132	6,500	6,500
2nd	57	57	92	92	6,500	6,500
1st	38	38	61	61	6,500	6,500

Standing ¼-mile	R/T:	18.0sec 77mph
	* JH:	18.9sec 75mph
Standing Kilometre	R/T:	34.0sec 92mph
	* JH:	35.0sec 92mph

Acceleration							
R/T:	3.9	5.8	7.9	10.7	14.5	20.2	30.8
* JH:	3.8	5.7	8.3	12.2	16.1	22.2	31.6

Time in seconds 0

True speed mph		30	40	50	60	70	80	90	100
Indicated speed mph	R/T:	30	40	50	60	70	82	94	105
Indicated speed mph	JH:	28¹	38	49	69	71	81	91½	102

Speed range, Gear Ratios and Time in seconds

mph	Top R/T	Top *JH	3rd R/T	3rd *JH	2nd R/T	2nd *JH	1st R/T	1st *JH
10-30	—	—	6.9	6.8	4.5	3.8	3.1	3.0
20-40	9.5	10.1	5.9	6.2	4.0	3.8	—	—
30-50	8.6	9.0	5.6	6.0	4.3	4.3	—	—
40-60	8.7	9.5	6.2	7.4	—	—	—	—
50-70	9.4	11.3	7.4	11.8	—	—	—	—
60-80	11.3	11.6	—	—	—	—	—	—
70-90	16.5	15.8	—	—	—	—	—	—

Fuel Consumption

Overall mpg	R/T:	27.5 mpg (10.3 litres/100km)
	JH:	32.0 mpg (8.8 litres/100km)

NOTE: "R/T" denotes performance figures for Ford Escort Mexico tested in *AUTOCAR* of 10 December, 1970.

* Performance figures for "JH" Mexico taken in undesirably wet conditions.

The cornering power is extremely high and the steering is just right, so that one can sense exactly what the machine is going to do.

There are many variations on the basic Ford Escort and still they come. At present, there is a demand for what might be called the family sports car, and that is exactly what this latest model is.

Ford already have the twin-cam RS 1600 and the Mexico, which are tremendous fun for playing at boy-racers round a circuit but rather lacking in refinement for road use. Few families would relish the high noise level and the booming of the body panels in the ordinary cruising ranges; the lack of flexibility and hard ride are a bore for duty-journeys and unacceptable for long-distance touring. In short, these cars are great fun and ideal for competitions but most of us have grown out of this sort of motoring, except in small doses.

The RS 2000 is not just an Escort shell with a Cortina overhead-camshaft engine dropped into it. Engine modifications include a really hefty aluminium sump, which greatly reduces the noise level. Most important is a new bell-housing, which puts up the natural boom period of the unit from 5400 rpm to over 6000 rpm, a speed which will be used much less frequently. The propeller shaft has been altered to give smoother running and the suspension has been re-calculated for the changed weight distribution and to give a more comfortable ride. An electric fan saves a lot of noise and a little power, too.

Though the engine is in standard tune, the performance is much greater than that of the Mexico and not far short of that given by the twin-cam machine. The gearbox is from the Cortina, fitted with a remote control with leverages proportioned to give short movements. The car is also higher-geared than the other two we have discussed, having a 3.54 to 1 hypoid, again with reasonably quiet high-speed cruising in mind.

The body furnishing is similar to that of other quick Escorts, with rather pleasant seats giving plenty of lateral location. As the new car is not yet on the British market, I tested a left-hand drive model but this differs little from the cars which will eventually be offered over here. The brilliant blue and white colour scheme is rather conspicuous and one might make better averages by attracting less attention. The whole production has been ordered by the German Ford agents until October and perhaps other colour schemes may be offered for less extrovert customers in Britain.

When I took over the RS 2000, I was immediately impressed by the smoothness and flexibility of the engine. This is a far nicer car

normal fast motoring. This makes for relaxed travel and if all hell does break loose above 6000 rpm, it scarcely matters for peak revs are at 5700, though 6500 rpm are allowed. With its high gearing, the car cannot get anywhere near the red in top, though its 112 mph maximum is highly satisfactory. It will easily exceed 90 mph in third, which is a useful overtaking gear. The gearchange is excellent and adds to the pleasure of driving the car. Though it is mechanically quiet, there is still a lot of wind noise at high speeds.

Certainly the best feature of this Escort is the way in which it dashes round corners. The cornering power is extremely high and the steering is just right, so that one can sense exactly, what the machine is going to do. In normal fast driving there is neither oversteer nor understeer and precious little roll. It is perhaps even better than the other hot Escorts in this respect and certainly the process of civilising it has not detracted from its circuit behaviour. The brakes stand up easily to hard driving and are well up to the performance of the car.

If the cornering is outstanding, the stability at speed is perhaps less impressive. There is

Ford's four-seater sports car: the RS 2000

to drive in heavy traffic than the other hot Escorts, which will appeal to most drivers as there is so much slow crawling nowadays. Perhaps the clutch pedal is a bit heavy in action, but all the controls are well arranged and the driving position is really good.

The engine has so much torque that there is no need to use very high revs during

sometimes a slight tendency to wander especially in side winds. Correction is easy and there is no need to lift the foot but it is best to pay full attention. The back axle tends to hop when racing starts are made and a limited-slip differential would be an advantage, but this will scarcely affect the normal road driver. In general, however, the road-

All the controls are well arranged and the driving position is really good.

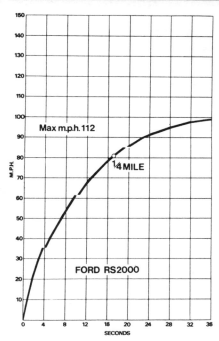

Max m.p.h. 112

¼ MILE

FORD RS2000

In normal fast driving there is neither oversteer nor understeer and precious little roll. Below, there are many modifications to the Cortina overhead camshaft engine.

The back axle tends to hop when racing starts are made and a limited-slip differential would be an advantage.

holding and handling are exceptional and no car could be easier to drive.

Though the efforts to make the car quieter and more flexible have been amply rewarded, the attempt to improve the ride has been less successful. The suspension is still very hard indeed and this may well put some purchasers off who like the car in other respects. The ride is perfectly satisfactory on motorways but on some country roads the occupants are well shaken up. Hard springing is tiring for the passengers on long journeys and it is to be hoped that work will continue on suspension development.

Obviously, the standard engine will receive the attention of the tuning specialists and exciting performance figures will no doubt be recorded. In normal touring trim, though, the car has enough speed and acceleration for most owners. It is not for its ultimate performance that the car is intended to appeal, and the excellent fuel economy will be just as important to many buyers.

The Ford Escort RS 2000 is a fast, economical car with an effortless high-speed performance. At the moment of writing the exact price is unknown, but this may well find its way on to the data panel before publication. If the suggested figure of around £1,500 proves true, you are going to get a lot of speed for your money. Perhaps the unsophisticated chassis design does not give a luxurious ride, but for getting round corners it's still pretty near the top.

SPECIFICATION AND PERFORMANCE DATA
Car tested : Ford RS 2000 2-door saloon.
Engine : Four-cylinders 90.82 mm x 76.95 mm (1993 cc). Compression ratio 9.2 to 1. 100 bhp (net) at 5700 rpm. Belt-driven overhead camshaft. Weber twin-choke downdraught carburetter.
Transmission : Single dry plate clutch, 4-speed all synchromesh gearbox with central remote control, ratios 1.0, 1.37, 1.97 and 3.65 to 1. Open propeller shaft. Hypoid rear axle, ratio 3.54 to 1.
Chassis : Combined steel body and chassis. Independent front suspension on MacPherson system with anti-roll bar. Rack and pinion steering. Live rear axle on semi-elliptic springs and radius arms. Telescopic dampers all round. Servo-assisted disc front and drum rear brakes. 165 SR 13 radial ply tyres on bolt-on disc wheels.
Equipment : 12-volt lighting and starting. Speedometer. Rev-counter. Voltmeter. Oil pressure, water temperature and fuel gauges. Heating, demisting and ventilation system. Heated rear window. Windscreen wipers and washers. Flashing direction indicators with hazard warning. Reversing lights.
Dimensions : Wheelbase 7 ft 10.5 in. Track (front) 4 ft 3 in, rear 4 ft 3.7 in. Overall length 13 ft 0.8 in, width 5 ft 1.8 in. Weight 2015 lbs.
Performance : Maximum speed 112 mph. Speeds in gears: Third 95 mph, second 62 mph, first 36 mph. Standing quarter-mile 17.1 s. Acceleration: 0-30 mph 3.6 s, 0-50 mph 7.4 s, 0-60 mph 9.2 s, 0-80 mph 17.0 s, 0-100 mph 37.2 s.
Fuel consumption : 28 to 32 mpg

AUTO TEST

FORD ESCORT RS 2000

No nonsense special

AT-A-GLANCE: New special Escort from Ford Advanced Vehicles with Cortina 2000 engine and much improved suspension. Super flexible performance, good economy and absolutely no tempérament. Better ride, less harshness, improved handling and brakes. Good value competition car with good road manners.

FORD ENGINEERS have been playing with Escorts ever since the model was introduced in 1968 and probably before. For serious competition, as opposed to just the brisk road driving offered by the Escort GT, there was first the Twin-Cam powered by the Ford-Lotus engine and then the very exciting 16-valve Cosworth-designed RS 1600. To save the cost of this complicated engine and cash-in on their successful World Cup rally to South America, Ford followed the RS with the Mexico powered by a push-rod "Kent" 1600 GT unit.

Both the Mexico and RS 1600 were the work of Ford's Advanced Vehicles Operation at Aveley and differed considerably from Escorts off the main production line at Hailwood. What has become known as the Type 49 heavy-duty bodyshell was developed from experience gained in rallies, side rails being strengthened, front strut housings reinforced and the wheel-arches flared to take larger wheels and tyres. Stronger Cortina-type front struts and larger Cortina front discs were fitted, together with Cortina rear brakes and radius-rod location for

the live axle. Front spring rates are the same as on the Escort GT and Sport but at the rear the leaves were stiffened by about 8 per cent. We tested the RS 1600 on 30 April 1970 and published a supplementary test of the Mexico on 10 December 1970; we subsequently ran an RS 1600 for 20,000 miles on long-term appraisal.

Ford is a company which listens to criticism and constructive comment and does something about it, so when production of the new overhead camshaft Cortina 2000 engine had built

NHK 247M

up enough for other installations to be considered, they set about improving the basic competition Escort and turning it into a much more civilized road car. Both the Mexico and RS 1600 suffer from a lot of suspension harshness and an unpleasant body boom at high-speed makes them far from restful on a long journey. Market research also showed that many buyers wanted RS 1600 performance at a lower price.

It is with these factors in mind that the RS 2000 has been developed. Contrary to what

you might expect from the RS label, it is not a new 2-litre version of the 16-valve BDA, but more a kind of 2-litre Mexico, dropped into the range of Ford AVO cars at a price mid-way between the other two models. Unlike the others, though, which continue in production as they were, the RS 2000 incorporates many worthwhile improvements which will be dealt with in detail later in this test.

The engine is a standard Cortina 2000 unit fitted with an electric rather than a fixed-drive cooling fan. This small difference increases the

Like the Mexico and the RS 1600, the latest car has the Type 49 bodyshell, with flared wheel arches. The contrasting side stripes are in plastic, but they cannot be peeled off

Inset: The heart of the RS 2000 is the 2-litre single overhead camshaft engine. A high-capacity export-type battery was fitted to the test car; the usual one is much smaller

FORD ESCORT RS 2000...

Above: The rim of the leather-trimmed steering wheel masks the smaller instruments on the right of the facia panel; the lamp alongside the cigarette lighter is the hazard warning repeater

peak power from 98 to 100 bhp (DIN), still at 5,700 rpm. This advanced unit, it will be remembered, features a single overhead camshaft driven by a cogged rubber belt and is fitted with a two-stage Weber twin-choke carburettor. Because of its larger capacity, the 2000 develops slightly more peak torque than the RS 1600 (108 lb.ft. at 3,500 rpm compared with 105 at 4,000), even though the latter has more top end power (115 bhp at 6,500 rpm). At the lower end, however, the torque curves separate by a much bigger margin and at 1,500 rpm for example the RS 2000 engine develops 93 instead of 73 lb.ft.

Standard too is the Cortina 2000 gearbox and because this has a lower bottom ratio (3.65 instead of the RS 1600's 2.97) a higher final-drive ratio of 3.54-to-1 is used (RS 1600 is fitted with 3.77-to-1). Thus the overall first gear ratio actually is lower (at 12.9 instead of 11.2), despite the higher final drive ratio, and the torque at the rear wheels at 1,000 rpm in bottom goes up by no less than 50 per cent.

It is not surprising therefore to find the RS 2000 a much easier car to drive than the RS 1600, especially as the clutch effort has been reduced as well. The extra bottom-end torque is most noticeable and it is not essential to keep the revs up in the way it is with the more highly tuned 16-valve unit. We found the RS 2000 would pull cleanly and strongly from as low as 1,000 rpm in top gear and a comparison of 30 to 50 mph in this ratio shows this car to be nearly 3sec quicker over this band.

During standing-start acceleration runs we were able to break traction from rest on a dry surface — something impossible with the higher gearing of the RS 1600 — and recorded a better 0 to 30 mph time (2.9 instead of 3.4 sec). To 40 mph the two cars were equal (4.8sec), and thereafter the RS 1600 pulls away, but only by a small margin. From rest to 100 mph in the RS 2000 is only 2.3sec slower, and the speed at the end of a standing kilometre is actually identical.

Gearchanging on the RS 2000 is faster and easier than with the RS 1600 because the lever is better placed and movements have been shortened. Typical Ford synchromesh is absolutely unbeatable and there is never any baulking. Second takes the car to 62 mph before maximum revs are reached and third is good for nearly 90 mph.

With a fairly tight engine in a relatively new car (only 2,000 miles of running-in) we lapped the MIRA banked circuit at 108 mph and clocked 111 mph on the best downwind leg. This mean is substantially less than the 113 mph of the RS 1600, although the difference is only of academic interest in this country. Compared with the Mexico, on the other hand, both top speed and acceleration are well up (Mexico: 99 mph and 0 to 60 mph in 10.7 sec).

When it comes to fuel economy, the advantages of a two-stage carburettor (instead of the two twin-choke Webers of the RS 1600) and higher overall gearing really start to show. At a steady 30 mph, for example, the RS 2000 covers 44.9 mpg against the RS 1600's 29.9 mpg and at 70 mph the figures are 31 against 26 mpg. This reflects noticeably in the overall consumption, our figure for the RS 2000 of 26.6 being much better than the RS 1600's 21.5 and only slightly worse than the Mexico's 27.5 mpg.

Above: Some of our larger drivers found the new seats on the narrow side, but they provide excellent support and do not get clammy in hot weather

Left: The light alloy wheels are extras, and it can be rather tricky trying to get the sleeve nuts to pick up on the stud threads

Noise, Vibration and Harshness

Ford have gained a lot of experience at dealing with these qualities of car design, and they have put this to good use in the RS 2000. We have found on Cortinas that some harshness is inherent in the 2000 engine and to reduce this the RS 2000 has a special aluminium bell-housing, a finned aluminium sump and a new rubber insulated propeller shaft. Attention to engine mounts and exhaust system hangers has put the natural boom period up out of the working rev range to around 6,000 rpm where it passes almost unnoticed among all the other commotion. The result is a vast increase in refinement, which combined with some special attention to sound deadening makes this a very quiet Escort and not a bit like the Mexico and RS 1600.

At high speed there is very little wind noise and without a body boom the cruising comfort is excellent. At 70 mph the engine is turning at only 3,750 rpm which makes very light work of motorways in this country. At 100 mph the engine is approaching its power peak, but still feels well within limits and easily able to keep up this pace all day.

Ride and Handling

The Ford works competition team had a lot to do with the improvements made to the suspension of the RS 2000. Front spring rates are 30 per cent stiffer than on other Escorts, partly to allow for the heavier engine and partly to improve the balance of the car. At the rear the rates are 6 per cent softer than on ordinary Escorts and 12 per cent softer than those of the Mexico and RS 1600. Damper setting are also revised to suit. The result is a much more comfortable ride without the harshness we complained about in the RS 1600 test and handling that is more consistent all the time. On the Mexico and RS 1600 we found there was a tendency towards ultimate understeer, which although it could be countered easily enough with the throttle, often led to untidy cornering characteristics especially when driving fast through unfamiliar bends. For this reason, it seems, keen rally types like the way the Mexico and RS 1600 are overbraked on the rear, as this helps them set the car up in advance of a corner.

On the RS 2000 rear braking has been reduced by using normal Escort instead of Cortina drums and the ride height has been lowered slightly, which combined with the revised spring rates makes the car much more consistently neutral. Throttle and steering can still be "played" against each other in a tight turn and we had tremendous fun at MIRA when we indulged in some really satisfying tail-out cornering, but that frantic scramble to scrub off speed for a bend which tightens unexpectedly has gone and generally braking can be maintained much deeper into a turn without the front running wide or the tail starting to go alarmingly light.

Stability at high speed is much better than on any other Escort, the well-known effects of sidewinds being less troublesome and the larger wheels and tyres, with more offset, seeming to have a greater self-aligning torque.

The large diameter front discs showed no signs of fade once their temperature had stabilized and from 30 mph the front wheels locked first to keep the RS 2000 in a straight line during panic braking. We recorded well over 1g with an effort of only 60 lb and the handbrake held securely facing either way on a 1-in-3 test hill. Restarting was very easy, thanks to the strong torque and low bottom gear.

Fittings and Equipment

Interior trim on the RS 2000 is just like any Escort two-door XL or GT, except that there is a black headlining, special seats, and an RS steering wheel with leather rim. The seats are completely new with excellent wrap-round frames and thick layers of soft padding, covered in durable Ford-type corded cloth. Headrests are built in to the seat backs, which can be adjusted for rake or reclined to lie right back. Pedals and steering wheel are well placed in relation to each other and the gearlever is slightly farther back than on the Mexico and RS 1600, which puts the knob in a much more easily reached position. Movements between ratios are short and very crisp; reverse is guarded by a push-down latch.

Left: A bracket holds the spare wheel steady on an angle; like most Fords, the boot can only be opened with the door key

Directly in front of the driver is a binnacle containing matching speedometer and rev counter and four small supplementary dials. There is only a total mileage recorder, no trip, and the steering wheel rim masks the smaller dials which are for fuel contents, oil pressure, water temperature and battery voltage.

The lamps switch is separate from the other rocker switches, these being to the left and right of the large central ashtray and the lamps switch being under the facia rail on the opposite side of the steering column. This prevents any confusion in the dark. A heated backlight is standard, as are hazard warning flashers.

A standard Escort heater is fitted, working on the air blending principle and demisting through two circular nozzles on the facia which can be rotated to direct fresh air in the driver's face instead. There is no independent fresh air ventilation system, but, stale air is effectively extracted through slots at the base of the rear window. Front and rear quarterlights are fixed. There is a two-speed booster fan which is reasonably quiet on its slower setting.

Another of the standard fittings is a pair of circular headlamps with twin-filament tungsten-halogen bulbs. These provided a really bright and long-range main beam with well-controlled dip pattern and plenty of illumination for speeds of 70 mph to be maintained after dark. On normal Escorts the wiper blades lift off the

screen at speeds over 60 mph, but special attention to those of the RS 2000 has raised this limit to nearly 90 mph.

Washers are operated by a pedal on the floor which is combined with an auxiliary spring-loaded wiper switch that can be flicked on its own for a single occasional wipe in light rain or drizzle.

The boot can be opened only with the door key. There is much more space inside now that the battery has been moved back to the engine bay and the spare wheel propped nearly upright in the left-hand wing recess. The boot floor is covered with a pvc mat, backed with felt. Tools comprise only a jack and wheelbrace, stowed in a black canvas bag.

Living with the RS 2000

After the latest price increases the Ford Mexico costs £1,348 and the RS 1600 £1,864. In between comes the RS 2000 at £1,586 including seat belts and delivery. The only extras on the test car were alloy road wheels, for which there was no price available, and low-profile 175/70 tyres are an alternative.

Paint and trim finish seemed to be above the normal Escort standard on the test car and we suspect that cars built at Aveley are treated rather specially. Two styles of decorative colour schemes are available, plain triple stripes along the waist, like on the 1300E, or the new pattern applied to the test car. The contrasting colour in

Reversing lamps are standard on the RS 2000, as is the electrically heated rear window; there are RS badges on the front wings and on the boot panel

FORD ESCORT RS2000 (1,993 c.c.)

ACCELERATION

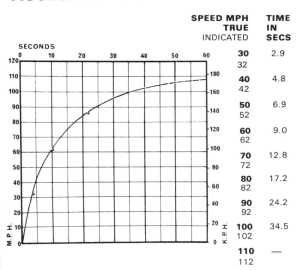

SPEED MPH TRUE / INDICATED	TIME IN SECS
30 / 32	2.9
40 / 42	4.8
50 / 52	6.9
60 / 62	9.0
70 / 72	12.8
80 / 82	17.2
90 / 92	24.2
100 / 102	34.5
110 / 112	—

GEAR RATIOS AND TIME IN SEC

mph	Top (3.54)	3rd (4.85)	2nd (6.97)
10-30	—	6.1	3.7
20-40	—	5.2	3.6
30-50	7.4	5.1	3.8
40-60	7.9	5.4	4.2
50-70	8.8	6.8	—
60-80	8.8	8.2	—
70-90	11.0	—	—
80-100	16.2	—	—

Standing ¼-mile
17.1 sec 80 mph
Standing Kilometre
32.3 sec 99 mph
Test distance
1,264 miles
Mileage recorder
accurate

PERFORMANCE

MAXIMUM SPEEDS

Gear		mph	kph	rpm
Top	(mean)	108	174	5,780
	(best)	111	179	5,940
3rd		89	143	6,500
2nd		62	100	6,500
1st		33	53	6,500

BRAKES
FADE
(from 70 mph in neutral)
Pedal load for 0.5g stops in lb

1	24	6	30-35
2	24	7	35
3	30	8	35
4	30-35	9	35
5	30-35	10	35

RESPONSE
(from 30 mph in neutral)

Load	g	Distance
20lb	0.41	73ft
40lb	0.85	35ft
60lb	1.05	28.7ft
Handbrake	0.36	84ft
Max. Gradient 1 in 3.		

CLUTCH
Pedal 35lb and 5in.

COMPARISONS

MAXIMUM SPEED MPH
Triumph Dolomite Sprint	(£1,869)	115
Alfa Romeo 2000 Berlina	(£2,499)	114
Ford Escort RS 2000	**(£1,568)**	**108**
BMW 2002	(£2,549)	107
Opel Ascona 1.9	(£1,567)	98

0-60 MPH, SEC
Triumph Dolomite Sprint	8.6
Ford Escort RS 2000	**9.0**
Alfa Romeo 2000 Berlina	9.9
BMW 2002	10.1
Opel Ascona 1.9	12.5

STANDING ¼-MILE, SEC
Triumph Dolomite Sprint	16.7
Ford Escort RS 2000	**17.1**
Alfa Romeo 2000 Berlina	17.2
BMW 2002	17.8
Opel Ascona 1.9	18.3

OVERALL MPG
Ford Escort RS 2000	**26.6**
BMW 2002	25.5
Triumph Dolomite Sprint	23.6
Opel Ascona 1.9	23.5
Alfa Romeo 2000 Berlina	21.8

GEARING
(with 165 SR-13 in. tyres)

Top	18.7 mph per 1,000 rpm
3rd	13.65 mph per 1,000 rpm
2nd	9.5 mph per 1,000 rpm
1st	5.1 mph per 1,000 rpm

CONSUMPTION

FUEL
(At constant speed — mpg)
30 mph	44.9
40 mph	43.0
50 mph	39.6
60 mph	35.4
70 mph	31.0
80 mph	26.7
90 mph	22.0
100 mph	17.4

Typical mpg . 28 (10.1 litres/100km)
Calculated (DIN) mpg 28.2 (10.0 litres/100km)
Overall mpg 26.6 (10.6 litres/100km)
Grade of fuel Premium, 4-star (min. 98 RM)

OIL
Consumption (SAE 10W/30) Negligible

TEST CONDITIONS:
Weather: Fine   Wind: 2-10 mph.
Temperature: 20 deg. C. (68 deg. F).
Barometer: 29.65 in. hg. Humidity: 80 percent.
Surfaces: Dry concrete and asphalt.

WEIGHT:
Kerb Weight 17.7 cwt (1,978lb-899kg).
(with oil, water and half full fuel tank).
Distribution, per cent F, 54; R, 46.
Laden as tested: 21.4 cwt (2,396lb-1,089kg).

TURNING CIRCLES:
Between kerbs L, 31 ft 0 in.; R, 30 ft 10 in.
Between walls L, 32 ft 11 in.; R, 32 ft 9 in.
Steering wheel turns, lock to lock 3.5.
Figures taken at 2,000 miles by our own staff at the Motor Industry Research Association proving ground at Nuneaton.

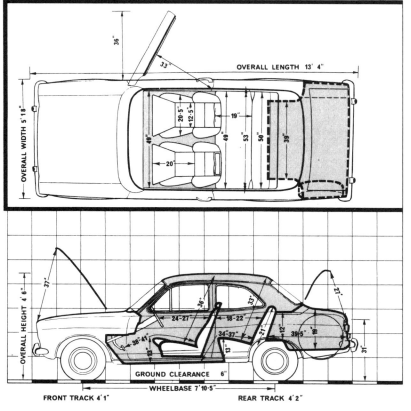

OVERALL LENGTH 13' 4"
OVERALL WIDTH 5' 18"
OVERALL HEIGHT 4' 6"
GROUND CLEARANCE 6"
WHEELBASE 7'10·5"
FRONT TRACK 4'1"
REAR TRACK 4'2"

STANDARD GARAGE 16ft x 8ft 6in.

SPECIFICATION

ENGINE

Cylinders	4, in-line
Main bearings	5
Cooling system	Water: pump, thermostat and electric fan
Bore	90.82mm (3.58in.)
Stroke	76.95mm (3.03in.)
Displacement	1,993 c.c. (121.6 cu.in.)
Valve gear	Single belt driven overhead camshaft
Compression ratio	9.2-to-1. Min. octane rating: 98 RM
Carburettor	Weber 32/36 downdraft
Fuel pump	Mechanical
Oil filter	Full flow, disposable can
Max. power	100 bhp (DIN) at 5,750 rpm
Max. torque	108 lb.ft (DIN) at 3,500 rpm

TRANSMISSION

Clutch	Cable-operated, diaphragm-spring 8.5 in. dia.
Gearbox	Four-speed, all synchromesh
Gear ratios	Top 1.0
	Third 1.37
	Second 1.97
	First 3.65
	Reverse 3.66
Final drive	Hypoid bevel, 3.54-to-1

CHASSIS and BODY

Construction	Integral heavy duty all steel body and chassis

SUSPENSION

Front	MacPherson struts, lower links, coil springs, telescopic dampers, anti-roll bar
Rear	Live axle, leaf springs, radius arms, telescopic dampers

STEERING

Type	Rack and pinion
Wheel dia.	14in.

BRAKES

Make and type	Girling disc front, drum rear
Servo	Girling vacuum type
Dimensions	F 9.63in. dia.
	R 8in. dia. 1.5in. wide shoes
Swept area	F 190.2 sq. in., R 75.4 sq. in.
	Total 265.6 sq. in. (246.4 sq. in./ton laden)

FRONT ENGINE, REAR-WHEEL DRIVE

WHEELS

Type	Pressed steel disc, four stud fixing Light alloy RS-type extra 5½in. wide rim
Tyres—make	Various, Dunlop on test car
—type	SP68 radial ply tubeless
—size	165 SR-13in.

EQUIPMENT

Battery	12 Volt 58 Ah.
Alternator	35 amp
Headlamps	Halogen 230/110 watt (total)
Reversing lamp	Standard
Electric fuses	7
Screen wipers	2-speed
Screen washer	Standard pedal operated
Interior heater	Standard air-blending
Heated backlight	Standard
Safety belts	Standard
Interior trim	Cloth seats pvc headlining
Floor covering	Carpet
Jack	screw pillar type
Jacking points	One each side under sills
Windscreen	Laminated
Underbody protection	Phosphate treatment prior to painting

MAINTENANCE

Fuel tank	9 Imp. gallons (41 litres)
Cooling system	12.2 pints (inc. heater)
Engine sump	6.7 pints (3.8 litres) SAE 10W/30. Change oil every 6,000 miles. Change filter every 6,000 miles.
Gearbox	2.4 pints SAE 80EP. No change
Final drive	2 pints. SAE 90EP. No change
Grease	No points
Valve clearance	Inlet 0.008in. (cold) Exhaust 0.010in. (cold)
Contact breaker	0.025in. gap; 38-40 deg. dwell
Ignition timing	4 deg. BTDC (static) 4 ±1 deg. BTDC (stroboscopic at 500 rpm)
Spark plug	Type: Autolite BF32. Gap 0.025in.
Compression pressure	156-185 psi
Tyre pressures	F 24: R 24 psi (normal driving) F 28: R 28 psi (high speed)
Max. payload	850lb. (385 kg)

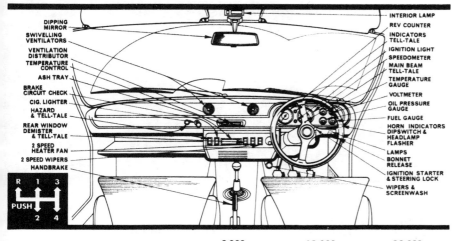

Service Interval	6,000 miles	18,000 miles	36,000 miles
Time Allowed (hours and mins)	3.36	3.42	4.48
Cost @ £3.30 per hour	£11.88	£12.21	£15.84
Oil Change	£1.23	£1.23	£1.23
Oil Filter	£1.61	£1.61	£1.61
Breather Filter	—	—	—
Air Filter	—	£1.58	£1.58
Contact Breaker Points	£0.45	£0.45	£0.45
Sparking Plugs	£1.39	£1.39	£1.39
Total Cost:	£16.56	£18.47	£22.10

Prices for British parts not available yet

---

both cases is provided by plastic *appliqué* with an adhesive so strong that only sanding will remove it. There was no trace of peeling around the edges on the test car. Ford shun any kind of rust-proofing after painting, so some proprietary treatment would be advisable if long life or much rough-road driving is being planned.

Complaints from the driver's seat were very rare, the only persistent one being about the lack of stowage space for oddments. There is a shelf under the facia each side, but that is all. Ford AVO expect to offer a central console soon to overcome this.

The RS 2000 is not meant as a full family car and the special front seats take away quite a bit of the back seat legroom. In fact, an adult can sit there only if those in the front put their seats in the most upright position. With armrest recesses in the rear trim pads there is enough width for three abreast, but the cushions are shaped for two and the raised edges tip the outboard passengers towards the middle.

The jack on all Escorts was improved just over a year ago and it now incorporates a flip-over handle for winding the screw pillar instead of a ratchet spanner. There is a single jacking point each side under the sill just aft of the centre of gravity. This location calls for a lot of jack winding to get the rear tyre clear of the ground. The sleeve nuts used with alloy wheels can be difficult to get started on their threads.

Under the bonnet the 2000 engine is a fairly comfortable fit, the only congestion in the layout being in the region of the bulkhead-mounted fuse box, which is masked by part of the throttle linkage. The distributor is easy to work on at the front of the engine, as we discovered when we experienced a most unusual insulation fault in the contact breaker during the test. The dipstick is at the back of the engine in a tube which solves the problem of replacing it in the dark.

Conclusions

Ford engineers have undoubtedly made a good job of improving the basic Mexico/RS 1600 package with this new RS 2000 option. Not only is it more tractable and refined but it behaves more consistently when driven hard and gives very good value in terms of fuel consumption. We make no secret of the fact that we find these high-performance Escorts tremendous fun cars and for the man who does not want the ultimate in competition machinery, the RS 2000 makes a superb road car. On acceleration, top speed and cornering power it can hold its own with much more exotic models and in this respect it is really good value. It seems so much our sort of car that we are adding one to our long-term fleet for full appraisal over 20,000 miles. □

MANUFACTUER: Ford Motor Co. Ltd., Warley, Essex.

PRICES

Basic	£1,332.76
Special Car Tax	£109.06
VAT	£144.18
Total (in GB)	**£1,586.00**
Seat Belts	Standard
Licence	£25.00
Delivery charge (London)	Free
Number plates	£5.50
Total on road (exc. insurance)	**£1,616.50**

Insurance (not decided yet, probably Group 6)

EXTRA (inc. VAT)

Alloy road wheels	price pending

GIANT TEST
Audi 80GT   Alfasud Ti   Escort RS2000

ANYONE WHO STILL BELIEVES IN THE concept of low-cost sports car is certain to have the rug of self-delusion pulled from under his feet by the members of this Giant Test trio. In performance, handling and roadholding—to say nothing of practicality—they simply demolish the traditional sports car ideal. Yet they are not sports cars, being boy-racer developments of family saloons.

Ford's AVO-made RS2000 is so totally divorced from the normal Escort saloon that it makes you wonder where they find the patience to keep trying to maintain the family resemblance. The RS2000 is the latest in a long, long line of race-and-rally-inspired products that have borne Mexico, GT and RS1600 badges.

Audi's 80GT is almost a contradiction. Its makers have always played it really cool when it comes to the performance image so beloved of the likes of Ford. Yet the GT

breaks totally from that conservative attitude by being unexpectedly hairy and surprisingly well developed—without the aid of a competition programme.

The Alfasud Ti is the first careful step in the long path of development that faces the Naples-built Alfa Romeo. When it's all boiled down, the Ti does not differ all that much from the bog-standard Sud, so manufacture of the hotter car causes few ripples in the production process. By starting with a sportingly-inclined base, Alfa have not had to do a great deal to the Sud to turn it onto the Ti path.

There is no longer any valid basis for attacking the price of these cars. With increases running totally out of control, £2000-plus is, comparatively speaking, no longer expensive. But for the record, the Sud costs £1717, the RS2000 £1964 and the Audi £2075. With the Audi you have to pay extra

for special shockers and alloy wheels; the sky's the limit with Escort options.

ENGINEERING, STYLING
In a way it comes down to front-wheel-drive versus rear-wheel-drive. The Ford could hardly be more conventional if it tried, whereas the other two thrive on being unconventional, the Alfa more than the Audi

The Escort is a very rigid metal box held off the road by wheels suspended on coil struts at the front with leaf springs at the rear, attached to a rigid axle located by radius arms. The difference between the RS and normal Escort is in the higher specification shockers and body strength, rather than anything clever. Ford have got their roadholding from stiffness and to hell with the ride. In this they have achieved what they set out to do.

Powered by Ford's current idea of the

44

Audi's main instruments are okay, but minor dials are in typical after-thought position on console, partly obscured by big wheel

Sud's wheel is adjustable for height, has its minor instruments angled towards driver to avoid viewing errors. Rim is covered in nasty plastic

Leather-bound wheel on RS is excellent, but rim blocks out dials on right, which are hard to read because of reflections. Fascia vents on RS and Ti are directional for demisting

niversal engine, the 2.0litre sohc unit of nto origin, the RS has by far the largest ngine of the trio. It is a big, understressed, nderdeveloped lump of a thing that relies n litres, not refinement. Nevertheless, you annot ignore 100(DIN) horsepower at 5750, 107lb/ft at 3750. It has a single carburettor nd a 9.2 to one compression ratio. The ansmission is a normal four-speeder with ose ratios, culminating in a 3.54 to one final ive that gives 18.7mph per 1000rpm in top. Brakes are normal, too. The front discs are 625in in diameter, aided by 8.0in rear ums. The dual hydraulic circuit is servo-ssisted. Rack-and-pinion steering is used nd the 5.5in wheels carry 165SR-13 radials.

Audi's 80GT has as much power as the S2000. However, you need another 750rpm the clock before you get it; there is me 10lb/ft less torque and it happens at 00rpm, anyway. But this is not a bad effort

from 1588cc. For the record, this engine is an overbored (79.5mm against 76.5mm) version of the 80GL unit, and although it retains the same 9.7 to one compression ratio, the double-throated Solex has bigger chokes. Mounted longitudinally in the chassis, the engine drives the front wheels through a four-speed gearbox that provides 17.3mph per 1000rpm in the over-driven top gear.

To cope with the extra power going to the gearbox, the clutch has been given a slightly larger diameter. And the 13in diameter wheels (cast alloy) have 5.0in rims (instead of the GL's 4.5) to carry 175/70 low-profile tyres. The servo-assisted disc/drum braking system remains largely unchanged, as does the rack-and-pinion steering. However, buyers can specify gas-filled dampers, just as can RS2000 customers. Both the test cars were thus equipped.

So the situation with the two big-powered

cars of this Giant Test is that the Ford is simply an engine-swap arrangement, whereas the Audi has been given much fuller treatment, involving the enlargement of an existing engine; the lessons of that will no doubt be transferred down the line into the more pedestrian models in due course.

Alfa Romeo have taken a different tack with the Sud Ti. They have mildly tuned the engine by altering the compression, camshaft and carburettor, so that it develops 68(DIN)horsepower at 6000rpm with 9.2kgm at 3200rpm instead of 63horsepower with 8.5kgm. Like the Japanese, Alfa Romeo are more fond of quoting the higher SAE figures than DIN, although the road performance suggests that there is nothing to be ashamed of in 68horsepower.

To ensure that the available power is well used, the Ti's gearbox has acquired an extra overdrive ratio (the Sud's transmission was designed with that adaption in mind) giving it a certain advantage over its rivals.

Like the Audi, the Sud's engine sits out ahead of the front wheels, but there similarities end abruptly. Instead of being an in-line four, the Alfa's engine is a flat four with a single overhead camshaft on each bank of cylinders. As with the Ford and Audi, the cams are belt driven. To most CAR readers, the rest of the specification should be familiar enough. However, to reiterate . . . inboard front discs (10.15in) and outboard at rear (9.17), coil strut, independent front suspension with rigid rear axle sprung-on coils and located with a Watts linkage and Panhard rod, rack-and-pinion steering and, in the case of the Ti, 165/70SR-13 tyres carried on 4.5in rims.

These cars are, of course, variations on existing saloons, so their styling represents no great departure. Perhaps the most substantial difference is in the Alfa, which is a four-door saloon in its Sud role, but becomes a two-door in the semi-sporting Ti application. It was originally intended to market both two and four-door Suds, but the two-door version was finally held over to become the Ti. With it goes a four-headlamp configuration, an air dam, a spoiler on the boot lid, elaborately pressed steel wheels, a matt-black grille and new badges. It looks slightly stubby, but not as aggressive as the Escort with its bulging wheel arches and dog's bone shaped, matt-black grille. Depending on taste, you can dress up the RS to look like a fairground organ but in the final analysis, there's not all that much to distinguish it from a normal Escort.

Nor does the 80GT shout that it, too, is different from the vehicle from which it was derived. Dosed with the matt-black paint— that great standby when all else fails—the Audi has an inconspicuous air dam under the nose, but the primary giveaway is the good-looking wheels. There's less of the boy racer image surrounding the GT's appearance, but more of it under the skin.

PERFORMANCE
All three cars give a quite different type of performance. Of course, the Ford's 2.0litres give it the muscle-car image. It's flexible and very responsive to the throttle, giving the impression as you drive through traffic in top gear that what you are really doing is holding back the horses against the moment when they are really needed. Which is exactly what is happening; but what you finally unleash is a harsh, noisy and generally unpleasant engine dogged by vibration periods that make absolutely no difference to the great lumps of torque and power that it tosses out on demand. This application shows the 2.0 Pinto engine at its worst. It has more in common with Japanese power plants than British or European units in that it is capable of revving to perhaps 6000 in the gears, but it feels so coarse that you never exploit the range that the tacho cunningly suggests is available.

A number of factors inhibit the RS's cruising speed, but the engine is the primary limiting factor. If you run in the 80-85mph region then you're striking the best compromise between vibration and speed.

Whereas the Pinto/Cortina is a plodding sort of engine, the 80GT's 400cc smaller unit delivers its biggest punches high up the rev range, in areas that are unthinkable in the Ford. Not that the GT is inflexible—it is more flexible than its 2.0litre rival, in fact—but it does not really get its teeth into the action until the tacho needle soars around the dial. The smooth and willing engine will dash the needle so deep into the red that it looks like a bank statement! And the results that you get for stirring up the GT are so remarkably good that only a handful of cars have any hope of matching it for acceleration. On a wet road there's an abundance of wheelspin right through to third gear, so you have to cool your hot-shoe tendencies when it rains or the road is loosely surfaced.

Nor is it a quiet car. The noise level is high above 85mph, and most of it comes from the busy mechanicals up front. The carburation is not all that pleasant; the second choke tends to come in with a jerk on occasion, but that seems to be a small price to pay for the sheer urge that it imparts. Although our top speed failed to measure up to the factory's claims, (a minor matter, really, for the noise level precludes continuous 109mph motoring anyway), we were immensely impressed by the genuinely usable power in the overtaking speed ranges. You can be out, passed and a speck in the distance before most drivers have managed to decide whether or not to stay in top or drop back to third. It's a sprinter, this Audi, and a damned good one at that. The one performance shortcoming is the fact that really high-speed cruising is beyond it on grounds of noise. In the whole kingdom of Wolfsburg there does not appear to be a five-speed gearbox—and there will be GT owners who would gladly see VW exchange that kingdom for an extra ratio.

There will probably be Sud Ti owners who would at times trade in their fifth gear for some of the Audi's power. But then they would regret it when they got on the motorway, for the Ti will cruise the go-faster stripes off either the Ford or the Audi. You can run the Alfa smoothly, quietly, relaxingly . . . and flat-out, at 100mph all the day long. Not for one moment can you pretend the Ti has anything like the acceleration of the other two. The insurmountable fact is that 68horsepower and 1200cc are not going to peel the rubber from the tyres in the Green Light Grand Prix for Cars and Light Commercials. Yet the sheer relentlessness of the Ti's cruising ability is enough to reduce other drivers to tears as they try to keep up.

RUNNING COSTS
If you can remember to keep your right foot out of the carpet, then the members of this

Audi's understeer changes to tail-out attitude as throttle is eased off. Basically, 80GT has excellent roadholding

Alfasud's roadholding is outstanding with minimum of roll and almost no understeer. Behaviour is superior to its two rivals

Easy-handling RS2000 is great fun to drive, but in these pictures is travelling 10mph slower than Alfasud Ti. Body roll is very well controlled, however

Recaro seats are feature of 80GT's cabin, but large boot is handicapped by high lip

Ti's seats are almost as good as Audi's and have excellent squab-tilting arrangements for back-seat access. Low-loading boot is unexpectedly large

Well-dimensioned seats in RS2000 effectively reduce seating to barely 2plus2. Boot also has high lip, but spare is well located, space is fair

trio will return quite good consumption figures. But the harder you tread the deeper you will have to dig into your wallet. However, based on the fact that once the novelty has worn off you can consistently get 30mpg from the 80GT, you will need to buy £216 of four star for every 12,000 miles of motoring, against £202 for the Escort and £187 for the Alfa.

The Alfa should also be lighter on tyres. Because it produces less power than the other two, it will chew off less rubber—if the driver does not spend all his time exploiting the handling and roadholding qualities. There are times, even on dry roads, when the GT and RS both demonstrate that they have more power than grip.

Servicing requirements are not particularly demanding, but in general Audi and Alfa component replacement costs are going to be higher than the Ford's.

HANDLING AND ROADHOLDING
All three rate very high marks indeed among the ranks of cars that offer their drivers outstanding roadability. But, as with the performance of the trio, they wrap their characteristics in distinctive packages.

Being the most conventionally designed of the group, the Ford behaves as you would expect it to. Its roadholding is inferior to the others (by some 10mph in our photographic corner) but the handling is totally predictable and thoroughly reliable. In other words, it is about as good as you are likely to get with a conventional design. As an old school car, all sideways and exciting, the RS2000 has few peers, but that does not make it stick to the road with the tenacity of the others. Unevenly surfaced corners bounce the tail out, despite the radius arms, and although it has a comforting degree of stabilising understeer, it is invariably the rear wheels that lose their grip first. With equal certainty, you can get them back again with a twitch of helm.

Braking is good without being sensational. When you really lean on the pedal at high speeds you have to be prepared for a touch of steering, this way or that, to keep it on the island, but it causes no real dramas. To cope with the heavy 2.0litre engine, the front suspension has been uprated enough to minimise nose dive, but the weight transfer leaves the back wheels feeling light.

With its much-vaunted outboard scrub radius front-end geometry, the Audi offers something close to foolproof straightline stopping, although the brakes themselves don't feel specially strong. In fact, they don't feel specially anything, even after you overcome the long pedal travel. But in other ways the 80GT is more positive. The roadholding is strong, building up to considerable understeer in tight corners that can be rectified by backing off the throttle to bring the tail around. In the wet, you have to play a tune on the accelerator pedal to maintain a comfortable balance and keep the front wheels from running too wide. But with

Engine compartments are
unspectacular, but provide reasonable
access to ancilliary components.
Only Alfa has front-hinged bonnet;
others are conventional. Audi (top),
Alfasud (centre), RS2000 (bottom)

the power available and the good spread of torque, you can nearly always drive the GT onwards through corners without the embarrassment of scrubbing off an irrecoverable amount of speed.

Oddly enough, the straight-line stability of the GT is not quite as good as we would have liked. The torque reaction tends to make it twitch slightly to one side of the other when you lift off or re-apply the power. We also noticed a slight self-correcting yaw in the front at speed.

Although it is not a specially sensitive car to handle, the 80GT is efficient in its roadholding, preferring long sweeping corners to tight ones where the understeer tries to build up to awkward, but not impossible, levels.

According to the rules of car design, front-wheel-drive also means excessive understeer. In the case of the Sud Ti, its designers either did not read the rules, or they changed them, for the car defies all the accepted theories by being just about neutral until, when the side loadings become too much, it slides its rear wheels. But, let it be said, when that happens you know for sure that you really are trying and there will be few other cars or people left in the hunt. In the wet it has thoroughly uncanny roadholding—and more of it than anyone has a right to expect! A sadistically-minded Ti driver could easily reduce his passengers to nervous seizure on twisting wet roads without even approaching the car's limits.

Or, to put it another way, the Ti has roadholding that would be outstanding even if it cost four and five times as much. If that is not enough by itself, the brakes are in the exotic-car class and certainly superior to all but a handful of the world's most sophisticated vehicles.

Disregarding the world and concentrating instead on the Ti's two rivals in this test, it has to be said that however good they may be in their dynamic qualities, the Alfa is better.

DRIVER APPEAL

Driver appeal is what these cars are all about, but Ford seem more aware of it than either Audi or Alfa. Not that Ford's efforts have been successful in all areas. For instance, the RS driver gets a handsome, leather-bound steering wheel through which he can clearly see the tacho and speedo, but the four minor dials are successfully shrouded by the wheel rim and usually have so much reflection in their glasses that they cannot be read anway. And the switch gear is spread around the fascia in an awkward, old-fashioned way.

Annoying though the minor controls may be, the major ones leave no room for doubt. The steering is light, responsive, high gear and provides a very good turning circle. Similarly, the gearchange is stubby and has short, precise movements from one position to the next; it's an exciting, urgent sort of machine that lets you take liberties with its roadholding because you can so easily sort

it out again. Really a fun car to drive but outdated in what it does.

Most of the kicks you get from the 80GT come from the engine performance. The Q-car aspect emerges when people discover that what they took to be the vicar's car is really a vampire with a big thirst for demolishing the ego of big-car drivers.

The controls are straightforward with a reasonably good but slightly rubbery gearchange. In typical German style, the steering wheel is too big, specially in view of the steering's over-light feel. As with the Ford and the Alfa, the main instruments are directly in front of the driver, the minor dials having taken up the after-thought position on the central console. Audi have not exactly gone overboard to enhance driver appeal and have well above the already efficient (with the exception of the push/push lighting pads) minor controls.

Apart from a rocker switch for the heated rear window, all the Alfa's minor controls are worked by the two steering-column stalks and you don't have to take more than two fingers off the rim to operate any of them. In addition to that, the steering wheel is adjustable; up and down to ensure sufficient thigh clearance, although the wheel itself is plastic covered and not specially nice to the touch. Minor instruments are ranged towards the centre of the fascia and are angled to eliminate parallex error; all good stuff.

Alfa have not tried to over-dress the Ti. It is simply and practically laid out. Where it scores with drivers is the way it appeals to the senses in an overall way, rather than strongly in individual aspects. Thus, the brakes, handling and steering are all beyond reproach, while the performance, as with all Alfas, is somewhat lower than the chassis capabilities.

COMFORT

In this area the Alfa scores again. The ride is superior to the other two and, despite intrusive road and transmission noise at low speeds, is a much quieter car overall. Even at 100mph you can talk to your passengers in normal tones. Four adults fit into the Ti comfortably, for the rear seat provides enough head and legroom for long distances, while the deeply-contoured, reclining front seats have head restraints and ample fore-and-aft adjustment. Trim is a cloth/vinyl combination and there are strange, felt-like carpets on the floors.

The Audi's accommodation is similar and its Recaro seats offer as much—or more—comfort as the Alfa's, while the check-pattern cloth trim looks better, too. With the optional gas-filled dampers, the GT's ride is very firm indeed and, coupled to the noise level, is a wearing sort of car to drive over long distances, however quickly you might cover them. In the suspensions's favour, though, is the quality of the damping. On our favourite series of humpbacks it behaved better than any car we have previously put over them.

Not far behind it were the Ti and RS. The

Ford's damping is almost as good as the Audi's but its ride is a lot worse, regardless of conditions. It's one of those cars that gives the impression that it is leaping from crag to crag, so no surface irregularities pass unnoticed by the inhabitants in their well-shaped, generously dimensioned front seats.

Perhaps it is these dimensions that effectively make the RS2000 a two-seater. With 5ft 10in tall driver at the wheel there is no usable legroom in the back. We are feeling charitable, so we will call it a two-plus-two, but that's all. Wind and mechanical noise levels are too high and the engine vibration periods can hardly help but be noticed by all the occupants: there's a certain crudity about it, and little comfort apart from that offered by the seats.

SAFETY
By far the safest thing about the this trio as a whole is their capacity for accident avoidance. Without exception they can be steered, braked, accelerated or handled out of situations that would bring down many a less agile car.

But there could be improvements. For instance, the lights on the RS2000 are not up to the performance and they just get by on the other two; the Alfa has a laminated screen as standard but the Audi's is toughened and so is the Ford's. The bumper bars cannot be taken seriously on any of these cars, and the Audi has particularly vulnerable winkers. Audi and Alfa include an exterior mirror.

We were all impressed by the immensely strong feel of the RS2000. It felt as though it had been carved out of steel rather than pressed in bits (a marked contrast to the normal Escort, which is sloppy by comparison). You get the impression that you could bounce the Escort off the scenery and it would stand up to it pretty well.

However, the forward mounting of the Audi's engine means that the accident has to squash quite a lot of material before it gets to the cabin. This applies also to the Alfa, with the added advantage that the flat-four engine is wider and distributes impact loads better.

CONCLUSIONS
Both the Audi and Escort have one big thing going for them: performance. The Ti cannot hope to match them in acceleration, yet it cruises at higher speeds than are realistic in its rivals. Fuel consumption is slightly better.

Ride and comfort are superior, the handling is not as good as the RS's but the roadholding is a long way in front, with the Audi trailing last on handling but between the two on roadholding. The Alfa's brakes are tremendously effective, too, There is little to fault in its dynamic qualities, nor in its compatability with the final component in its concept: the driver.

If you can live with adequate rather than startling performance, then the Alfa is the answer. And you can use the difference in price to take your bank manager to lunch against the day when you want an Alfetta. ●

Escort

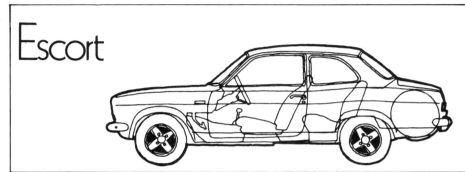

Alfasud

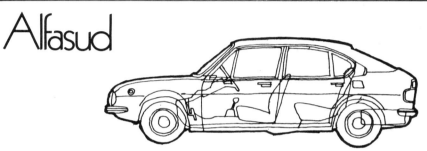

Audi

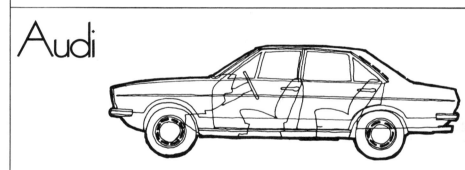

SPEEDS IN GEARS

	FIRST	SECOND	THIRD	FOURTH	FIFTH
Escort	0-30	0-60	15-85	20-100	
Alfa	0-30	5-50	15-72	20-90	30-102
Audi	0-31	0-54	10-83	15-104	

PERFORMANCE

	0-30	0-40	0-50	0-60	0-70	0-80
Escort	3.5	5.3	6.8	9.4	12.8	16.2
Alfa	4.1	6.1	9.2	11.8	17.1	21.5
Audi	3.4	4.8	7.1	10.9	14.8	18.8

FUEL CONSUMPTION

Escort 26-30mpg, Alfa 27-35mpg, Audi 23-33mpg

Ford Escort RS 1800

1,845 c.c.

Successor to RS1600 in Escort II form brings added refinement and economy but little loss of cross-country journey potential. Still very much an enthusiast's car with taut ride, excellent handling and brakes. Still lacks refinement in many areas despite the very high price

Black quarter bumpers, round headlamps and the front bib spoiler make the RS1800 immediately distinguishable

THERE was much consternation among the owners of the early Ford RS1600s, when the coming of the new Escort became a certainty, as to whether the BDA-engined model would continue in the new model's line-up. Not only does it do so – the new car is such an improvement on its predecessor as to be almost unrecognizable as coming from the same basis.

The new RS Escort starts its life as an Escort Sport and progresses down Ford's Halewood production line as such until it reaches the point in production where it can be removed for fitment of the Rallye Sport parts that differentiate it from all the other Escort models.

These parts start with the Ford-produced BDA engine which has grown in capacity from the 1,601 c.c. version fitted to the original RS1600. In its current form, the capacity is 1,845 c.c. from which 115 bhp is produced at 6,000 rpm, compared with the 120 bhp that was extracted from the smaller unit. Combating the lower output in terms of performance is a worthwhile increase in torque from 112 to 120 lb. ft. produced at the same revs as before (i.e. 4,000 rpm). The internal design of the engine is unchanged; the

drop in power results from the adoption of a single Weber progressive twin-choke 32/36 DGAV carburettor in place of the twin Weber 40 DCOE units that had always been fitted on the RS1600.

In terms of both performance and the general impression of the old and new cars on the road, there is really precious little difference. Perhaps the older car has a slight edge in performance right at the top end of the rev range; but on the road, the new car's higher gearing and improved torque output fully compensate. What one is really saying is that the RS1800 is just as exciting as was the RS1600. This gave a unique combination of mass-produced reliability and out-and-out performance the like of which was unknown except in special one-off cars produced by tuning establishments, often without guarantee or adequate after sales service.

It is interesting, however, to consider how many more manufacturers are now represented in the field of the really high performance family car than was the case when the RS1600 first appeared on the scene. Back in April 1970, we could only pull together an assorted collection of comparison vehicles ranging from the esoteric Lotus Elan

+2S to the Triumph Vitesse 2-litre, whose prices varied enormously from the Vitesse at £1,001 to the Lotus and the Alfa Romeo 1750GTV at close to £2,500. In 1975, however, there are a number of serious competitors with the RS1800, not only in performance but also in price. We have chosen competitors in this test from Audi, Renault, Toyota and Triumph – but to these could have been added examples from another half-dozen companies that have also produced the kind of four-seater sports car that was once almost Ford's domain. Thus it is necessary to be more critical of the RS1800, and if one says that it only gives best in a few areas to the strength of the opposition, one is acknowledging Ford's understanding of what is needed in this market sector.

As the old RS1600 got longer in the tooth and new rivals appeared by which to judge, it became obvious that what the RS1600 lacked was a desirable level of refinement. The Audi 80GT and of course the BMW 2002Tii both showed that blistering performance *could* be allied to perfectly acceptable road manners and it is good to report that the new RS1800 is much improved in this respect. The ride, though still taut, is

Ford Escort RS1800

much improved and where the old car had to be driven in exuberant tail-out attitudes for ultimate performance, the latest version is just as quick without any of the previously exaggerated necessity for ragged edge

displays. Sound levels too are now much reduced and only at speeds approaching the maximum does the wind and engine noise become seriously obtrusive.

Internally, the new car has an air of refinement that was totally absent on the original car – but then it really should be when the high price is considered. Typically, Ford have weighed up the likely market for the car and offered the two versions that

will suit the two distinct potential buying groups. For the man who wants the basic starting-off point for a serious rally car, Ford offer a version without unnecessary trimmings. To this, the club rally man can add his own choice of seats, additional tuning equipment etc. For the other class of buyer, there is the RS1800 Custom, the version tested, which has, in effect, a

---

Comparisons

MAXIMUM SPEED MPH
Triumph Dolomite
 Sprint (o/d)............(£2,937) 115
Toyota Celica GT..........(£2,345) 113
Ford RS1800 Custom......**(£2,990) 111**
Renault 17 Gordini........(£2,994) 111
Audi 80GT ....(£2,476) 106

0–60 MPH, SEC
Triumph Dolomite Sprint (o/d) 8.7
Ford RS1800 Custom **9.0**
Toyota Celica GT 9.3
Audi 80GT 9.5
Renault 17 Gordini 9.8

STANDING ¼-MILE, SEC
Triumph Dolomite Sprint (o/d)......16.7
Ford RS1800 Custom...........**16.9**
Toyota Celica GT 17.1
Audi 80GT 17.2
Renault 17 Gordini 17.4

OVERALL MPG
Toyota Celica GT.................29.8
Audi 80GT 29.5
Ford RS1800 Custom **26.5**
Renault 17 Gordini 25.2
Triumph Dolomite Sprint (o/d)......23.6

Performance

ACCELERATION SECONDS

True speed mph	Time in Secs	Car Speedo mph
30	2.9	32
40	4.7	41
50	6.6	51
60	9.0	62
70	12.4	72
80	16.6	83
90	22.0	94
100	32.9	105

Standing ¼-mile
16.9sec 81 mph

Standing kilometre
31.4sec 98 mph

Mileage recorder:
2.6 per cent over-reading

GEAR RATIOS AND TIME IN SEC

mph	Top (3.54)	3rd (4.46)	2nd (6.41)
10–30	—	7.1	4.6
20–40	8.8	6.6	3.9
30–50	8.2	6.2	3.9
40–60	8.4	6.2	4.4
50–70	8.9	6.6	5.6
60–80	9.6	7.8	—
70–90	11.8	10.3	—
80–100	17.2	—	—

GEARING
(with 175/70HR13in. tyres)
Top ....18.5 mph per 1,000 rpm
3rd ....14.7 mph per 1,000 rpm
2nd ....10.2 mph per 1,000 rpm
1st ....5.5 mph per 1,000 rpm

MAXIMUM SPEEDS

Gear	mph	kph	rpm
O.D. Top (mean)	111	179	6,000
(best)	114	184	6,150
3rd	96	155	6,500
2nd	66	106	6,500
1st	36	58	6,500

BRAKES
FADE (from 70 mph in neutral)
Pedal load for 0.5g stops in lb

1	30	6	40
2	30–25–30	7	40
3	30–35	8	40–45
4	30–35	9	40–45
5	35–40	10	40–45

RESPONSE (from 30 mph in neutral)

Load	g	Distance
20lb	0.25	120ft
40lb	0.55	55ft
60lb	0.90	33.4ft
75lb	1.00	30.1ft
Handbrake	0.35	86ft
Max Gradient	1 in 4	

CLUTCH
Pedal 32lb and 4¾in.

Consumption

FUEL
(At constant speed – mpg)
30 mph....................46.0
40 mph....................44.0
50 mph....................41.2
60 mph....................36.0
70 mph....................30.8
80 mph....................27.0
90 mph....................22.2
100 mph...................18.9

Typical mpg 28 (10.1 litres/100km)
Calculated (DIN) mpg 28
 (10.1 litres/100km)
Overall mpg 26.5 (10.7 litres/100km)
Grade of fuel Premium, 4-star (min 98RM)

OIL
Consumption (20W/50) Negligible

TEST CONDITIONS:
Weather: Clear and dry
Wind: 5–15 mph
Temperature: 14.5deg C (58deg F)
Barometer: 29.9in. Hg
Humidity: 60 per cent
Surface: Dry concrete and asphalt
Test distance 700 miles

Figures taken by our own staff at the Motor Industry Research Association proving ground at Nuneaton.

All Autocar test results are subject to world copyright and may not be reproduced in whole or in part without the Editor's written permission.

Dimensions

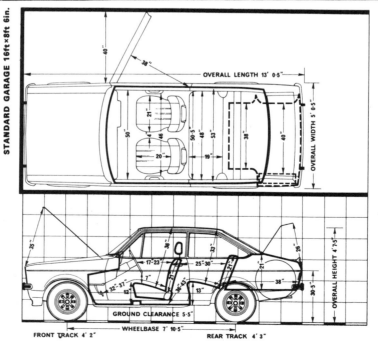

TURNING CIRCLES:
Between kerbs
L, 31ft 6in.; R, 31ft 10in.
Between walls
L, 32ft 9in.; R, 33ft 2in.
Steering wheel turns, lock to lock 3

WEIGHT:
Kerb Weight 18cwt (2,016lb–915kg)
(with oil, water and half full fuel tank)
Distribution, per cent
F, 53; R, 47
Laden as tested:
21¼cwt (2,380lb–1,080kg)

custom pack including all the items of trim and comfort that the keen road-only driver would want. These items include the comfortable bucket front seats, inertia reel seat belts, vinyl roof, the sensible centre console as well as the outward visual identifying treatment that has become a questionable hallmark of the highest-performance Escort models.

Performance and economy

Fortunately, in the RS1800, it is possible to have performance with quite reasonable economy. As well as its ability to accelerate from rest to 60 mph in just 9sec, and to cover a standing ¼-mile in 16·9sec, the RS gave an overall fuel consumption of 26·5 mpg and on several occasions, brim-to-brim figures approaching 30 mpg were recorded. This is a great improvement on the previous car whose overall consumption worked out at only 21·5 mpg. Such things are difficult to quantify, but it may just be that the new car's added refinement and quietness gave less encouragement to try hard *all* the time which was certainly the case with the earlier car. Proof of the valuable added torque is the improvement in the top gear acceleration figures. In the middle range, the smaller-engined car certainly has the edge, however, and in the region from 30 to 80 mph it was quicker in third gear than its successor.

When taking the acceleration figures through the gears, the feeling on the road that too great a gap exists between first and second gear is confirmed. While

Specification

Ford Escort RS1800

FRONT ENGINE, REAR-WHEEL DRIVE

ENGINE
Cylinders	4, in-line
Main bearings	5
Cooling system	Water; pump, fan, thermostat
Bore	86·75mm (3·42in.)
Stroke	77·62mm (3·06in.)
Displacement	1,845 c.c. (111·9 cu. in.)
Valve gear	Belt-driven twin ohc, bucket operation of valves
Compression ratio	9·0 to 1. Min octane rating: 98RM
Carburettor	Weber 32/36 DGAV
Fuel pump	AC Mechanical
Oil filter	Full-flow, renewable element
Max power	115 bhp (DIN) at 6,000 rpm
Max torque	120 lb. ft. (DIN) at 4,000 rpm

TRANSMISSION
Clutch	Sdp; diaphragm spring, cable operation, 8·5in. dia
Gearbox	Manual; 4-speed all synchromesh single rail
Gear ratios	Top 1·00
	Third 1·26
	Second 1·81
	First 3·36
	Reverse 3·37
Final drive	Hypoid bevel; 3·54 to 1
Mph at 1,000 rpm in top gear	18·5

CHASSIS and BODY
Construction	Unitary in steel

SUSPENSION
Front	Independent; MacPherson struts, coil springs, anti-roll bar
Rear	Live axle, half elliptic leaf springs, radius rods, telescopic dampers

STEERING
Type	Rack and pinion
Wheel dia	14in.

BRAKES
Make and type	Girling, discs front, drum rear, divided circuit, self-adjusting rear brakes
Servo	Girling vacuum
Dimensions	F 9·63in. dia
	R 9·0in. dia, 1·75in. wide shoes
Swept area	F 190 sq. in., R 96 sq. in.
	Total 286 sq. in. (269 sq. in./ton laden)

WHEELS
Type	Steel, ventilated disc 5½in. J wide rim
Tyres – make	Pirelli CN36
– type	Radial ply tubeless
– size	175/70HR13in.

EQUIPMENT
Battery	12 Volt 55 Ah.
Alternator	45 amp a.c.
Headlamps	Tungsten-halogen, 110/100 watt (total)
Reversing lamp	Standard
Electric fuses	7
Screen wipers	Two-speed continuous, two-speed intermittent
Screen washer	Standard, fingertip stalk operated
Interior heater	Standard, air-blending
Heated backlight	Standard
Safety belts	Standard, inertia reel
Interior trim	Cloth seats, pvc headlining
Floor covering	Carpet
Jack	Screw pillar
Jacking points	One each side
Windscreen	Laminated
Underbody protection	Zinc phosphate primer. Pvc coating in wheel arches

MAINTENANCE
Fuel tank	9 Imp gallons (41 litres)
Cooling system	12·5 pints (inc heater)
Engine sump	7·2 pints (4·1 litres)
	SAE 20W/50. Change oil every 6,000 miles. Change filter every 6,000 miles
Gearbox and Overdrive	2·4 pints. SAE 80EP. Check every 6,000 miles
Final drive	2·4 pints. SAE 90EP. Check every 6,000 miles
Grease	No points
Valve clearance	Inlet 0·005–0·007in. (cold) Exhaust 0·006–0·008in. (cold)
Contact breaker	0·025in. gap; 38–40deg dwell
Ignition timing	4deg BTDC (static)
Spark plug	Type: Motorcraft AGR 12. Gap 0·025in.
Tyre pressures	F 22; R 22 psi (normal driving)
Max payload	1,058lb (481kg)

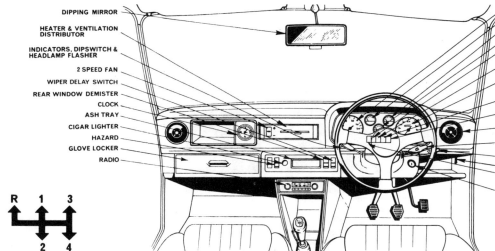

DIPPING MIRROR
HEATER & VENTILATION DISTRIBUTOR
INDICATORS, DIPSWITCH & HEADLAMP FLASHER
2 SPEED FAN
WIPER DELAY SWITCH
REAR WINDOW DEMISTER
CLOCK
ASH TRAY
CIGAR LIGHTER
HAZARD
GLOVE LOCKER
RADIO

REV COUNTER
FUEL GAUGE
WATER TEMPERATURE GAUGE
OIL PRESSURE GAUGE
OIL PRESSURE WARNING LIGHT
MAIN BEAM TELL-TALE
SPEEDOMETER
IGNITION LIGHT
INDICATOR TELL-TALE
SWIVELLING VENTILATOR
LAMPS
WIPERS & SCREENWASH
BONNET RELEASE
INDICATOR TELL-TALE
IGNITION STARTER & STEERING LOCK

R 1 3
2 4

Servicing

	6,000 miles	18,000 miles	36,000 miles
Time Allowed (hours)	3·6	3·8	4·8
Cost at £4.30 per hour	£15.48	£16.34	£20.64
Engine oil	£2.40	£2.40	£2.40
Oil Filter	£2.63	£2.63	£2.63
Air Filter	—	£2.46	£2.46
Contact Breaker Points	£0.58	£0.58	£0.58
Sparking Plugs	£2.38	£2.38	£2.38
Total Cost:	£23.47	£26.79	£31.09

Routine Replacements:	Time hours	Labour	Spares	TOTAL
Brake Pads – Front (2 wheels)	0·6	£2.58	N/A	—
Brake Shoes – Rear (2 wheels)	1·2	£5.16	N/A	—
Exhaust System	0·7	£3.01	N/A	£24.43
Clutch (centre + driven plate)	2·3	£9.89	£14.54	£24.43
Dampers – Front (pair)	1·5	£6.45	N/A	—
Dampers – Rear (pair)	1·8	£7.74	N/A	—
Replace Half Shaft	0·5	£2.15	N/A	—
Replace Alternator	0·5	£2.15	N/A	—
Replace Starter	0·5	£2.15	£19.21	£21.36

Ford Escort RS1800

the old car was barely capable of 60 mph in 2nd, the new car can reach no less than 66 mph at the (unmarked) maximum recommended reading of 6,500 rpm on the clear rev counter. Compensation for this is found in the ideal relationship of the top three gears that give steadily reducing rev drops with each upward change and permit the right choice of gear to be made for any medium or high speed corner.

An undoubted contributor to the improved economy of the new car is its higher gearing compared with the RS1600. In top gear, the latter gave 17·7 mph per 1,000 rpm while the RS1800 gives 18·5. Apart from reducing engine speed when cruising, this means the maximum speed exactly coincides with the maximum power output – in contrast to the RS1600 which was unable to reach its higher power peak in top gear. One could, of course dwell for ever on the performance of which the car is capable, even in standard form, and quite considerable further power increases are possible at reasonable cost. Over 200 bhp is available with reliability from this unit and surprisingly, even at such high specific outputs, the engine remains docile.

Roadholding, handling and ride

Where the original RS1600 needed driving all the time, the new car is much more relaxing at all speeds. Negative camber on the front wheels and radius arms that were too short meant that the RS1600 lacked natural stability and was instantly affected by camber and road surface changes. By contrast, the new car is much more-forgiving of any changes in road surface and is markedly better in a sidewind.

While it required an experienced and forceful driver to extract the best from the natural

Above: Although the facia is similar to other Escorts, there are three small central gauges instead of the large combined one, and a small pocket in front of the passenger, by the clock

Below: The cloth trimmed front seats are deeply shaped to hold their occupants; the catch on the side allows them to tip forward. The steering wheel had a padded, leather trimmed rim

oversteering tendencies of the RS1600, the new car has rather softer rear suspension and increased roll stiffness at the front which results in a change to predictable understeer nearly all the time. Admittedly, although at low speeds on slippery surfaces it is still possible to hang the tail out, under most conditions, the changes in suspension settings allow the nose to be pushed wide by the application of as much power as space and courage permit. Lifting off the accelerator in mid-corner brings about a gentle tightening of line at the front of the car with no tendency for the rear of the car to run wide. However, while the characteristics are now inherently safer and more predictable, it is much less easy to be tidy when cornering hard and one finds it necessary to work quite hard to get the best from the car. Contributors here are the Pirelli Cinturato CN36 tyres whose astonishing grip in wet or dry conditions does mean that the car is difficult to slide at will. As well as giving good grip in cornering, these tyres also grip well under acceleration braking. It was only possible to get the car away from rest with the right amount of wheelspin by quite brutal treatment of the clutch and when recording the maximum braking of 1g, there was no trace of wheel-locking.

Brakes

The brakes impressed under all the tests through which they were put. No trace of fade was experienced either on the road or in the accelerated fade test. Immediately after this test, the brakes proved able to match their optimum retardation when cold with exactly the same pedal pressure – the sort of consistency that inspires great confidence on the road. Only 75lb pressure was needed to give 1g optimum stopping and only a little over half this gave 0·5g check braking – ideal response. The self-adjusting rear drums helped the handbrake to give 0·35g emergency braking on its own although it

The RS1800 badge and side striping are painted on, and the rear spoiler is made from a flexible high-density foam, with a smooth, shiny surface. Special pressed steel wheels are fitted. The aerodynamic aids front and rear can be seen clearly

could not hold the car on a 1-in-3 slope as the rear wheels were dragged downhill. Facing up the slope, the brake held well and a restart was successfully made despite the high bottom gear.

Comfort and fittings

Ford's award-winning facia panel gives the driver a matchless and glare-free view of the comprehensive instrumentation, the only omission on which is the absence of kph markings on the speedometer. The instruments are all clearly viewed through the thick leather-rimmed steering wheel whose high-mounted position is a disadvantage only to very short drivers. Average and tall drivers find the driving position ideal with all controls in easy reach and a pedal layout that allows comfortable heel-and-toe operation.

The gearbox is a joy to use with short precise movements in a narrow gate, and reverse a simple pushdown-out to the left-forward action. The gearbox and its ratios are only used in the RS1800 in this country, the box being of German manufacture.

The Custom Escort RS has bucket seats with fabric trimming of the wearing surfaces as standard. The seats are comfortable and adjust comprehensively but like all bucket seats, they are a compromise. Slim or short drivers may lack lateral support since even the biggest of drivers are catered for by the width of the seat backs between the wrap-round side support sections. Built into the tops of the front seats are head restraints, trimmed to match the fabric portions of the seats themselves. In the rear of the car, the fabric facings are repeated and the seats themselves are comfortable. There is, however, too little kneeroom and the driver and his rear seat passengers have to compromise over the space available.

The custom pack includes good stowage space; as well as the central console, there are map pockets on the backs of the front seats.

Living with the Escort RS1800

The new Escort shape allows the driver a more commanding view all round than in the earlier car. The rear pillars, especially, are narrower and the car is definitely easier to drive in traffic. The two-speed windscreen wipers clear the screen effectively and provide intermittent wiping by a facia-mounted switch which effectively gives two-speed delay wiping.

Following recent Ford trends, the indicator stalk is now on the left, continental-style, while the controls for the lights and wipers are on stalks to the right of the wheel. A grumble that we have always had with

Above: The engine is not very exciting to look at, with the carburettor air cleaner covering the carburettor and distributor

Below: The spare wheel stows away neatly in the left-hand wheel arch. The boot space is good, but the lid has a key-only lock

this system remains in that it is all too easy to flick the lights switch to an "on" position without removing the ignition key without noticing that this has been done. Either the switch should have the "off" position at the top or the movement of the lights stalk itself should be more definite.

At night, the halogen light units give a splendid throw of light up the road on main beam and a carefully-controlled beam pattern when dipped.

The controls for the heater are positioned in the centre of the facia where they are within reach of both driver and front seat passenger. They are simplicity itself to operate with just

an unintentionally speed-sensitive upper temperature control and a lower distribution slide lever. To their left is a switch whose up and down movement controls a silent low speed for the fan, and a rather noisy fast speed. Output from the fan on its highest speed is good and it

can be used to boost the two fresh air vents at the extremity of the facia as well as the heater outlets. Further over on the facia towards the passenger is a small open facia pocket which has a clock built into its right-hand side. Beneath this pocket is a glove box whose lid cannot be locked but which is strongly supported in the open position.

The boot on the new version of the Escort is more useful than that of the superseded model thanks to a more regular shape that has the spare wheel stowed vertically in the left wheel arch, in contrast to the earlier RS1600 which had the wheel lying flat in the centre of the floor. The tool-kit of jack and wheelbrace is accommodated behind the retaining strap for the spare wheel.

The changes in the induction arrangement have done little to aid access beneath the bonnet. The two twin-choke Webers that previously prevented access to the distributor have been replaced by a massive air cleaner that presents the same problem. However, all other items are easy to get at.

Conclusion

In conclusion, one could not do better than to echo the comments that closed the very first test of the Escort RS. It *is* hard to think of a sporty driver that would not be delighted by the performance and appeal of the RS1800, but equally hard to see how very many will justify paying quite so much money for the privilege. Admittedly, this RS is more readily identifiable from the rest of the Escort tribe than its predecessor but as this has been accomplished in a rather gaudy way, it may attract the attention of the wrong sort of people.

If, however, you have the money to afford it, there is no doubt that the RS1800 has that rare dash of vigour and persistent demand to be driven quickly that marks out the true sports car, whether the roof comes off or not.

With the added refinement that is apparent in the latest model, the appeal has certainly been widened without loss of character and with the changes to the engine, economy has been added to the appeal. Thank you, Mr Ford, for continuing to supply the needs of those who do not think that the family car should just be a means of getting from A to B. □

MANUFACTURER:
Ford Motor Company Limited, Warley, Essex

PRICES		Total on the Road (exc	
Basic (Custom model)	£2,527.50	insurance)	£3,036.68
Special Car Tax	£210.63	Insurance	Group 7
VAT	£219.05	EXTRAS (inc VAT)	
Total (in GB)	£2,957.18	Push-button radio*	£66.65
Seat Belts	(standard)	Vinyl roof*	£31.02
Licence	£40.00	*Fitted to test car	
Delivery charge (London)	£33.00	TOTAL AS TESTED ON	
Number plates	£6.50	THE ROAD	£3,134.35

The 1600 Sport — Mexico replacement — shares the new body shell and offers greater visibility and comfort.

An all-round improved "Mexico"

Having tried all the various versions of the new Ford Escort in the Algarve, I have now lived with the 1600 Sport for a week in England. In the Escort range of some 22 models, the 1100 is the economy or fleet car, the 1300, in standard or GT form, is perhaps the best all-rounder, and the 1600 Sport is directed towards the more performance-conscious driver, having greater power and more sporting handling at the expense of a harder ride.

In effect, the car replaces the Mexico, which was tremendous fun when regarded as a competition-type car but not really acceptable for everyday motoring. The Ford engineers have done an immense amount of work on the body booming problem and the suspension, though harder than that of the other Escorts, does not have the spine-jarring firmness of the Mexico. It shares the new body shell, having a greater window area and hence a better all-round view for the driver, with the less powerful models. The headlights are reinforced with a pair of spotlights, which considerably improve the spread of light but are likely to suffer in any minor contretemps.

As in the earlier Escorts, the design is completely conventional, with MacPherson front suspension and a live axle behind. The new Ford single-rail gearbox is used and the engine has the same bore as the 1300, with a crankshaft having a longer throat. Fords' own automatic transmission may be specified, but the test car had the excellent manual box.

The front seats are comfortable and give good lateral location. Though the Escort is a small car, the rear passengers have more knee and head room than would be expected. The driving position is excellent, unless one is very tall, the controls being well placed, and the pedals invite heel-and-toe. The stalks under the steering wheel seem to differ from those of other cars — at first I tended to wipe the screen when I wished to signal a turn. However, I soon got things sorted out. The instruments are well placed and easily read. The interior of the test car was neatly trimmed in black, with an off-white roof that would not show the dirt. The interior door cappings repeated the external paint colour, but I would prefer a wooden or fabric covering, if it were my car, the brilliant red looking odd inside.

The engine starts at once on the automatic choke and does not tend to race or stall while warming up. In contrast, it idles rather unevenly, which can become irksome at the traffic lights. Once on the move, its behaviour is impeccable, and its low speed torque is excellent, which encourages top-gear driving in the interest of fuel economy. Its manners are far better than those of previous Ford engines, during the relatively low speed driving which we are forced to endure. After a long period of pottering, the first speed burst may reveal a tendency to misfire at around 6000 rpm, but the engine soon clears itself.

The maximum speed is almost exactly 100 mph, which is highly satisfactory. Though the gear ratios are not particularly close, the engine's capacity for high revs allows 60 and 80 mph to be exceeded on second and third gears respectively. The car feels very lively and the acceleration figures, aided by the quick gearchange, are excellent.

Though the engine has what one might call an efficient sound, it is not objectionally noisy, even when quite hard pressed. The reduction in booming of the body panels is remarkable and though there is still an incipient boom period as one passes through the 3000 rpm band on the over-run, the painful booming at high cruising speeds has been eliminated. Road and wind noises have also been greatly reduced; the Escort is still not the most silent of cars but the greater refinement is very impressive, nevertheless.

Perhaps the car does not feel quite such a racer as the Mexico did, but it certainly has improved stability in a side wind. If very sharp corners are taken with a lot of power on, the inside rear wheel tends to spin rather easily. Though this would be a nuisance on a competition car, it is of little consequence for normal road driving. The one exception is the ascent of mountain passes with

The Sport can be identified from behind only by its matt-black bumpers and over-riders.

Road test

Particular attention has been paid to prevention of body-boom. Below: functional dashboard.

hairpin bends, when a fast climb might be spoilt by wheelspin. I drove the car flat out up a straight but bumpy hill and though the back axle appeared to be bouncing a good deal, the traction was surprisingly good. In general, the handling inspires confidence and the cornering power is quite high.

The ride is still fairly hard — the Sport has an extra spring leaf compared with other Escorts —

Latest versions of the 1.6 Kent series engine show impeccable behaviour.

but the car levels-out nicely on fast roads. On country lanes, the occupants are shaken about a good deal, and over really bad surfaces one just has to grin and bear it, but at least it is a plain up-and-down movement without pitching. On the better British roads, the ride is quite comfortable though not luxurious.

As regards fuel economy, the 1600 Sport is well up to the average in its class. The man who doesn't

really hurry should safely attain 30 mpg or a little more. Even the driver who risks a bit of 100 mph motoring occasionally should achieve 27 mpg or so. The car seems well engineered, the only faults on the test vehicle being a door that had to be slammed really hard and a piece of bright metal decoration that peeled off the rain gutter and made an alarming noise. The latest Escort, in 1600 Sport form, is an economical small car of remarkably high performance.

SPECIFICATION AND PERFORMANCE DATA

Car Tested: Ford Escort 1600 Sport 2-door saloon, price £1,860 including car tax and VAT.
Engine: Four-cylinder 80.98 x 77.62mm (1598cc). Compression ratio 9 to 1. 84 bhp DIN at 5500 rpm. Pushrod-operated overhead-valves. Weber twin-choke downdraught carburetter.
Transmission: Single dry plate clutch. 4-speed synchromesh gearbox with central change, ratios 1.0, 1.418, 1.995, and 3.337 to 1. Hypoid rear axle, ratio 3.54 to 1.
Chassis: Combined steel body and chassis. MacPherson independent front suspension. Rack and pinion steering. Live rear axle on semi-elliptic springs. Anti-roll bars front and rear. Servo-assisted dual-circuit disc/drum brakes. Pressed-steel sport wheels fitted 175/70SR-13 tyres.
Equipment: 12-volt lighting and starting. Speedometer. Rev-counter. Water temperature and fuel gauges. Heating, demisting, and ventilation system with heated rear window. Flashing direction indicators with hazard warning. Reversing lights. Cigar lighter.
Dimensions: Wheelbase 7ft 10.5ins. Track 4ft 2ins/4ft 3ins. Overall length 13ft 0.5in. Width 5ft 0.5in. Weight 1987lbs.
Performance: Maximum speed 100 mph. Speeds in gears: Third 85 mph, second 62 mph, first 40 mph. Standing quarter-mile 17.8s. Acceleration: 0-30 mph 3.4s, 0-50 mph 7.5s, 0-60 mph 10.2s, 0-80 mph 21.0s, 0-90 mph 37.5s.
Fuel consumption: 27 to 32 mpg.

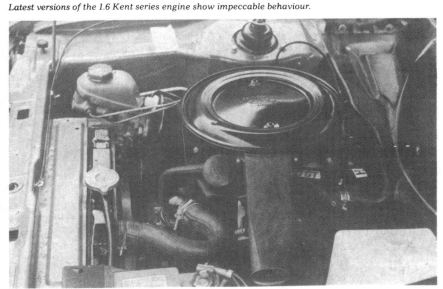

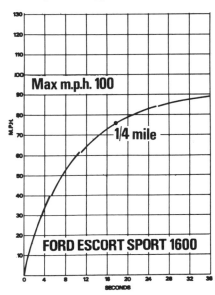

Max m.p.h. 100

1/4 mile

FORD ESCORT SPORT 1600

Testing the ESCORT II/RS1800...

RS-REFINED

ABOVE: The RS1800 comes as a two-door, with luxury trim which includes special wheels and rear spoiler. LEFT: The dash layout is identical to the base-line cars, except for tacho and some additional gauges. Plus there's a sporty steering wheel, special seats and centre console. FAR RIGHT: RS1600 — this is the car the RS1800 replaces. The 1600 and a number of other special models carried off a great many victories for FordSport teams around the world. Correspondent Andrews says the RS1800 is a 'boulevarde special' compared to the old 1600.

RIGHT: This is a specially tricked-up version to show what the car looks like in rally trim. After early successes in British rallies Ford expects big things of the RS1800 in competition.

THE ASSIGNMENT seemed straight-forward enough — just drive and compare the recently released Escort RS 1800 to the RS 1600, its predecessor. But actually it became more — it became a report on a breed of car that is soon to vanish due to legislation and assorted ecological problems. The report had to be relative in terms of today's thinking, and with this in mind I felt need to be more critical of the new car than perhaps I would have been a year ago.

When the RS 1600 was released over five years ago it was a real fireball sock-it-to-me mini road burner. Today with new values (and price structures), its lack of refinement couldn't really be justified because new cars are being released that have that blistering performance with acceptable road manners. "Horror!", cry the enthusiasts bemoaning the gradual disappearance of real drivers' cars. But we have to be realists — the writing *is* on the wall. Ford has even finally realised this and decided to update its high performing bombshell. In fact one gathers that the only reason Ford still makes the RS model is so it can

homologate its tweaked (up to 220 BHP) versions for people like Dave Brodie (now into Capris) and Roger Clark — who is already successfully campaigning his BDA.

Well the new car is quite frankly a disappointment — this new kid on the block is actually the same old recipe dressed-up in a new wrapper. It's the direct development of the BDA 1600 MK II (with the alloy block and head) which was the road-going version of the Cosworth FVA F2 engine. Why disappointing? Well, to answer this best, refer to the chart overleaf. In a straight comparison with other competitive models the RS 1800 doesn't fare well at all. Where once there was no direct equivalent now there are too many — and the old recipe just doesn't cut the mustard any more! By end of 1971 the RS 1600 cost £stg1517 — less than four years later it nearly doubles its price to £stg2900.

Some things have changed noticeably in that time. Where as once you had to be a really avid sports car driver to enjoy the RS 1600, today its revitalised brother is more civilised — but not much! The old model was

probably the most uncompromising product ever to be publicly offered by a major manufacturer. Yet for all its rip-snorting hypertension and temperament the car was still a good basic platform for serious racers to work on. It was too tame to race off the showroom floor yet not really suitable for modern traffic conditions.

Today the RS 1800 is even harder to justify when it isn't even the quickest in its class! In fact unless it's bought to build into your special-stage rally supercar (which it does become) it becomes superfluous even in Ford's own lineup as the newly released Capri 'S' 3000 GT out-performs it for more than £stg400 less money — and the Escort still hasn't the looks or the pose value of the all-black hatch-back V6.

So where does it leave the RS 1800? More sophisticated cars like the Lancia Beta Coupe, Alfetta 180C, Fiat 124, R17 Gordini and Scirocco either outperform it or underprice it — or both! And dig the Celica GT price tag in UK. Twin cams, 5-speed box et al, need I go on ... In face even though the Citroen CX2000 is in a different category I could not resist the price

SPEEDSTER, OR RALLY SPECIAL?

HOT BEHIND the release of the 'cooking' Escort II comes the sporty RS1800 version, and Ford have delivered it into a highly competitive market area up against cars like the Scirocco, Alfasud Ti and Lancia Beta. How does it shape up? Our roving European correspondent Paul Andrews says only just ...

ESCORT II/RS1800

comparison by listing it — a mere £stg205 more.

But enough diversions, most people buy the RS 1800 for its performance so let's investigate the powerplant and how it motivates. It has an alloy block and head whereas the original RS 1600 had an iron block. The old bore and stroke was 80.98 x 77.62 now it's 86.75 x 77.62 mm for 1840cc. The dual 40 DCOEs have been replaced by one dual choke (progressive) 32/36 DCAV Weber which accounts for 86kW at 6500, down 3.7kW on the old car. Torque is up though with 163Nm at 4000rpm — the RS 1600 and 150Nm at 4500. All this has made the engine more civilised but taken away the old car's punch, as the 1800 suffocates at 6000 rpm sounding very asthmatic and coarse. Down low it shines, yet neither car is still happy in top gear at less than 50-60km/h.

The old car was meant to be blasted around, in high revs and on the cam.

The new car with the changes, plus 30km/h per 1000rpm top gearing (old car was 27.5) and extra weight has lost its sparkle. The 1800 also has a lower compression — down to 9:1, which actually helps cold weather starts and staying in tune. One thing is for sure though, and that is you can pick the heritage of the reskinned car. All one has to do is open the bonnet to see the same old inner panels — and it still is not self-suporting on a £stg3000 car!

Engine access to the ancillaries is worse than before even though the dual Weber manifold is gone — because the car now has a big air cleaner (and silencer) complete with temperature controlled intake that limits work space.

The handling has had a little attention, but its not really 1975 stuff. The suspension is specially stiffened with Armstrong competition struts at front and Girling gas-filled dampers and radius arms at back. This is the basic difference between your new RS 1800 and 1600 sport models. Now with the South Ockendon operation (AVO) closed the RS model goes into mainstream production at Halewood. The rack and pinion steering has always been good and accurate — though it now hasn't the old kickback problem. Handling is fairly precise and predictable but it didn't appeal to me, having been spoilt on cars like the Alfasud Ti — a car that has phenomenal roadholding but not at the expense of its ride characteristics. The old RS1600 was a "jaw-breaker", and the new car isn't a great deal better!

The Pirelli CN36 175/70 x 13 on wide rims obviously have something to do with its attitudes for they are particularly adhesive and at slow speeds hide the understeer. Only once near the limits can you tell because you are working! The nose runs wide and will break away first, back off and you're in business again but watch the wet roads and roundabouts. Whereas the old car virtually enticed you to rush around "hanging the tail out", displaying ragged-edge antics for cornering thrills, the RS 1800 is not as quick but does its job with less fuss until you reach its limits.

Then it goes messy and you have to act seriously or it can become quite unenjoyable, particularly if, as in Australia, owners basically are used to cars that require opposite lock. The stability on the open road is much better than the RS 1600 as it's not

affected by crosswinds or surface irregularities — possibly an aerodynamic factor as one car is very rounded, the other rather square and stiff. Ford engineers have made the rear suspension softer and increased the roll stiffness at the front which has resulted in a calculated understeer nearly all the time. The old car went from mild understeer to controlled oversteer; — definitely hairy but most rewarding if that's your bag (as it used to be mine!)

The gearbox is the German-built single-rail shift with shot-peened internals (this box, minus the 'nicer' ratios is used on the Mustang II and Pinto). The RS 1800 through the gears gets 58-106-153—182km/h — not as close as the older version, which peaked second at 93km/h and third around 145km/h for a smoother, more correct flow pattern. Both boxes, nevertheless, are fun to use with positive action, although the old one was a little smoother and the syncros unbeatable.

The brakes still have the same surface area but they work much better (or seem to) and the pressure is definitely less. The Pirellis have a lot to do with the braking capacity, which uplifts the Escort to an excellent rating. Other tests at MIRA have shown 1g deceleration readings with no fade after up to 20 stops from speed with less than five percent pressure increase. That's no comparison for the RS 1600, which needed a heavy, size-thirteen boot. The old car needed the four-wheel-disc kit that was available, or twin boosters.

Once inside the car some features become immediately obvious — the airy feeling with 23percent more glass and a lower beltline and slimmer pillars

Car	Cost	C.C.	kW	G/box	Top speed	0-100 time	400M	mpg	length (cm)	width (cm)	boot (cu.ft.)	Power to weight ratio (kg/kW)
1971 RS 1600	£1517	1601	89.5	4	185	8.45	16.65	26-29	396	152	8.0	10.7
1975 RS 1800	£2990	1840	83.5	4	182	8.7	16.9	26-29	396	154	8.9	11.9
Lancia Beta Coupe	£2697	1756	82.8	5	190	9.0	17.2	25-30	401	166	9.5	12.9
Alfetta	£2970	1779	90.2	5	180	9.5	17.3	24-28	429	163	11.5	13.1
Capri 'S'	£2543	2994	103	4	198	8.4	16.5	20-25	427	169	7.2	12.5
Fiat 124 coupe	£2676	1756	85	5	179	9.2	17.6	26-31	411	167	6.8	13.1
Celica GT/S	£2345	1588	82	5	182	9.3	17.2	26-30	419	163	8.0	12.3
R17 Gordini	£2896	1605	80	5	180	9.8	17.5	27-32	427	163	11.0	14.2
Alfa 2000 GTV	£2999	1962	112	5	185	8.9	16.8	21-27	409	160	6.8	11.1
Dolomite sprint	£2937	1988	95	5	186	8.4	16.7	23-27	413	154	9.4	11.5
Vauxhall Firenza	£3048	2279	98	5	190	8.3	16.5	19-24	427	163	10.5	11.4
BMW 2002	£2999	1990	75	4	175	9.4	17.3	24-27	427	156	7.2	13.4
Datsun 240 K	£2678	2392	97	4	180	9.7	17.3	21-26	442	163	11.0	13.4
VW Scirocco	£2392	1971	64	4	175	9.4	17.5	27-34	389	162	9.0	13.4
Citroen CX 2000	£3195	1998	76	4	180	11.0	18.0	25-31	461	175	12.5	16.6

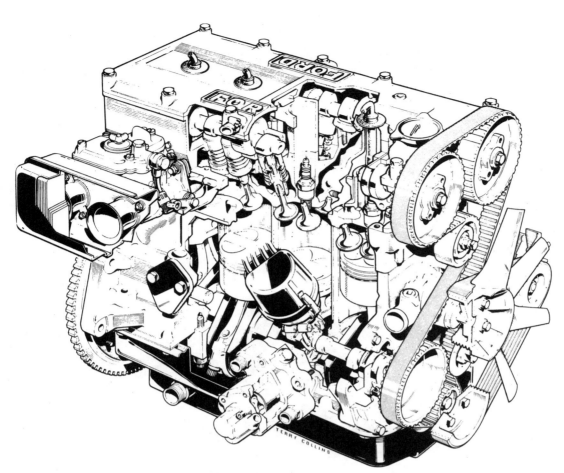

are all good features. The instrument panel is greatly improved but as yet hasn't a totally-integrated look — the ashtray and radio still seem like afterthoughts. The award-winning instrument cluster is fine, not suffering the RS 1600 problem of the steering wheel hiding the secondary instruments — yet the speedo doesn't have km/h readings!

The new interior is better — the RS 1600 was too basic. The buckets of the RS 1800, strangely, aren't as good as the *road* seats on the new 1600 Sport which have been put up for a design award (they deserve it). The RS Escorts always have been 2+2s due to the big rally seats. These recliners just take up too much room, losing the 2in space gain the reworked package (the base cars don't suffer this problem).

There is a lot of space in the cabin, but with cars like the Alfasud around it's not over-generous by comparison. These big front seats, for all their *looks* and size, actually are too low, lack underthigh support for very tall drivers, and the bolsters are too wide for slim drivers.

The RS 1800 now has the Cortina stalks on the column, a big improvement: left for headlight flasher and horn, right has washer/wiper and lights, but they are located too close to each other. Also the fiddly rocker switches of the old car have been re-sorted so that you don't grope in the dark for them!

On the road the new car is less noisy, but it's no LTD. Noise and Vibration Harshness (NVH) has been improved

over the RS 1600, which was like a fire-breathing dragon with a hangover. Wind noise grows at speed, particularly due, I think, to the seals at the top of the doors lifting. At 90mph the exhaust still drones enough so you can't hear the radio. The old car at this stage was like a summit conference at the UN between ermergent nations! The halogen lights are good, yet the car doesn't get the extra lights that are featured on the 1600 sport. The wipers are efficient in the rain, as is the demisting and heating. The heater's booster fan is still too noisy. The fresh air vents now actually do a good job — excellent compared to the old car.

Some random thoughts: finish and fittings of the RS 1800 are better — so they should be for the money and competition it's up against. The doors click shut now and general quality is improving — the quality controllers have a big responsibility. The car doesn't feel like £stg3000 worth — its not obviously luxuriously fitted, rather it's sensible — like a mid-range German car. The striping and spoilers don't really suit the boxy uninspired design that looks (so help me God) like it was styled in Tokyo or Osaka! The car will sell because it offends nobody but there's the easy way out, right? Good for sales, I guess. The bumpers I thought were especially treated chip-resistant epoxy painted, but I've seen Escorts with scratched bumpers already and it reveals chrome-plating underneath!

One sensible improvement is that the

new car only needs one key — not three; door, ignition, boot as before.

In summary, the car probably will sell well because it's a Ford, has a fairly good dealer service backup, parts aren't scarce, you can get a ton of 'trick' bits for it and build up a 200kW road, rally or circuit car and really it still is rapid — it just doesn't have that much breathing space to sit on its laurels! I guess people in UK don't really check around before buying. I was stunned after doing my research into the RS 1800's competitors as to the fantastic selection that's now available for similar money. Now, after this report — the figures in the chart speak for themselves — even though I enjoy blasting down narrow country lanes at sunrise holding good rpm in the gears, I can't honestly say that the Escort would be choice 'numero uno'. Best value would go to the Celica or Datsun. Best performance to the Lancia, Capri or Firenza, most fascinating to the CX 2000. And, one can't overlook the potential of cheaper cars like the Scirocco or Alfa Ti.

So where does this leave the new RS 1800? Only you, Mr Potential Buyer, can really answer this and what you decide will shape future trends. A lot can happen to an 'open' category in four years, Mr Ford, er, Mr Ford . . . I said. What's that? You might drop the RS model and introduce a turbo V6 Capri? Like the Broadspeed? . . . now you're talking. If you can't match the competition on technical sophistication you cover them in tyre smoke!

Front and rear spoilers are a distinctive feature of the new RS2000 – but do they serve any useful purpose?

ROAD IMPRESSIONS — FORD ESCORT RS2000

A sophisticated partner

Ford have a habit which must infuriate their competitors — that of always being just "right" in their marketing. It has never been more evident than with the Mk 2 Escort RS2000 which became available last Monday on the British market. It is a surprising improvement over the original two litre sohc Escort and a vehicle which must be particularly galling to Vauxhall, for it's just what the Firenza "Droop Snoot" *should* have been. Ford have taken the GM frontal treatment idea, as applied to a small car, and have successfully styled it into the conventional Escort. In the flesh it looks most purposeful — not in the slightest "grafted" even though it is constructed of glass reinforced plastic with a soft rubber grille, headlamp bezels and bumper rubbing strip. It is a five minute task with a starhead screwdriver to replace. Less successful, in this writer's opinion is the bootlid mounted spoiler which certainly does spoil. It would perhaps be a less offensive appendage if finished in the body colour and not boy-racer black. The car's external identification is completed with garish side striping and lettering plus the welcome continuation of the Mk 1 RS2000's four spoke alloy wheels. Altogether a pretty effective packaging job, rear spoiler aside, and aesthetically very pleasing at the front.

Superb seats and driving position leaves little to be desired.

of nooks and crannies for personal item stowage, an oddments bin, centre console, deep shelf and generously sized locker in all.

Significant improvements

Seating position comfort, coupled with Ford's universally accepted steering column stalk controls, the perfect gearchange and vastly improved vision of the Mk 2 shell all gives the driver a very cossetted existence and after a four hour 250 mile run, the longest drive that time permitted with this car, its driver felt perfectly capable of twice that stint again. Little things like properly effective wiper blades (Ford wipers always used to squeak over the screen annoyingly); a wiper delay and very acceptable full beam headlamp illumination all play an important part in keeping the driver's peace of mind and concentration. The most severe criticism from this area was a lack of graduation in the heating controls.

This car fits into the range between the competition orientated Mexico (rear spoiler, standard flat front) and the alloy engined RS1800. The RS2000 is the "smoothie" of the trio and is likely to attract amongst its clientele purchasers who would have run a personalised "tuned" car a few years ago and, hopefully, may also appeal to those who consider the British sports car to be a joke that should finally be laid to rest.

Within reason the RS2000 must be approaching the perfectly equipped small car inside. The quality of finish evident on an initial walkaround is also reinforced. This may have something to do with the fact that the RS2000 is produced on German Escort lines and also, more tangibly, to the extensive use of plastic injection moulded trim items of a remarkably accurate fit. An otherwise sombre all-black interior is lifted from the depths of depression by grey cloth seat facings — the front seats being a pair of the reclining items from the RS 1800 "Custom Pack" (of German manufacture) offering superb comfort and excellent location. On this two-door shelled car the inertia seat belts are attached well behind the shoulder and find their correct position and tension perfectly.

As would be expected of recent Ford practice, the instruments — speedometer with trip, rev counter, fuel, water, oil and clock are all positioned for a quick scan and are perfectly legible. Thankfully, a battery voltmeter (or battery ruined gauge) was not considered necessary. Bolstering the other, expected, top-range Escort trim items is a massive allocation

How times have changed when appraising a small high performance saloon car. When such vehicles were the domain of the tuners, the usual en-route grouses were normally of a much greater magnitude — such as engine explosion, suspension collapse, or that perennial "strong smell of petrol within car — untraceable".

On the road, this Escort really shows where the manufacturer has channelled his time and money. We have waited quite a number of years for Harley Copp's "NVH" programme to show through, but as all road impressions of the Mk 2 Escort have proved, this model is a significant improvement over its predecessor. On the RS2000 this assault against noise, vibration and harshness appears to have been particularly successful, bearing in mind this model's projected spheres of operation. The old Mexico and RS were something approaching purgatory the way they jolted and rattled down the road; this car is positively "soft" by comparison.

Happier handling

More surprisingly, not only is the ride improved and the noise level considerably reduced, it is also a better handling car. The limit of road holding may or may not compare, for it is only of the most superficial interest. A complete idiot can drive either the old or the new car quickly — such is the level of handling and failsafe characteristics — and a skilled driver can drive it very quickly. The difference is in how the car reacts. There is slightly more understeer evident, but this can be controlled or got rid of more predictably and certainly more smoothly. The competition-bred twitchiness has been reduced, wheel lifting and tramping is much less evident on twisty going and, all in all, the driver enjoys a much more peaceful time behind the wheel. By the time the old car was beginning to induce driver symptoms of buzzing head and aching arms, the new car is still a perfect partner. By no means is the car less "sporting"; in fact it is quite the reverse, being that bit more sophisticated with creature comforts and a little less point-and-squirt. Progress is less likely to attract adverse attention and is more likely to be safer, especially when tackling long distance cross-country routes.

Although it feels as though the sharp-edge of performance has been lost (this example had covered only 750 miles on collection); unfortunately there were no suitable opportunities over the Christmas period to take performance figures under controlled conditions and it may well be that the car is deceptive in this respect.

Braking, steering and the four speed single rail gearbox are all close to perfection and require no other comment except that a fifth gear could be put to good use — but not if it means putting-up

Distinctive front styling blends well. Twin headlamp installation is impressive.

with a ZF box. Going under the bonnet is quite a treat; the engine compartment is particularly well ordered, a large battery and high output charging taking care of the RS's comprehensive electrical systems. A large capacity windscreen fluid reservoir strategically positioned above the exhaust manifold is another welcome sight. The luggage compartment is similarly well-ordered, being nothing more than a large carpeted void, the accessible upright spare wheel naturally taking a little extra room due to its wide section but still leaving a more than adequate expanse.

Obvious restrictions

Where are the vices? There is not much to report. The most obvious single fault is inadequate rear seat legroom (dismal) with such, correct, emphasis being given to the front seat occupants. One rear seat passenger can be accommodated in a position bordering on claustrophobic, while a second passenger would have to be quite a good friend, for leg room behind the driver's seat (when

set for Mr Average) is, virtually, non-existent. Noise level variation between front and rear passengers heads is also quite marked, those unfortunates in the rear reporting an annoying exhaust resonance. Their visibility is also a little restricted by the front seat headrests. Price could also just about be considered a vice; there are many other enticing cars available for similar money, but no really direct competitors (£2,857, ex-works).

As a well made high performance small car, the RS2000 is likely to find quite a few friends. However, they might not turn out to be the expected rally or motor racing men.

Instead, for the young, high mileage, professional asked to choose from big four products for his company wheels, the RS2000 could be just the right tonic to prevent the onset of sedentary rot. For what it is, this car sets new standards and the competition, on present form, would find it hard going to catch up. It is, however, extremely unlikely that any will even bother.

IAN SADLER

Good — the front section is quite functional and lamps stay clean.

Not so good — rear spoiler causes number plate and rear lamps to opaque.

BRIEF TEST
FORD ESCORT RS 2000

Will Ford win where Vauxhall failed? Their "droop-snoot" has been a long time coming but was worth waiting for. It's not as economical as we'd expected and the ride is jittery, but there is refinement, excellent performance and taut handling. Good value if you want an entertaining four-seater

When the current Escort came on sale in early last year the well-known Ford Advanced Vehicle Operation mini-production line had been dismantled, though the engineering establishment itself remained. Where were the Rallyesport cars to be built and was the 1600 Sport a compromise replacement for the aging Mexico? These were just a few of the questions posed about Ford's range of hot Escorts.

The first teaser was answered by the arrival of the RS1800 (*Motor* w/e July 12, 1975) an updated, refined replacement for the old RS1600, which was assembled in the mainstream plant at Halewood, yet still bore the stamp of the FAVO engineers right down to its heavy-duty shell. But there were more changes in the pipeline, and by the time the long-awaited "droopsnoot" RS2000 made its British debut at Earls Court last October, the proposal had already been made to close FAVO's doors altogether, integrate the select band of engineers into other departments and to manufacture all Rallyesport cars—the RS1800

the RS2000 and the new Mexico announced only last week—in Germany initially. The Sport evidently was not a replacement for the old Mexico and happily once again there is a full complement of sporting Escorts from which to choose.

This test concerns the most luxurious model fitted with the biggest engine, the RS2000. Like the other two variants it starts life as a Sport, being pulled off the production line at the appropriate moment for the fitting of its bigger, ohc engine, the strengthened pick-up points, and all the other items that make up the package. Like them it is fitted with a pair of radius arms to locate the rear axle in place of the combined anti-roll bar location system usually provided.

Since those first Halewood RS1800s came into being, considerable work has been done on the suspension in an effort to improve both the ride and the handling. The resultant improvements are now enjoyed by all three cars which have the same spring and damper settings.

The RS2000 is better equipped

Above : familiar shell and familiar engine, but note strengthened strut mountings and new " 4 into 2 " exhaust manifold. Left : large ears on the seat-backs give good lateral support, but prevent sufficient tilt

Left : the minor instruments could give more information, but the main ones are excellent. Below : the driving position is good and the steering full of feel

than the less expensive Mexico in particular having reclining backrests for its rally-type front seats and in place of a bib spoiler it wears a large foam-filled plastic snout, whose wind-cheating shape adds a further 6in to the car's overall length. Contained within it are four very powerful Cibie lights.

Powering this latest RS2000 is an uprated version of the 2-litre Pinto engine currently available for the Capri, Cortina and Granada. By using a " four into two " exhaust manifold coupled to a big bore system with special absorption silencer, the output of the Escort unit has been pushed up from 99 bhp to a claimed 110 bhp. While this figure seems a shade optimistic, there is certainly evidence of more power than before. The top speed for instance is more than 108 mph (our mean figure was taken on a very windy day and is if anything on the conservative side) the previous car managing only 106.6. Outright acceleration is also decidedly brisk, 60 mph appearing in just 8.5 sec and 100 mph

Flexibility has always been a feature of the Pinto unit and top gear acceleration is equally impressive, the 30-50 mph increment taking 8.4 secs and 50-70 mph even less at 8.0 secs. With this new-found performance the RS2000 is hard on the heels of Triumph's Dolomite Sprint and together they make most rival cars appear decidedly pedestrian.

We found the RS2000 a first-time starter, one dab on the throttle being sufficient to set its automatic choke. The warm-up was uneventful even with the air-filter on its summer setting—to ensure a supply of cold air and hence the maximum output—and full power became available within a very few miles. Driving in town one soon becomes aware of a low speed booming, an exhaust-excited vibration that is evident in top gear until above about 28 mph. This is bad enough to discourage low-speed slogging and thus partially negate the excellent low-speed torque. At higher revs the engine is a little buzzy.

While the power does not come in at any particular engine speed

the unit really gets into its stride at about 2400 rpm. Maximum power occurs at 5500 rpm and we found little point in revving over 6000 rpm by which time the engine is still smooth but sounding a little strained. Apart from an occasional hesitation on the opening of the second choke of the Weber carburetter, the engine proved totally viceless.

Together with its Mexico stablemate, the previous RS2000 was the classic example of the way a large-capacity engine in a light bodyshell can offer an outstanding combination of high performance and excellent economy. The Pinto engine has proved particularly economical to run in the past, returning excellent overall figures in the Capri, Cortina and Granada. Whether Ford have upset the carburation with their new exhaust system remains to be seen (it is the only change to the engine), but the new car is nothing like as economical as its predecessor. In fact we tested two models—the first being rather down on power—and they returned almost identical figures, the mean of which is a disappointing 23.5 mpg. With a touring figure of 27.6 mpg (itself actually lower than our previous overall consumption value) there is little scope for much improvement if the performance is used. By careful avoidance of the second choke something nearer 30 mpg might be possible, but there is no doubt that in this respect the RS2000 has lost its edge over its competitors. With the modest 9 gallon tank its maximum range is now under 250 miles.

Utilising a special version of the Cortina 2000 single rail shift gearbox with a short-throw lever, the RS2000 enjoys Ford's flick-switch gearchange at its best. If one were to be pedantic, then a slight spring bias to the third/fourth plane would make life even easier, but in other respects this aspect of the box almost defies criticism. It is complemented by a light progressive clutch that encourages smooth changes even from the most ham-fister of drivers.

Unlike the competition-biased RS1800, the " droopsnoot " does not feature a special set of close ratios and first is on the low side, there being a detectable " hole " between it and second. We also felt a car with such excellent flexibility could pull a higher overall ratio. It would certainly lead to more relaxed cruising and perhaps better economy.

At the front, apart from a change in castor angle effected by fitting an anti-roll bar (which locates the wheels in the fore-and-aft-plane) of a slightly different shape the suspension is as on the Halewood RS1800s. For the rear, however, stiffer, flatter (by half an inch) leaves are used in order to make the handling more neutral. Their effect is immediately apparent too, the car being far better balanced than before ; lacking the determined understeer of the early 1800s or fairly sudden, if controllable,

oversteer of the old 2000. Now medium pace corners are taken with initial understeer followed by a gentle transition to oversteer. Vicious use of the throttle will induce an easily held tail-out posture in the wet, or harmless spinning of the inner wheel in the dry. Fast or slow the car remains fun to drive and very safe. The adhesion of the fat Pirelli tyres is excellent at all times.

Bumps, however, have an adverse affect on the stiff suspension causing the car to weave slightly on an undulating straight or even be thrown a little off line on a rough corner. At present the cars coming in from Germany are fitted with Fichtel and Sachs front struts and Boge dampers at the rear, as opposed to the Armstrong struts and Girling Monotube dampers found on the old Halewood cars. While they are said to give the same handling characteristics, the Boge units apparently give a rougher high-speed ride than the Girlings. Conversely the Girling units make the ride less comfortable at low speeds. Certainly as tested, the ride was always firm and did deteriorate slightly with speed — an unusual phenomenon. Though there is little of the crashing and banging sometimes associated with ultra-stiff suspension, most of our staff felt the ride was bordering on the uncomfortable.

With its competition background one would expect a sporting Escort to feature powerful, fade-free brakes. The RS2000 does. No matter how much punishment you subject them to, they come back for more, the pedal remaining firm and reassuring in its action. But there is a slight rearward bias so that premature lock-up of the back wheels will sometimes occur when braking hard on a bumpy surface. It seems Ford have solved their previous problems of " pulling," though, for even in a " hands-off " test the RS2000 would pull up square each time.

Apart from the small amount of additional boot space absorbed by the extra bulk of the 175/70 HR 13 spare tyre and its 5½J alloy wheel, the only other item affecting the accommodation of this hot Escort is the seating. Luxurious, fully-reclining rally-type bucket seats are standard on the RS2000 and while offering considerable comfort to front seat passengers, their thick backrests do steal legroom from those in the rear. The side bolsters that provide the excellent lateral support make entry to the rear more difficult still, because they prevent the backrest from being tilted forward very much.

Though we were unanimous in our praise for the heavily contoured seats, some felt that they gave too much thigh support for the driver — an unusual criticism, as it's usually the other way round — forcing the knees up unnecessarily. In other respects the driving position is hard to fault. The pedals are conveniently arranged, the neat RS steering wheel comfortable to grip and all important minor controls where they should be, on Ford's now

Together, the foam-filled plastic snout and flexible rear spoiler are said to give a significant reduction in drag. Note also the powerful set of Cibié lamps that point the way. Below: the stalk controls are good but the light and wiper ones should be swapped round

common tri-stalk system. Though good, we feel the layout would be further improved by the reversal of the light and wash/wipe stalks. At present the smaller lights stalk is hidden, cannot be found in a hurry, and can easily be knocked on by accident when removing the ignition key from its slot below.

In common with the Mexico and RS1800, the 2000 features a full array of instruments with circular water temperature, oil pressure and fuel gauges joining the award-winning speedometer and rev-counter in a neat binnacle ahead of the driver. While the minor gauges are skimpily marked, all the dials are easy to read day or night; for the latter they are illuminated by a subtle green glow.

All current Escorts enjoy a new-found level of refinement and this is certainly evident in the RS2000. Wind noise is well suppressed up to 100 mph when the tops of the doors start to bend outwards and their seal is broken. But road noise is quite prominent, there being considerable bump-thump on rough surfaces. The engine is quite quiet at its mid range, but excites the aforementioned boom low-down and begins to sound busy when revved. If driven moderately the 2000 is a quiet car overall, if pushed hard, as indeed it asks to be, it becomes considerably noisier.

If the performance is impressive for less than £3000 then so is the level of equipment. Inside one finds a passenger sun visor with vanity mirror, three grab handles, two coat hooks, reclining bucket seats with built-in head rests, three ashtrays, a clock, cigar lighter, a heated rear window, hazard warning lights, and the newly instituted intermittent wipe facility for the wipers.

Oddment space is well catered for, with a glove tray in the facia, a lidded box below it, another cubby ahead of the gearlever and a small parcel shelf above the driver's legs as well as one behind the rear seat.

Outside, low-profile tyres adorn

RS alloy wheels, and exceptionally powerful Cibie lights are housed in the impact-absorbing snout. On the bootlid is an equally flexible spoiler and inside it a carpet covers the floor of the illuminated luggage area. Most 2000s will come with contrasting broad stripes on their flanks, but slimmer, Sport-style coachlines can be specified.

We were generally impressed by the finish of our German-built vehicle. The style of the unusual nose may not be to everyone's taste, but it is neatly tagged on to the standard steel wings. The attachment of the rubber wrap-round pieces to the usual Escort bumper at the rear is less dainty. We thought the trim well executed, the paint finish pleasing and found the car to have a solid, lasting feel about it.

At £2857, the RS2000 is £413 dearer than its stablemate the Mexico. It is also notably quicker and better equipped, the wheels alone accounting for over £150 of the difference. At under £3000 it is also slightly cheaper than close competitors such as the Colt Galant, Audi 80GT, and R17 which are also slower. It is also one of the best-handling saloons around. If Ford could win back some lost economy and improve that jerky ride without spoiling the fine handling and roadholding they would make a good car even better.

PERFORMANCE

CONDITIONS

Weather	Dry, wintry; wind 5-20 mph
Temperature	48° F
Barometer	29.8 in. hg
Surface	Dry tarmac

MAXIMUM SPEEDS

	mph	kph
Banked circuit	108.2	174.1
Best ¼ mile	112.5	181.0
Terminal speeds :		
at ¼ mile	83	134
at kilometre	102	164
Speed in gears (at 6500 rpm) :		
1st	33	53
2nd	61	98
3rd	88	142

ACCELERATION FROM REST

mph	sec	kph	sec
0-30	3.0	0-40	2.2
0-40	4.4	0-60	4.0
0-50	6.2	0-80	6.1
0-60	8.5	0-100	9.3
0-70	11.4	0-120	13.0
0-80	15.3	0-140	18.8
0-90	20.7	0-160	29.0
0-100	29.7		
Stand'g ¼	16.8	Stand'g km	31.4

ACCELERATION IN TOP

mph	sec	kph	sec
20-40	9.2	40-60	5.7
30-50	8.4	60-80	4.9
40-60	8.1	80-100	5.2
50-70	8.0	100-120	5.0
60-80	8.4	120-140	6.1
70-90	10.0	140-160	11.8
80-100	14.2		

FUEL CONSUMPTION

Touring	27.6 mpg 10.2 litres/100 km
Overall	23.5 mpg 12.0 litres/100 km
Fuel grade	98 octane 4 star rating

Tank capacity	9.0 galls 40.9 litres
Max range	248 miles 399 km
Test distance	1204 miles 1937 km

* Consumption midway between 30 mph and maximum less 5 per cent for acceleration.

SPEEDOMETER (mph)

Speedo	30	40	50	60	70	80	90	100
True	30.5	41	50	59	68	77.5	87	96

Distance recorder : 3.6 per cent fast.

WEIGHT

	cwt	kg
Unladen weight*	18.1	919.5
Weight as tested	21.8	1107.5

* With fuel for approx 50 miles.

Performance tests carried out by Motor's staff at the Motor Industry Research Association proving ground, Lindley.

Test Data: World copyright reserved; no unauthorised reproduction in whole or in part.

GENERAL SPECIFICATION

ENGINE

Cylinders	4 in line
Capacity	1993 cc (121.67 cu in.)
Bore/stroke	90.82/76.95 mm (3.57/3.02 in.)
Cooling	Water
Block	Iron
Head	Iron
Valves	Ohc with finger followers
Valve timing :	
inlet opens	24° btdc
inlet closes	64° abdc
exhaust opens	70° bbdc
exhaust closes	18° atdc
Compression	9.2 : 1
Carburetter	Weber 2v downdraught
Bearings	5 main
Fuel pump	Mechanical
Max power	110 bhp (DIN) at 5500 rpm
Max torque	118.5 lb ft (DIN) at 4000 rpm

TRANSMISSION

Type	4-speed manual
Clutch	8.5 in. dia, sdp, diaphragm spring

Internal ratios and mph/1000 rpm :

Top	1.00 : 1	18.6
3rd	1.37 : 1	13.6
2nd	1.97 : 1	9.4
1st	3.65 : 1	5.1
Rev	3.66 : 1	
Final drive	Hypoid, 3.54 : 1	

BODY/CHASSIS

Construction	Unitary, all steel

Protection	Full electrostatic coat primer

SUSPENSION

Front	Ind by MacPherson struts, coil springs, and anti-roll bar
Rear	Live axle supported by semi-elliptic leaf springs and pair of radius arms

STEERING

Type	Rack and pinion
Assistance	None
Toe-in	2.0-4.0 mm
Camber	0° 40'
Castor	1° 45'
King pin	7° 20'

BRAKES

Type	Disc/drum
Servo	Yes
Circuit	Split, front/rear
Rear valve	No
Adjustment	Self-adjusting

WHEELS

Type	Ventilated steel disc, 5½Jx13
Tyres	175/70 HR 13
Pressures	24 F ; 22 R

ELECTRICAL

Battery	12V, 57 Ah
Polarity	Negative earth
Generator	Alternator
Fuses	7
Headlights	4 Cibié Halogen, 55/115W

Make: Ford

Model: Escort RS2000

Makers: Ford Motor Co Ltd, Warley, Essex

Price: £2441.88 plus £203.49 car tax plus £211.63 VAT equals £2857.00

THE RIVALS

One domestic and four imported sporting saloons which compete against the Escort

FORD ESCORT RS2000 £2857

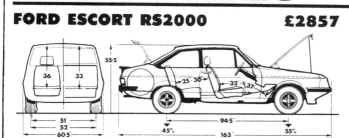

The most luxurious of Ford's trio of sporting Escorts. Outstanding performance combined with excellent handling and roadholding make it very much a driver's car. Economy is fair, though poor compared with other Pinto-engined cars. Generally well finished and very comfortable for front seat occupants. Poor rear legroom. Ride firm but not uncomfortable. Well equipped and good value for money.

Power, bhp/rpm	110/5500
Torque, lb ft/rpm	118.5/4000
tyres	175/70 HR 13
mph/1000	18.6
weight (cwt)	18.1
max speed, mph	108.2
0-60mph secs	8.5
30-50 mph in top, secs	8.4
overall mpg	23.5
touring mpg	27.6
fuel grade (stars)	4
boot capacity, cu ft	8.9

AUDI 80GT £2910

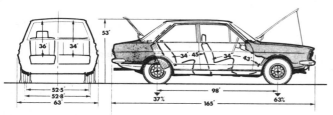

Most powerful version of Audi 80/Passat range. Enjoyable car with excellent driving position, adequate performance and good handling up to the limit. Lacking in refinement though, with poor ride, harsh, hesitant engine and body boom. Interior is comfortable and rear seat accommodation good. Like RS2000 is well equipped with bucket seats and alloy wheels as standard.

Power, bhp/rpm	100/6000
Torque, lb ft/rpm	97/4000
tyres,	175/70 HR 13
mph/1000	17.4
weight (cwt)	16.9
max speed, mph	101.5
0-60mph secs	10.9
30-50 mph in top, secs	8.5
overall mpg	26.6
touring mpg	32.1
fuel grade (stars)	4
boot capacity, cu ft	10.5

LANCIA BETA COUPE £3136

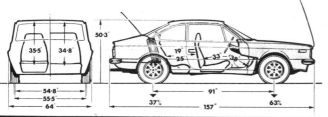

Stylish coupe version of successful front-wheel drive saloon. Lusty performance from 1600 cc engine coupled with excellent handling and roadholding make it another car with strong driver appeal. Well built and comprehensively equipped, though instrumentation is confusing. Accommodation is indifferent and engine fussy when revved.

Power, bhp/rpm	108/6000
Torque, lb ft/rpm	102/4500
tyres	175/70 SR 14
mph/1000	18.4
weight (cwt)	19.5
max speed, mph	107.2
0-60mph secs	10.1
30-50mph in top, secs	10.2
overall mpg	24.3
touring mpg	30.8
fuel grade (stars)	4
boot capacity, cu ft	8.5

RENAULT R17 GORDINI £3113

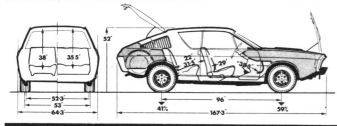

Performance version of a proven coupe. A high compression ratio and fuel injection ensure eager performance from 1600 cc. Excellent ride but driving position is poor and instruments difficult to read. Engine harsh and vibratory. Standard equipment includes cloth upholstery and five-speed gearbox.

Power, bhp/rpm	108/6000
Torque, lb ft/rpm	100.5/5500
tyres	165 HR 13
mph/1000	18.9
weight (cwt)	21.0
max speed, mph	111.1
0-60mph secs	9.9
30-50mph in top, secs	11.7
overall mpg	23.2
touring mpg	—
fuel grade (stars)	5
boot capacity, cu ft	8.6

COLT GALANT GTO £2995

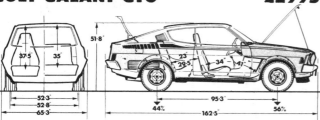

Exceptionally well-equipped competitor from Japan. Only fair performance for the price, but flexible engine coupled to excellent five-speed gearbox. Comfortable driving position and comprehensive instrumentation. High-speed handling not as precise as most British and European opposition and steering woolly by our standards. Ride disturbed and rear seat accommodation poor.

Power, bhp/rpm	125/6200 (SAE)
Torque, lb ft/rpm	126/4000 (SAE)
tyres	185/70 HR 13
mph/1000	20.1
weight (cwt)	19.8
max speed, mph	107.4
0-60mph secs	11.7
30-50 mph in top, secs	9.8
overall mpg	23.2
touring mpg	31.7
fuel grade (stars)	4
boot capacity, cu ft	7.5

TRIUMPH DOLOMITE SPRINT £3083

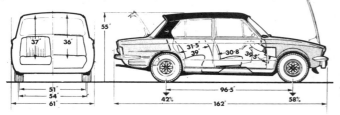

Quickest of the bunch. Reputation supported by recent win in the RAC Touring Car Championship and consistent placings in national rallies. Has a well equipped, luxuriously appointed interior but old-fashioned chassis giving only average handling and an indifferent ride. Accommodation for four or five adults makes this the most commodious car of the group, though best not very big.

Power, bhp/rpm	127/5700
Torque, lb ft/rpm	122.1/4500
tyres	175/70 HR 13
mph/1000	23.7 (O/D)
weight (cwt)	19.8
max speed, mph	112.7
0-60mph secs	8.4
30-50 mph in top, secs	8.0
overall mpg	23.0
touring mpg	26.1
fuel grade (stars)	4
boot capacity, cu ft	9.4

SPECIFICATIONS FOR

FORD ESCORT RS 2000

RATIOS:

	Gearbox	Overall	km/h per 1000 rpm	mph per 1000 rpm
First	3.65:1	12.92:1	8.2	5.1
Second	1.97:1	6.97:1	15.0	9.4
Third	1.37:1	4.59:1	21.8	13.6
Fourth	1.00:1	3.54:1	30.88	18.6
Final drive	3.54:1			

CHASSIS AND RUNNING GEAR:

Construction . . . . unitary, all steel
Suspension, front . . . . MacPherson struts, anti-roll bar
Suspension, rear . . . . .live rear axle, semi-elliptic springs, radius arms
Dampers . . . . telescopic front and rear
Steering type . . . . rack and pinion
Turns I to I 3.5
Brakes, type . . . . disc/drum, split hydraulic system

DIMENSIONS:

Wheelbase . . . . 2400 mm (94.5 in.)
Track, front . . . . 1295 mm (51 in.)
Track, rear . . . . 1321 mm (52 in.)
Length .4140 mm (13 ft 7 in.)
Width . . . . 1270 mm (5 ft 0.5 in.)
Height . . . . 1444 mm (4 ft 7.5 in.)
Fuel tank capacity . . . . 40.9 litres (9 gallons)
Kerb mass (weight) . . . . 9195 kg (2027 lb)

TYRES:

Size 175/70 HR13
Make fitted . . . . Pirelli Cinturato

SPECIFICATIONS

MAKE . . . . .FORD
MODEL . . . . Escort RS 2000
BODY TYPE . . . . Two-door Sedan
COLOR . . . . Red
PRICE:
Basic $7700
As tested $7700
OPTIONS FITTED . . . . None
ENGINE:
Cylinders . . . . .four, in line
Valves . . . . single overhead cam
Carburettor . . . . Weber 2v downdraught
Fuel pump . . . . mechanical
Oil filter . . . . .full flow
Compression ratio . . . . 9.2 to 1
Bore x stroke . . . . .90.82 x 76.95 mm (3.57 x 3.02 in.)
Capacity . . . . 1.993 litres (121.67 cu in.)
Power at 5500 rpm . . . . .82 kW (110 bhp)
Torque at 4000 rpm . . . . 160 N-m (118 lb/ft)
TRANSMISSION:
Type . . . . four
Clutch . . . . single plate
Gear lever location . . . . .floor

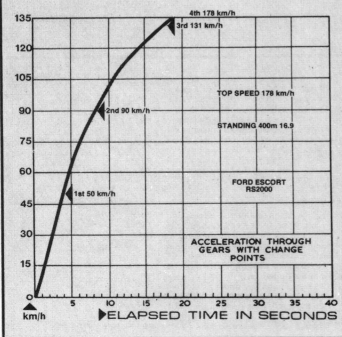

ACCELERATION THROUGH GEARS WITH CHANGE POINTS

TOP SPEED 178 km/h

STANDING 400m 16.9

FORD ESCORT RS2000

PERFORMANCE

TEST CONDITIONS:

Weather . . . . fine
Surface . . . . Castlereagh Dragway
Load . . . . .two persons
Fuel . . . . Super
Power-to-mass (kerb) . . . . 11.21 kg/kW (18.43 lb/bhp)
Piston speed at max power . . . . 14.11 m/s (2770 ft/min)

SPEEDOMETER ERROR:

Indicated km/h	50	70	90	110	130
Actual km/h	50	68	87	107	127

FUEL CONSUMPTION ON TEST — Distance and conditions:

Check one . . . . . . 9.8 km/l (27.7 mpg) over 1073 km (670 miles)
Check two . . . . . 8.99 km/l (25.3 mpg) over 307 km (192 miles)
Average . . . . . . 9.6 km/l (27 mpg) over 1380 km (862 miles)

MAXIMUM SPEEDS:

Fastest run . . . . 178 km/h (111 mph)
Average all runs . . . . 178 km/h (111 mph)

IN GEARS:

First . . . . .50 km/h (31 mph) (6000 rpm)
Second . . . . .90 km/h (56 mph) (6000 rpm)
Third . . . . .131 km/h (82 mph) (6000 rpm)
Fourth . . . . 178 km/h (111 mph) (5950 rpm)

ACCELERATION — Through the gears:

0-50 km/h . . . . .3.6 sec
0-70 km/h . . . . .5.7 sec
0-90 km/h . . . . .8.2 sec
0-110 km/h . . . . .11.9 sec
0-130 km/h . . . . .16.9 sec

IN THE GEARS:

	Second	Third	Fourth
30-60 km/h	3.1 sec	4.7 sec	7.9 sec
40-70 km/h	3.6 sec	4.7 sec	7.4 sec
50-80 km/h	3.2 sec	4.8 sec	7.0 sec
60-90 km/h	3.5 sec	5.0 sec	7.1 sec
70-100 km/h		5.2 sec	7.0 sec
80-110 km/h		5.5 sec	7.1 sec
90-120 km/h		5.7 sec	7.4 sec
100-130 km/h		7.0 sec	8.3 sec

STANDING START — 0-400 m (¼ mile)

Fastest run . . . . . . 16.8 sec
Average all runs . . . 16.9 sec

THIS FORD IS NOT RS...

...or how we came to hate FoMoCo (for a while)

The everlasting hate and loathing we felt for Ford Australia for only importing 25 Escort RS2000s came to an abrupt and complete halt when we learned of its hush-hush plans to build its own 2-litre cars here. We give you a taste of the fine sports sedan that's coming next year . . .

THERE ARE a couple of dozen swearwords you can apply to a motor manufacturer without repeating yourself and we called the Ford Motor Co of Australia every one of them, the day we gave back their Escort RS2000 test car.

It wasn't that the car was a dog — which is usually what makes staffers stare blackly into their Reschs and explete. It was the fact that the car is so damn good — yet only 25 Australians were going to own an RS2000 and most of them only as a means to a checkered flag. What a cheap trick, we thought, to import 25 cars to reap the publicity for the rotten old 1300s (which were still being sold at the time) with cars that looked similar but were about as much

like the ordinary family barges as a skateboard is to a Saturn Five.

That was before we gleaned, from sources close to the top of Ford Australia, that the country was almost certain to get its own Escort RS2000 — without the racy name and perhaps without the wedgy flexible nosecone, but having the same Cortina/Pinto four-cylinder single overhead cam engine and gearbox plus suspension mods to make it handle.

To be technical about it, no-one from Ford has yet looked us in the eye and said yes there will be an Aussie Escort 2-litre, but they've said everything but. Ford is "aware" that the RS is a great little car, Ford "realises" that it has the components — access to 2-litre drive-components and a surfeit of two-door bodies — to build its own RS2000s. But Ford also has "other projects" on its hands at present and it will need to get these out of the way before it can turn to "jobs like a 2-litre

Escort". Would they call it RS2000? A positive, no-nonsense "No". No ifs or buts.

So our conclusion — and it's not a guess — is that there will be a 2-litre

Escort arriving in the first half of next year and costing around $6500 on today's levels. It won't be an RS2000 and it may not even look like one. It's far more likely to be called the Escort GS. Great news. It's only rivalled by the probability of GMH producing a big-engined Gemini, also next year (see accompanying story).

We know it's good news because we recently had the Ford RS2000 test car laid on us for around a week which was plenty long enough for us to (1) find out that it's a lot faster in a straight line than an Alfetta GT (2) get all bitter and twisted about (what we thought was) its lack of a future here (3) start arguing about whether it would out-corner the aforementioned A-R and (4) speculate on whether it would still be worth owning after the assorted hacks and leadfooted hangers-on who always drive Ford test cars and left their pound of Pirelli on the blacktop. That all means we thought it was very good.

It's SO good, that it's hard to believe it's such a simple car to build. Take one two-door Escort body, equip it with black innards and equipment to Ghia standard (heated rear window, German bucket seats, full instruments, console, AM/FM radio, glove-box, clock, sporty

steering wheel) and drop in one Cortina 2-litre engine, standard except for the exhaust system which is organised for better gas flow and a bit more poke at higher revs. Give it wide steel wheels, Pirelli rubber, anti-roll bars and firmer suspension settings front and rear and let it loose to terrorise the around $10,000 2-litre Italians and Germans.

The differentness of the RS2000 starts with its appearance. It has a plastic wedge-shaped nose which is made of an unbreakable plastic material which absorbs the average parking biff and just pops back into shape. It looks fine, they say it cuts the wind a bit better than the standard snout and it houses four quartz halogen headlights which turn night into day when asked.

The nose has a dummy grille which actually admits almost no air to the radiator. The bulk of the cooling flow goes into a discreet hole behind the numberplate and below the rubber bumper. Just behind that there's a neatly shaped "cow-catcher" spoiler which transforms the car's appearance and which only lamebrains can run into kerbs. There's a rear spoiler made of rubber which runs across the bootlid and a black stripe which runs along each side about wheel-arch level. Door frames are blacked out, there are RS2000 badges on the rear sides and bootlid and a discreet badge behind the front wheel.

Incidentally, before driving this car we were convinced Ford had two sporty Escorts in Europe — the 16-valve RS1800 for the enthusiasts and the plastic-nosed, Cortina-engined 2000 for the five-tenths play-racers and

RS2000's plastic nose-cone protects you from parking station biffs and looks pretty cool as well. It deforms easily under hand pressure.

boulevardiers. Sure, we'd read tests which said the 2000 was good, but we all know you can't trust the bulk of the Pom press with a home-made car. And the reliable guys hadn't driven an RS2000 recently. We now know that both are top-flight cars. Here endeth the descriptive rhubarbing . . .

Screw yourself into the RS2000 and it's just like a black Ghia except for the shift lever which is a short, knobbly affair which the 2000 shares with the RS1800. All the rest of it is familiar. The European bucket seats with their wraparound backrests leave the local cut-down Cortina ones for dead, the steering wheel still seems too high and to protrude too far from the dash but all-round visibility is good and the interior is quite well laid out, etc . . .

Unfamiliarity starts when you push in the clutch and start the engine. For one thing you expect an Escort clutch to be feather-light, not firm like this one and you aren't quite prepared for the extra vibration and exhaust pipe rort that happens when the blue 2-litre four kicks over.

If you begin by driving sedately — as some road-testers have been known to do — you find that the engine doesn't need to go above 2500-3000 rpm in the gears because there's plenty of torque in the unit. The torque peak is actually at 4000 but the curve must be pretty flat. The engine isn't conspicuously smooth, but with its good breathing (from the free-flow exhaust) plus the light body it hauls about it's pleasantly lively and responsive to small throttle alterations.

So you let it get a bit angrier and that's when you discover performance. Enough performance to get it down the standing 400 m course in just 16.8 seconds which is better than all but the

Continued on page 78

Escort seats are cloth-covered and grippy. Interior is all-black, well equipped and attractive. Spec level is similar to that of Aussie-made Escort Ghia.

Escort RS2000 driving position is comfortable enough, courtesy of the supportive European-made bucket seats, but steering wheel (padded rim, small diameter) is high and rather close to the driver.

Improved trio of RS Escorts tested

JUST OVER five years ago Ford were busy establishing, and producing the first high performance Escorts, from a new Advanced Vehicle Operation at South Ockendon in Essex. Almost a year ago, in January 1975, it was announced that the last F.A.V.O. Escort had been made at Ockendon, but that there would be more Escort RS types, based on the new Escort shape (all the Ockendon cars were encased within the earlier Escort body shape) and these cars have now materialised. As before there is a four valve per cylinder derivative (the 1845 c.c. RS 1800), a 2 litre Cortina-engined model (RS2000) and a 1.6 litre capacity for the Mexico, but this time that model has the s.o.h.c. motor as well. To complicate matters further there is the far cheaper, but much less sporting, Escort Sport, sold through all Ford dealers in either 1300 c.c. or 1600 c.c. crossflow engine capacities.

We have tried all three of the successors to the F.A.V.O. Escorts and were relieved to find that the cars still do offer considerable improvements over the normal production Escorts, though the RS1800 has an even more dubious roadgoing future than the rorty RS1600 had. As before all these Rallye Sport Escorts will be sold through a 70 strong network of selected Ford RS dealers.

Both the RS2000, which now carries the distinctive twin headlamp "beak", and the Mexico, are excellent road cars. This makes it particularly sad that they are likely to be the last such Escorts to offer genuine engineering improvements over mass production models. The process began with the closure of F.A.V.O.'s separate production facility. Today the RS2000 and Mexico are manufactured in West Germany at one of Ford's major car plants in Saarlouis. Thus the old practice of extra attention to paintwork and quality (in effect a second complete quality control check) can no longer be counted on as part of the extra purchase price.

The second rather disturbing point is that the team of engineers, who developed all the cars from the original RS1600, through to the three models driven for this test, are currently under pressure to disband and accept alternative employment on a variety of projects. This does make one wonder what the future of such cars will be, and it seems likely that Ford will attempt to slide smoothly from beneath their original high performance ideals. Thence, into a series of matt black paintwork S designated models, like those currently offered as replacements in the old GT lines: i.e. Granada S and Capri ditto.

Such a move might well result in better profitability for a company that is already embarrassingly efficient in money matters, compared to other British-based manufacturers. Incidentally the man in charge of F.A.V.O.'s activities these days is former German competition manager Michael Kranefuss, who succeeded Stuart Turner in that task, and the job of Competition Director for Ford in Europe. Turner is now the Public Relations Director for Ford in Britain.

After establishing who does what and to whom, let us explore the cars. First, the components they all share. Number one is the bodyshell, which is the normal Escort unit carrying strengthened mounting plates to the top of the front struts, and a stronger rear

Mexico (above) is a pleasure to drive quickly and has more civilised noise levels throughout the speed range, which culminates in a maximum of 105 m.p.h. Nose-to-nose the RS1800, in white, and the extended RS2000 front end make an interesting contrast. The new front ensures that the 2000 is the only new shape Escort to have an aerodynamic drag factor that is as low as the earlier Escorts.

crossmember to carry the nearly vertical rear shock absorbers. The floorpan, including the re-aligned dampers, is exactly as in the late model Escorts of the previous shape.

The RS2000 uses a bodyshell that is further modified in respect of the front wings, which are cut back 10 cms. and properly flanged to accept the polyurethane nose. This streamlined front adds about 20 lbs. and carries quadruple Cibie 5 in. headlights compared to the 7 in. diameter Lucas H4 units installed on the Mexico and RS1800. The latter two cars carry deep glassfibre front spoilers, while the 2000's is part of the new front end treatment: all three have polyurethane, boot-mounted spoilers. The cars are all stable in a crosswind but it would be preferable to have the back spoiler painted in the body colour on all models, instead of just the 1800.

As with all Escorts, the suspension system comprises MacPherson strut i.f.s. and leaf sprung live axle. Working with the objective of improving the ride a little, and bettering an already sporty set of handling mannerisms, the F.A.V.O. engineers have transformed the feel of their cars. At the rear the bent bit of wire which serves as a roll bar and traction arms (similar in concept to a Capri) went out in favour of twin axle location rods. Front end castor angles were decreased and specialist damping from Armstrong (front) and Girling (rear) ensures the cars have a lot more feel for fast driving. Just about every combination in spring rates has been tried in the various Escorts over the years and the final compromise on these cars was arrived at with 130 lb. front rating and 115 lb. sq. in. rear leaves. Theoretically the minor changes in front end weights should

have little effect. The 1800 is lightest, the Mexico carrying 30 lb. less over its MacPherson struts than the 2000.

All three models have 9.63 in. diameter front disc brakes (as fitted on Capris of 2 litres) and 9 in. by 1¾ in. back drums. A larger capacity servo-assistance unit is incorporated.

An Escort Sport axle, carrying a 3.45:1 final drive ratio is common to the range, but there are very important gearbox differences. The Mexico and RS2000 have Cortina ratios:- first, 3.65:1; second, 1.97:1; third, 1.37:1 and direct 1.0:1 fourth. The RS1800 has the same top gear (and therefore an identical 18.6 m.p.h. per 1000 r.p.m. figure) but closer ratios that trace their ancestry back to the American Pinto 2.3 litre "Compacts." Spacing on the first three gears is:- first, 3.36:1; second, 1.81:1 and third 1.26:1.

In practice this means the 1800 has the long ratios of a competition car, first carrying you to 37 m.p.h., second to 70 m.p.h. and third to 97 m.p.h. Very nice indeed, but the other two Escorts are quite sporting on gear speeds of 32, 60 and 84 m.p.h. appearing at the optimum gearchange points for our track tests. On the road one tends to settle for lower gear speeds on the overhead camshaft cars. It is a disgrace to report that Ford are still penny-pinching by *not* indicating a redline on the tachometer. This is stupid, especially in the case of performance cars like these, which most definitely do not have indestructable engines when liberties are taken! We used up to 6200 r.p.m. on the Mexico and RS2000, and 6500 r.p.m. for the RS1800.

RS Escorts

Which serves well enough to remind us that instrumentation is common to all three models. Based on the usual Escort style, the single pane viewing panel covers a speedometer, tachometer, and a clearly visible trio of minor gauges for oil pressure, water temperature and fuel contents. The pressure gauge is not marked with figures, but the markings are consistent with 20-40-60-80-100 lb. per sq. in. readings. Doubtless German customers can interpret in possible kilogramme indications. Our 1800 had a genuine leather rimmed steering wheel, the others used the same wheel, but with a sticky synthetic plastic of some description.

From the outside it can be seen that Ford have rummaged in their Child's Book of Fancy Striping again, producing a different combination for each model. The RS2000 is the luckiest, with just a single black stripe, while the RS1800 owner gets pretty colours, but they were peeling beautifully as well!

Interiors are those of the RS2000 (top) and Mexico. The latter has effective bucket seats, but lacks the centre console and clock of the 2000, which can be seen in understeer action above.

Only the RS2000 has the aluminium 6J by 13 in. wheels as standard. Mexico and RS1800 owners have steel 5½J wheels, or they can spend £117 for a set of five such alloy wheels. All the test cars were served by 175/70 HR x 13 Pirelli CN36 radial ply tyres. As a further aside on costs it is worth remembering that the prices we quote in the panel do not include delivery charges, now back in the Ford armoury at £35, or inertia reel seat belts, which cost £27.

We drove the RS1800 within two separate test weeks, one in blazing June when the performance figures were taken, while the second occasion was over Christmas. On the later date the car had been totally rebuilt, following a multi roll-over accident at a test track session for another magazine. It was hard to tell that JJN 981N was indeed the machine we had tried in Summer, for then our impressions had been of a superb road car, imbued with enough spirit to make a respectable weekend competition car. Over Christmas it struck as a harsh and noisy beast, with brakes that vibrated and a poor driving position.

The four cylinder d.o.h.c. engine is a development of the 1601 c.c. Cosworth Ford four valve per cylinder unit. The alloy cylinder head and block are retained but the larger 86.75 m.m. bore accounts for the extra capacity when combined with the original 77.62 m.m. stroke. A single Weber 32/36 DGAV twin choke carburetter was installed instead of the double 40 m.m. side-draught units previously obtained from Dellorto or Weber. Quoted output is down just 5 horsepower on the RS1600 with 115 b.h.p. at 6000 r.p.m. Torque is increased from 112 lb. ft. to 120 lb. ft., though you still need 4000 r.p.m. to obtain that peak.

As with the other RS Escorts, the gearbox is fitted with a new linkage to halve the movements of the stubby gear lever. As we now demand a super gearchange from Ford as a right, this merely puts a little dressing on the package, for one very soon accepts the lightning changes that result.

The competition-orientated ratios are superb: the gears have some spare torque capacity, owing to extra width and the shot-peening process. Se-cond gear is very effective at hurling the car along narrow gravel roads, third gear's nigh-on 100 m.p.h. ability adding to the fun with pan-ache. Unfortunately top brings out the beast in the machine under motorway conditions. Engine noise over 70 m.p.h. is a throwback to the days of hot Mini Cooper S types.

On the test track, or under country road conditions, the 1800's advantages are crystallised in sheer speed. Where the RS2000 is quietly trying to shove its way past 105 mph, the 1800 is bellowing grimly past 110, intent on recording its eventual maximum of 115 m.p.h. Under the same conditions the Mexico is very hard put to exceed 100 m.p.h.

Nobody has said anything officially about the 1800's future, but insiders have said to us that no Ford mainstream plant wants to build it, and the engines are known to be in short supply in this specification. I have seen just one privately registered car on the road, and Ford have their homologation for the model in International Group 2 form, so it looks as though it will be quietly dropped. Potentially the 1800 could be matched up against the Dolomite, but Triumph's ingenious single camshaft 16-valver holds such an edge in cost that Ford look certain to lose money on every RS1800 sold on a competitive price footing with the Triumph.

Settling into the RS2000 was a positive relief. The production seats do not have the disconcerting support roll under the knees, which is a feature of the 1800's comfort pack seat. You sit higher in the car, watching the bonnet fall away into the smartly-mated contours of the nosepiece. An automatic choke brings the 2000 smartly to life and the mildly modified Cortina unit punches the car along swiftly with a minimum of effort. There is practically the same torque claim (119 lb. ft.) as the 1800 at the same engine speed, while maximum power is said to be minus 5 horsepower, compared to the Cosworth 16-valve unit. However, that maximum is allied to a very flat torque delivery, which peaks at 5,500 r.p.m. So it is very much easier to drive a 2000, and much quieter, than the stretched BDA.

Brakes on this car were superb on any road surface and were very nearly up to the standard of the best all-disc systems. Handling at low speed was slightly marred for this writer by the heavy steering but since his wife (a frail lady, not prone to hammer-throwing or sudden games of hockey) specifically said that it was no trouble to park, further comment seems unneccessary.

On the move the 2000 isn't quite so dodgem-like as the RS1800 in its ability to weave and sprint round slow corners, but the high speed (80 m.p.h. plus) handling appears to exhibit none of the understeer that afflicted the 1800 on its return from crash repair. Over B roads the 2000 covers distance just as fast as the 1800, and is a delight to drive, sweeping round the quicker corners with safety and considerable style. In town the 2000 attracts no unwelcome attention, its quiet exhaust masking very accessible, and frequently exploited, sprinting potential. Under the same conditions the 1800 is a clumsy car to drive by comparison.

At night the 2000 has a clear plus over the single headlamp units. Mr Cibie provided definition and range, while Jo Lucas manages as good a dip beam, but a rather woolly main beam.

Both the Mexico and RS2000 have fresh exhaust down and tail pipes, which accounts for their extra quoted power when compared to the standard engines installed in Capris and Cortinas. The 2000 used to have an electric fan, but that has been dispensed with to save money. We are told that such a fan is worth another 5 to 6 b.h.p., which would take the 2000 right into the 1800's performance territory at low cost.

Although the Mexico lacks the 2000's beaky snout, it is very similar in its driving mannerisms. Comparatively quiet – it is the first Mexico we can recall noticing wind noise above the commotion of the engine at 70 m.p.h. – the Mexico is a very well balanced little car that feels a lot tauter than the others, for no logical reason.

In this form the single overhead camshaft motor (87.65 mm by 66 mm versus the RS2000's 90.8 mm by 76.95 mm) gives 95 bhp at 5750 r.p.m. and 92 lb. ft. torque at 4000 r.p.m. This is enough to produce exactly the same sort of 0-60 m.p.h. times as recorded by earlier Mexicos and there's no doubt that the car does feel as comparatively slow as one would expect, when driving it directly against the more powerful versions. On the road the Mexico needs a little more anticipation than you need in the 2000, but it will show very good cross country averages, and keep the driver very entertained within the standard seats, which are of pronounced bucket configuration. Since the Escort Sport is just under £2000, many readers will wonder if the overhead camshaft, better seating, suspension, and braking are worth having. I think they will prove worth every new penny to anyone who enjoys his motoring. Comparing the Sport to the Mexico is about as fair as assessing the Mini Cooper S and the Mini 1275 GT for sporting appeal!

Altogether I covered the best part of 1000

RS1800 is generally a little more tail-happy than the 2000, but all three RS Escorts have more understeer and slightly softer rides than before. The RS1800 displays the tail spoilers used on all three cars, below, with its 1845 c.c. engine underneath. Both 2000 and Mexico use outwardly similar s.o.h.c. motors, as shown beneath.

miles in each of the RS Escorts, so there were some pertinent general comments to arise. First of all oil consumption was virtually negligible in the s.o.h.c. cars and 250-300 m.p.p. on the 1800. Secondly the 1800 shrieked for five star fuel, and had a tendency to pink on that when sulking too. Thirdly, we had trouble with all three cars! The 1800 overheated and the starter motor ring gear came loose. The RS2000 ruined a crown wheel and pinion, the result of oil surge at the test track, so it's very unlikely to happen on the road. Then, the poor Mexico arrived with a severed pipe to the carburetter emission control system. The latter was easily corrected, but it did make a nonsense of our fuel consumption figures at the time!

When it comes to picking and choosing I feel there's only one effective British opponent, and that is the £3086 Dolomite Sprint. The Fords look more modern and handle far more crisply, but the Triumph has the edge in civilisation, ride and a superb engine.

I think we can dismiss the 1800 as a competition special, and report that the Mexico and RS2000 have a valid place in the British market, alongside the Dolomite. We should give those F.A.V.O. and competitions engineers a pat on the back for improving already good cars. As for the imports, I would recommend a run in the Audi 80 GT (£2965) and an investigation into the new Asconas and Mantas from Opel, we have yet to drive. – J.W.

Performance	RS1800	RS2000	1.6 Mexico
MPH	seconds	seconds	seconds
0-30	3.2	3.0	3.2
0-40	4.7	4.9	5.5
0-50	6.5	6.9	8.1
0-60	8.6	9.8	11.1
0-70	11.3	13.2	16.2
0-80	15.4	19.2	23.0
Standing ¼ mile	16.2	17.0	17.8
Fuel economy (m.p.g.):	21-24	23.6-27	26.3-28
Prices (£, inc taxes):	3049	2857	2443.50

FORD'S RS SPECIALS

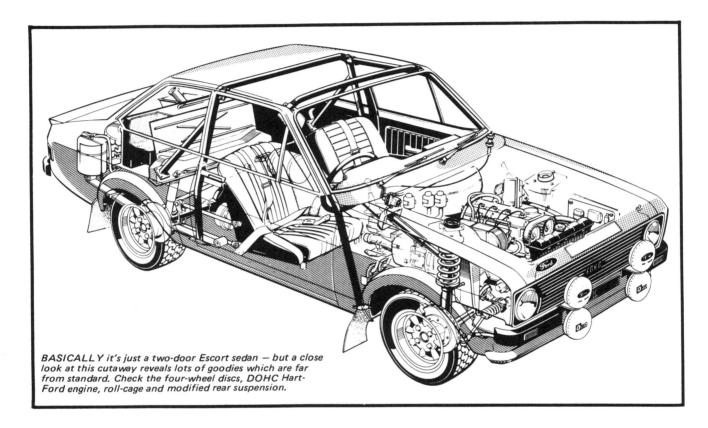

BASICALLY it's just a two-door Escort sedan — but a close look at this cutaway reveals lots of goodies which are far from standard. Check the four-wheel discs, DOHC Hart-Ford engine, roll-cage and modified rear suspension.

Ford's Escort-based RS series is leading the company right into a boots' n' all rally effort that is taking it to the top of the ladder – fast. With a contingent of the giant –killing RS 1800s entered for the Southern Cross we decided to take a look under the skin and find out why these bright rising stars are so good . . .

SINCE Ford first imported a limited number of RS2000 Escorts into Australia there has been speculation that they would be backing motorsport again. The new European look Escort is a real success story already and the addition of the RS2000 version adds further to the range but only to a very select group of Australian enthusiasts.

But this car is only the 'tip of the iceberg' of the Escort range of goodies available to enthusiasts in England. We had the opportunity recently to see the behind the scenes activities of Ford's competition department in England and road test the ultimate production line RS1800 Escort.

Added interest follows Ford's announcement that they will be entering two UK works prepared RS1800 Escorts in the coming Southern Cross Rally at Port Macquarie NSW. Drivers will be Roger Clark and Timo Makinen, two of

the quickest and most experienced rally drivers in the world today.

The team will be backed up by mechanics, team mangers and loads of spares all from England. Ford Australia will also assist with service crews and preparation.

Escorts currently dominate the rally scene in the UK but here in Australia with no factory participation they are rarely seen in major events against the many Datsuns and Lancers. However this may change having seen the meticulous preparation the works Escort's are currently going through at Boreham.

The Group 2 rally Escort RS1800 is basically the same as the regular production Escort RS1800 although the Group 2 rally car incorporates modifications and refinements to cope with the extraordinary demands of international rallying.

Under-body protection is increased by the addition of a light weight alloy shield which covers the underside of the engine and gearbox. The twin overhead camshaft 1800cc, 16-valve, 4-cylinder engine has its capacity increased to 2-litres and with the addition of two twin choke 45mm Weber carburettors — replacing the single twin choke, down draught Weber — with modified camshafts engine power output is increased to an average 171.5kW at 8,200 rpm.

Brian Hart prepares and tunes all the works engines and power goes to 183kW on some engines. Additionally, the engine's lubrication system is changed to the dry sump type with the oil reservoir located in the boot of the Escort.

The four-speed gearbox is changed to a ZF five speed and a limited slip differential is incorporated in the rear axle. In order to produce high rates of acceleration with a comparatively low maximum speed the ratio of the final drive unit is also changed between a 5.1 or 5.3.

Last year no less than 8 different types of Dunlop tyres ranging from extra wide, hand-cut racing tyres to narrow snow tyres were available to the drivers in the Ford 'works' team. The Minilite alloy, extra wide wheels are enclosed within special wheelarch extensions and both the front and rear suspensions systems incorporate gas/oil filled Bilstein shock absorber units.

Rear axle location is also improved and modified by the addition of extra suspension links. In order to provide maximum protection for the occupants of the rally Escort RS1800 a special steel safety cage is built into the car and mounted to the body at 14 points.

Full aircraft type seat harnesses are provided for both driver and navigator, a special fireproof bulkhead is built across the rear of the car between the boot and the passenger compartment, and the long range fuel tank which is mounted in the boot is filled with plastic foam to prevent fuel spillage in the event of the tank being ruptured.

All fuel and brake lines are routed through the inside of the car for protection while the front and rear brake systems are on separate circuits.

The ignition can be switched off from either inside or outside the car and a special fire extinguishing system is fitted. In case of fire the system automatically releases a special gas which extinguishes the flames but is not dangerous to the occupants of the car.

The international rallies have formed a particularly important part of Ford's Escort development programmes. The many improvements which have been brought about in suspension, brakes, lights, comfort and durability in today's production car have been developed in competition. Additionally, the specialist components which are fitted to Ford 'works' rally cars are available to the pri-

vate owner who wishes to compete in competition.

Ford performance parts are marketed throughout Britain and Europe through the network of Ford Rallye Sport Dealers. The Ford Rallye Sport Club concentrates more and more on providing technical information for its members who wish to take part in motor sport competition.

A series of facts sheets which can be incorporated into a comprehensive binder to make up a complete volume on rally preparation is distributed to members. This new facts service is designed to enable the private entrant to keep pace with the works drivers.

As a further part of its activity, the Ford Rallye Sport Club has established a comprehensive film library of motor sport films. These include the 1973 Scottish, the 1972 Safari and the Ford instructional film on rally driving. New additions to the library include the filmed report of the 1975 Lombard-RAC rally and the 1975 Scottish.

With an annual turnover now exceeding $30,000 and almost half of it going for export, the Ford Rallye Sport Club's clothing range now extends from Timo's Lombard-RAC rally winning hat to marshalls' golf-style umbrellas. The range of clothing also includes light, medium and heavyweight jackets, T-shirts, key rings and badges.

All this gives you an idea as to how enthusiastically Ford follow up their motorsport involvement. What hope for Australian Ford enthusiasts? Lets wait until after the Southern Cross rally!

DRIVING IMPRESSIONS

WE COLLECTED the RS1800 Escort from Ford's head office at Brentwood in Essex, and headed straight for Boreham where the work's cars are prepared and serviced. The standard road going RS1800 not only has good under the bonnet performance but it handled like a sports car. Very tight, smooth with the comfort of a touring car.

Imported from Germany the overall

THE INTERIOR of Roger Clark's car shows masses of rally aids screwed onto a standard Escort dashboard. Makinen's car is much more complicated, with a great deal more equipment.

THIS is the shell of Roger's car for Australia's Southern Cross rally. The body is specially stiffened with additional welding and the rear suspension is modified.

AT THE rear there's additional links to tighten axle location. Note Panhard bar and disc brake. Ahead of the axle there's radius rods and alloy plates to protect the differential.

THE BDA 2000cc engine for Roger Clark's car — it's prepared by tuner Brian Hart, one of Britain's top engine specialist, and produces 183kW (245bhp).

finish was excellent with full bucket contour seats and cloth trim.

The original engine began as a Cosworth FVA enlarged from 1600 to 1800cc using an aluminium block and head housing four valves per cylinder. The current capacity is 1854cc with a 10.1 compression ratio and 93kW at 6500 rpm plus 162 Nm torque at 4000 rpm.

We were expecting racing type engine characteristics, rough idle, hard to start and not working under 5000 revs. How wrong we were! The new engine uses a single twin choke Weber which provided easy starts, extreme flexibility even in London's peak hour traffic. Putting the foot down in top gear at 60 km/h gives smooth fuss-free acceleration.

The works rally Escorts run a 5 speed gear box but the road going RS1800 has a smooth shifting 4 speed. A standard 3.54 differential unit is used instead of an LSD. This proved quite satisfactory for city and highway driving. Top gear performance was extremely flexible, pulling from 1500 rpm, most uncharacteristic for a race bred engine.

We drove the Escort RS1800 over 1100 km which included a one day trip up the M1 freeway from London to Leeds, across to North Wales then through the tight twisting mountain roads of Wales down to Cardiff and to Bristol. Arriving back in London in time for peak hour traffic jams.

Throughout the trip the BDA engine ran quietly cruising at 112 km/h and showed 4300 rpm at 128 km/h with rapid acceleration right up to 190 km/h. Even with the single twin-choke Weber the Escort will reach 0-95 km/h in 8.6 seconds but using all gears to the limit helps, as over 3500 rpm there was a definite surge of power.

A performance car like the RS1800 tempts one to use the gears far more frequently, reving it out to 6500 and driving it like a sports car. Even driven hard the BDA return 25mpg.

Roadholding throughout the tight Welsh mountain roads was excellent. Ford's involvement in competition has paid off with this road machine. Suspension is very similar to works rally RS1800 we saw inside Boreham.

The live rear axle had additional radius arms and heavier leaf springs with Bilstein gas shockers all combining to stop any rear axle movement. Up front the McPherson struts are again Bilsteins, heavy duty springs and anti roll bar.

The ride is firm and sure, no body roll or rear axle hop, just complete contact

LOOKING deceptively domestic the RS 1800 is a real Q-car. Minimal exterior jazz-up hides 171kW engine and five-speed gearbox which gives the little car a top speed of 185km/h and acceleration of 6.9seconds from zero to 100km/h.

with the bitumen at all times. Completely predictable with power at your foot to give some added on-off cornering assistance. Unfortunately time did not allow us the opportunity to try out the RS1800 on the dirt, but from all reports, it is just as responsive.

Interior layout was well designed with tachometer and speedo clearly layed out directly in front of the neat vinyl padded wheel, along with an oil pressure temp and fuel gauge clearly marked white on black. Driver comfort rates very highly with excellent contoured hip hugging fabric covered seats.

Visibility was excellent, and a 12 hour trip in the Escort proved that the seats really work.

So how much does this ultimate little sports sedan cost, in UK you pay $4905 for the standard version or with extra door trimmings, reclining seats, head restraints, inertia seat belts, carpeted boot, centre console and glove box, it costs $5118.

So what price here in Australia? We don't like to guess but if ever the little tourer comes out here, you'll have to stand in line. ∎

FORD ESCORT RS1800 SPECIFICATION

BASIC VEHICLE:
Escort RS1800, 2-door, 4-seater saloon of unitary steel construction. In rally form the car has a top speed in excess of 115 mph/185 km/h, and accelerates from 0 to 60 mph/96.5 km/h in under 7 seconds.

Engine
(Alloy block, 4-cylinder in-line, water-cooled)
Bore ....90.00 mm
Stroke ....77.7 mm
Cubic capacity 1,977cc
Compression ratio ....11.5 : 1
Power output ....171kW at 8,200 rpm
Maximum torque ....226 Nm
Maximum engine speed.......................8,500 rpm
Fuel supply ....Twin 45 DCOE or 48 DCOE
Weber carburettors

Gearbox
(ZF, five forward synchronised ratios)
First ....2.3 : 1
Second ....1.8 : 1
Third ....1.36 : 1
Fourth..1.14 : 1
Fifth ....1.0 : 1
Rear axle ratio...5.3/5.1 : 1

Brakes:
Front, 241 mm diameter ventilated discs; rear, 254 mm diameter solid discs with twin calipers; twin brake servos.

Wheels:
Alloy 13 ins diameter, rim widths 5, 6, 7 or 8 ins, Dunlop competition tyres.

Shock absorbers:
Bilstein gas-filled.

Steering:
Rack and pinion, geared 2½ turns lock to lock. Sports steering wheel with leather rim.

Lights:
Cibie head and auxiliary lamps with quartz halogen bulbs.

THIS FORD IS NOT RS . . .
Continued from page 70

best-tuned 5-litres and MUCH better than a 3.3 to 4-litre de-toxed six. The power is so utterly controllable that the car never seems to be going terribly fast.

The engine pulls quite well to its 5500 rpm power peak, but the last 500 rpm to our arbitrary limit of 6000 rpm (no redline is marked on the tacho) is a waste of time. There's very little justification for going over 5000.

The gear ratios aren't all that well chosen — perhaps because they're a compromise between genuine high-performance gears and a practical set for town-running. The top three are as for high performance open-road work which is fine because you almost never get back to one out of town anyway. But first is quite low to get the car away from traffic lights without clutch judder or slip and to let it crawl among the jams, efficiently. Consequently there's a big gap between first and second which is noticeable even though the engine's power spread covers it fairly well.

The best way you can describe the performance is "adequate", but not the kind of unenthusiastic adequate you're likely to see on your brat's report card. We mean the kind that says there's power on tap whenever you need it — enough for any purpose this side of drag racing. Top speed is around 180 km/h (115 mph) and at that speed — close to 6000 in top the car is stable and pretty quiet. Surprising.

Come to think of it, the car's quiet all through the range. You can always hear the engine, but the hard, annoying noises are filtered out so it becomes a pleasant cross between growl and hum. Wind noise is very subdued right up to the top speed and road noise is kept out quite well, though on rough surfaces the suspension noises can be a bit intrusive. In small car terms it's a quiet car; in performance car terms it's BLOODY quiet . . .

The steering, roadholding and braking of the Escort

RS2000 deserve to be described in poetry. They are just wonderful — and that's something for Ford Australia to take very much to heart. If it builds a 2-litre Escort it won't be worth much unless it has roadholding as well as poke. And if that means it has a firm ride — so be it.

The RS can be fairly hurled in to bends without any drama at all. It seems to be able to absorb the cornering loads thrust upon it by the most senseless driving technique and when it is used with reasonable skill — it's just plain blinding. Body roll is minimal, understeer is non-existent. Oversteer isn't evident either, largely because the car's outside wheels cling so well that it finally picks up an inside rear wheel when cornering hard.

The RS is a revelation to drive on twisty roads. You simply don't slow down for the bends and you watch pursuing traffic melt away into the distance in your rear-vision mirror. At the limit, we suppose, it would break rear-first but though we drove it *bloody* fast, we rarely approached its limits. Steering is pin-accurate geared just right and quite light. It transmits its messages with perfect reliability.

The brakes are only disc/drums but they resist fade and lockup very well. They pull the car up straight and short, but they can be made to fade in the end. But that does take persistence.

The ride is quite firm — which is apparently what is needed to make a car with unsophisticated suspension handle so very well. It's not a bouncy ride, in fact it's no worse than an Alfa GTV or Berlina, and because the seats hold your bod so well you're not affected by it too much. One of our test drivers — Mr Editor Robinson, it was — claimed he was "getting too old" for such a ride, but then that's probably an indictment of the man himself, not the car . . .

In a year's time, you and I will be able to buy 2-litre sporty Escort two-door sedans — and not for the $8500 that Ford was asking for its batch of 25 imports (though it was undoubtedly less than that for FoMoCo's friends on the tracks). That, friends (you too, Robinson Esq.) is the best piece of Australian sporty sedan news for many a long day. *

RS2000 BEST ESCORT YET?

OF all the 'new' Escorts the RS 2000 took the longest time coming. Photographs were shown early in 1975 and a car appeared at European motor shows during the year, the production version only just hitting dealers' showrooms in the past few months. Now the RS 2000 is on sale the range is said to be complete and Ford fans can now choose between three RS models, the Mexico and RS 1800 in addition to the larger capacity 2000.

The RS 1800 is really only for competition — you have to be mad to buy a twin overhead camshaft, sixteen valve, 115mph version of a basic family small car for anything but rallying or racing. Ford know this, which is why you'll have one hell of a job finding an RS 1800 in your Rallye Sport man's showroom. But the RS 2000 is there and it's Ford's idea of the ultimate road car on the Escort shell.

The formula is fairly simple. All three RS model Escorts share the same basic body, chassis and trim package. The difference comes in the power unit and the level of luxury. All cars have uprated Escort II suspension with twin radius arms locating the live rear axle instead of an anti roll bar and the servo assisted brakes of 9.63 in disc at the front, 9 in drum to the rear. The same rear axle is used with a 3.54 final drive. Standard wheels are 5½J steels with a 6J alloy as an option, in all cases 175/70-13 radial tyres being used.

The RS 2000 power comes from the single overhead camshaft big four of 1993cc as used in various Cortina, Granada and Capri models but a re-designed exhaust manifold and system puts the power up to 110 bhp at 5,500 rpm, a ten per cent gain over the more lowly versions. Gearbox is the same as that used in the Mexico (but not RS 1800) being the standard two litre Ford model with 8.5 in diameter clutch.

Visually the RS 2000 is way apart from the other two RS models because of its polyurethane moulded snout that most certainly gives the car a distinctive look. The finish on this plastic nose is excellent and it is virtually impossible to tell that it is not made of metal as the rest of the car. Any suggestion of improved aerodynamics must be questionable but the absorbing quality of the nose is likely to be of value in low speed accidents. Expect to see more British cars with front end treatment like this before long.

At the rear the RS 2000 gets a boot lid spoiler this time manufactured in thick, squidgy, rubber. Just like those dirty great wings on roadgoing Porsche Carerras!

Interior gets the full treatment. Carpets, centre console, full instrumentation and cloth covered Recaro recliners in the front. All in sporty black, of course. The black theme carries on outside the car in fact with bumpers and window frames in matt anodised finish.

The RS 2000 drives like an RS 1800, and no doubt like a Mexico but I have yet to try one of those. On the wide alloy wheels the steering is heavy at all speeds until you get right on the cornering limit (when it lightens considerably and quite suddenly) and the stiff suspension coupled with the rack and pinion steering transmits most road irregularities to the — black — chunky steering wheel.

Driving the RS is very much like driving an old type sports car, MGB or TR6. The difference is that Ford's performance saloon car does things a lot better than most of the traditional sports cars. The engine is torquey and willing, high revs being unnecessary for quick motoring; which is a good thing because the engine, just like a 2.0S Capri I tried recently, gets very harsh above 4500 rpm. The RS needs to be *driven*, you can't expect it to do the work for you. You need to drive by the seat of your pants, have to be alert all the time, need to place the car accurately on the road and be prepared to counteract the twitchyness that is there when travelling quickly on anything but the smoothest surface.

Ford say the spring and damper settings have been selected to 'provide the ultimate in handling with the usual compromises to ride quality'. To my mind the ride has suffered (it's too harsh and choppy for a family day out) but that doesn't matter. The RS 2000 is built for people who enjoy driving and are prepared to accept small inconveniences for the pleasure of getting some real motoring. Otherwise go out and buy a Marina or Cortina Mk III.

Speeds tend to be academic nowadays with all our nasty limits. Ford claim a top of 111 mph and 0 to 60 mph acceleration of 8.5 seconds, which compares with the RS 1800 figures of 115 mph and 8.2 seconds and must be quick enough for most people. The good thing about the RS 2000's performance is that it is effortless. Sound proofing is good (until that engine speed gets high) and wind noise extremely low.

The RS 2000 which, it would appear, is currently being assembled in Germany rather than this country is a car which quite obviously has had a lot of thought put into its development. Which is probably why it has had a longer gestation period than most of the other Escort 2's. In production line form it would seem there's little doubt that — although it is primarily a road car — you could run one in a club road rally and do well with very little preparation. It's also already homologated for Group One and should be highly competitive.

It's only the little things that annoyed me. The jerky clutch on the test car. The fact that the, very good, Recaro seats were so big there was no room to adjust the rake knob without opening the door and the fact that rear seat leg room was cut to the absolute minimum. The steering column mounted indicators, wipers and light controls all seem to be in the wrong places and are awkward to operate. Finally, there's a particularly nasty chrome strip running along the interior trim on each door which is most definitely out of character . . .

You can't really find heavy criticism with the RS 2000. It's a super car and one in which a lot of *real* drivers will enjoy some *real* driving. My only worry is that somehow I can't personally justify spending a cool £2857 on what is, after all, only a Ford Escort. Perhaps I can't keep pace with inflation. **PD**

FOR YEARS THE MAKERS OF WARMED-OVER family saloons have kept to a familiar formula: take the lightest (and generally cheapest) version of a hack model, endow it with extra performance and a stiff suspension, slip in some extra instruments and a thick-rimmed steering wheel, and let it loose on the roads at a premium of several hundred pounds — taking care to add enough matt black paint, distinctive badgework and stripery to convince the buyer and his neighbours that the extra outlay is worthwhile. The formula has been very successful but it has not produced many memorable cars. The car makers' chief aim has been to circumvent the High St hot bits supplier by fitting the go-faster equipment 'in house' and collecting the profit thereon, rather than producing performance models with genuine design refinements. The best hot saloons — Lotus Cortina, Mini-Coopers, BDA Escorts — have invariably been produced for competition and their inspiring road performances have been by-products of that.

Ford's Escort RS2000 has been the exception to the formula. Overshadowed for the first years of its life by the Escort Twin-Cam — RS1600 and RS1800 — the 2000 has always been primarily a pokey saloon for the road, rather than a tamed track car. But suddenly the field is becoming more crowded. The Golf GTi is on the scene and the new Lotus Sunbeam is imminent. Fiat have recently put two new sporty versions of family cars on the market,

Giant Test

Fiat's refined 131 Sport tangles with Britain's top hotshoe special, the Ford RS2000, and proves that backstreet brawn Italian-style is the thing to beat the pugnacious little 127 Sport (complete with 10percent more power) and the 2.0litre Mirafiori Sport, a natural and deadly enemy for the RS2000. With the release of this model, the 131 finally realises its full potential. Because it was spawned during the oil crisis of '73 the first 131 had an extremely conservative specification; in fact, it only received its rightful engine (the DOHC 1.6litre) last year in the model Fiat's admen are pleased to call the Supermirafiori. Now with 2.0litres under the bonnet, Bertone-designed aerodynamic additions reminiscent of the Abarth-Fiat rally cars, a fresh round of suspension development and a standard set of Pirelli P6 radial tyres — the finest available for it — the car reaches what must be its ultimate affordable form, the 131 Sport. At £4635 it is £220 more expensive than the RS2000 Custom which offers a similar level of equipment. But the prices, specification and performance are certainly close enough to compel an enthusiast of one model to take a serious look at the other.

Of course, Ford's strength is the fact that the Custom is the best-equipped of two RS2000 models; there is a basic model nearly £500 cheaper which has identical dynamic qualities but lesser trim, seats and steel wheels instead of the Custom's elegant four-spoke alloy ones. Fiat are not too worried about a price disadvantage. While this test was being prepared they increased the 131 Sport's price to its current level from previous parity

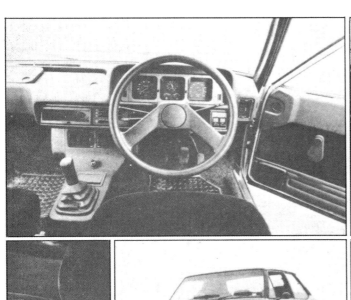

FIAT 131 SPORT

Instruments are very good (though speedo optimistic) and are made legible for all by height-adjustable steering wheel. Stalk controls could be better. Gearchange must be one of the best in class. Wet weather grip of Pirelli P6s puts Fiat ahead of all corners but steering is not very sharp at straight-ahead. Velour seats add to a feeling of luxury but driver's seat cushion is low in relation to pedals. Rear room is not a strong point but is adequate for smaller adults and much better than Escort. Fiat engine is venerable DOHC 2.0litre which is spirited but too loud. it pulls well from low speeds, however, especially since allied to well spread ratios of five-speed box. Boot is capacious and uncluttered but has lip over which luggage must be lifted. Details: Fiat lacks infinite adjustment of seat squabs; clutch pedal rubber falls off easily: dangerous in wet weather

FORD RS2000

Ford dials do the job well enough although award-winning binnacle has become boringly familiar. Small wheel is nice to use; gearchange is foolproof, column stalks don't fit hands very well. Escort is chuckable and precise in dry but its Pirelli CN36s are outclassed in the wet and for ride and noise suppression. Steering is pin sharp. Standard Recaro seats give comfortable, secure driving position but foot room is at a premium. Rear room is a joke for all but amputees. RS2000 uses warm Cortina 2.0litre SOHC engine which gives it slightly better acceleration than Fiat but it still sounds like a Cortina. Rev limit not marked but 6000rpm is the natural redline. Boot is deep and surprisingly roomy but smaller than Fiat's. Loading lip is high and spare wheel intrudes. Details: Custom model has alloy wheels (Fiat's are steel) but only a four-speed gearbox — one slot too few

Giant Test

with the Escort Custom's. And they point out that the market for high-performance saloons of around 2.0litres has expanded from 18,000units in 1976 to an estimated 30,000 for this year. And despite the price hike, their car is still £800 cheaper than an Alfetta 2000L and £1000 cheaper than a BMW 320, both of which have a comparable performance with the Fiat (and Escort), although the Alfetta is a rather different kettle of fish.

STYLING, ENGINEERING

In their lowest forms both cars are simple, box-on-two boxes family cars so the primary elements of their styling are simple, neat and not even a little bit emotive. The Fiat, conceived during the oil upheaval, is Italy's Marina; a 'just transport' car. It concentrates, within the natural restrictions of having a rear-drive layout, on being an efficient people-carrier with a large passenger cell, a low waistline, a short bonnet and boot, thin doors and pillars and a large area of glass. The present Escort is the product of a comprehensive but cheap-as-possible re-skinning job designed to turn a car which was selling well in Europe but nowhere else into a car which could sell well everywhere. It worked. The car now has a lot of glass and clean, chiseled styling but its old basic design gives it a narrow body and higher waist than the Fiat.

It is careful detail styling that turns a pair of boring traffic jammers into the two best hotshoe specials currently available in Britain (the Golf GTi is only available LHD to special order). And they need their distinctiveness. Fast cars which don't look the part are for occasional daydreams but not for buying. Both Ford and Fiat are artfully toughened-up without the changes costing real money. The Escort gets its deformable plastic wedge nose with quad headlights, integral 'chin' spoiler and a duct for radiator air under the black front bumper. The slatted grille that contains the Ford emblem is but a dummy although most tyre kickers don't realise it. Apart from that the Ford is plain, with painted window frames, an absence of chrome, decals on flanks and bootlid (which also has the RS rubber spoiler) and the highly visible alloy wheels. It all makes a squat wide-chested little tool, poised for rushing off in. The Fiat is low, too, on its no-nonsense Pirelli P6s. It has a grey plastic nose spoiler which runs back to join grey plastic mudguard flares over the four wheel arches. At the front they double as wheel-well liners which help keep the corrosives out.

To some eyes the Fiat is dowdy and unimpressive. There is a preponderance of grey plastic and the pressed-steel wheels, buried rather too far inside the wheel arches, are finished in dingy gunmetal. The idea has been to make the Sport like a no-frills, performance-is-everything track car. In Italy the model is called the Mirafiori Racing. But the idea has not worked very well, especially since the special gunmetal grille looks more like the front of a Japanese transistor radio than a car. Henry wins clearly in the styling stakes, and proves once again his skill in making ordinary cars look aggressive.

In mechanical layout both cars are two-door versions of utterly conventional saloons, with bigger engines shoe horned in. But the essential thing is that neither is a hot rod. The Ford has had years of development, including the Escort II facelift and in the first place it was built in Ford's advanced vehicles workshops where they know there is more to building a fast car than the old transAtlantic technique called LJDIA (Let's Just Drop In A...). And neither the Fiat nor Ford 2.0litre engine is all that much bigger or hard to accommodate than the 1.3 and 1.6litre engines of the cheaper versions. Each has its engine conventionally mounted north-south, driving the rear wheels through a live axle. The Fiat puts its power through a five-speed gearbox; the Ford makes do with four. Both have MacPherson strut front suspensions. The Escort's rear axle is suspended by leaf springs with radius arms to keep them under control, while the Fiat uses the coil springs, trailing links and Panhard rod which are favoured these days by those designers who persist with non-independent rear suspensions.

The most interesting mechanical feature of either car is the Fiat's engine. It is all-Italian, has twin overhead camshafts (still a rarity in medium cheap cars), it sounds good and the sight of its two cast cam covers separates it from mass-produced mediocrity, though mass-produced it definitely is. It is a familiar engine which powers several other Fiat and Lancia Beta models. It is undersquare which probably helps put its torque peak lower in the rev range than the Escort's, it breathes through a twin-throat downdraught Weber carburettor and produces 115bhp at 5800rpm. Maximum torque of 123lb/ft is derived at 3600rpm. The RS2000 engine is Ford's trusty SOHC 1993cc unit, most commonly found in Cortinas. It comes complete with dingy paint job, tin rocker cover and 110 honest horses developed at 5500rpm. Peak torque is 116lb/ft at 4000rpm. Like the Fiat, the Escort is Weber-fed. It has assorted internal tweaks which lift its power output 17percent above the Cortina's 95bhp.

The biggest visible difference between the cars is their size. The Fiat is comprehensively the bigger. It has 4in more wheelbase, is 4in wider, 5in longer, has around 35percent more boot space, carries 2gal more fuel, is bigger in all cabin dimensions except headroom, and weighs a hefty 324lb more, if the makers' claimed weights are derived the same way. That goes a long way towards offsetting the price difference between the cars because the Fiat offers at least as much metal for the money as the Ford.

PERFORMANCE

That is precisely what both of these cars were built for. Both are genuinely fast cars and streets ahead of the Mini 1275GTs and Datsun SSSs of this world. Despite the power and torque advantages and the extra speed in its gearbox, the Fiat is the slower of the two, doubtless because of its greater weight and frontal area. The Escort is the rocket. Using a rev limit of 6000rpm (none is marked on the tacho) it will run to 60mph from standstill in just 9.3seconds which is a shade slower than an Alfetta GTV and Saab Turbo and on a par with a BMW 320i, all much more expensive and supposedly better-bred cars. In top gear (which gives 18.6mph/1000rpm) it is geared for 112mph and the speedo will indicate that in neutral conditions, though error knocks this back to a real 107-108. Key to the Escort's fast getaway is its torque, light weight and its tall second and third gears. Second and third are good for 60mph and 90mph if you stretch a small point with the self-imposed rev limit. The Escort offers all those things that are pleasant about big-engined cars. It is very flexible (although the tall second and third ratios can sometimes be a hindrance in town pottering) and the throttle has a real metering function instead of being wide-open-or-shut as in many small cars. Indeed, it is a very sensitive control which, if not used smoothly, can turn progress into a succession of fits and starts.

The Fiat goes well, too, although it does not have quite the same feeling that there are cubic inches under the bonnet. In acceleration its better gear spread keeps it in touch with the Escort's performance until 70mph where it starts to lose out noticeably. But it is only 0.8sec slower from 0-60 which is not a big enough margin for the seat of the average pants to discern. The Fiat redline is clearly marked at 6000rpm and there is a warning sector beginning at 5500. At these speeds the twin-cam is much louder than the Ford. Top speed is about the same as in the Ford although after a long, long run the Fiat will indicate a lot more because the speedo acts as though it were made by the Brothers Grimm. It is 6mph fast at 80mph and the error builds up as the car goes faster. This can lead you to believe at first that the 131 Sport is a kind of miracle car — the first time you see it sustain 70mph through a corner where previous experience tells you 60mph is a very good effort. It is really doing 64mph which is very good, but not as sensational as all that...

Fuel consumption cannot be of major interest to the buyers of these cars — except if it is so disastrous that it affects a buyer's ability to withstand the running costs. Neither car consumes fuel furiously, but neither is particularly economical. Driven gently (difficult) both will return up to 30mpg but systematically driven into the ground they will return only 21-22mpg. Most drivers should get about 26mpg.

The dominant sound in the Fiat is its engine. The ride is quiet, thanks to the combination of suspension development and space-age tyres, and there is little wind noise. But the engine produces lots of induction roar, some mechanical clatter from the top of the engine and a drone from the exhaust that is well-bred but far too loud. There are booms, too. One at 80-83mph is a particular nuisance because you have to drive either above it (which can be upsetting to policemen) or below it (upsetting to your trip average). The noise is much more annoying on motorways than on back roads where you are running up and down through the gearbox. When pressing on, the noise can be very nice although nothing would be lost if there were less of it. Ford's engine is quieter (though not impressively so by other standards than Fiat's) but it has more wind and road noise. Neither car is quiet; neither is deafening. The Fiat has an excellent gearchange. It is precise, beautifully spring-loaded towards the third-fourth plane and requires only short, rhythmical, flicking movements between ratios. The synchromesh is unbeatable. This is allied to a clutch which is unusually smooth and predictable, so that gearchanging is something a driver looks forward to. The Escort's change is smooth and precise, too, but somehow it doesn't have the precision-engineered, snap action of the Fiat's.

HANDLING, ROADHOLDING

Fiat can probably thank their own development engineers for the 131 Sport's advantage in this area — and Pirelli's engineers for the size of it. The P6 tyres are fitted to 5.5in wide steel rims as standard and in wet and dry grip, ride comfort and quietness they are simply a cut above any production tyre you care to name with the possible exception of Michelin's TRX. But it is clear that Fiat have put a great deal of development into the 131 Sport to make it suit the tyres as well as it does. It is well-known — at least to CAR readers — that these tyres function best on cars with minimal amounts of camber change because they have flat, wide treads which must be kept in complete contact with the road. The Fiat behaves beautifully. It corners neutrally, long past the stage where other cars — or differently-shod Fiat 131 Sports; in other countries, the Pirellis are only optional — would be displaying extreme slip angles or departing into the scenery. And when breakaway finally arrives it gives plenty of warning, the tail moving out far more gently than the driver has a right to expect. The slow, measured breakaway is evident in the wet; it is evident even on hard-packed snow.

Because it grips so well it takes some effort to get the 131 Sport to demonstrate its on-the-limit cornering characteristics but eventually the tail does move outward in that fine fashion. It can be provoked out, if the driver insists, with power on slower bends but it is happiest in the neutral mode. Fiat's adoption of the Pirelli P6 and the suitability of its car to them is a tribute to its development engineers and shows how well the various arms of Fiat — including Ferrari and Abarth — are now working together. When you're beyond the limit, the handling is first class: sharp, precise, obedient and safe and the car can be balanced to your tiniest whim at all times. For the chassis, it is impeccable.

The best you can say is that the Ford is not disgraced. It does a good job on its Pirelli CN36s but the limits are just not as high. It rides more harshly and makes more noise about it, its grip is not as good and it will understeer or oversteer much more easily. It is the same nimble, chuckable car it has always been and it does have the advantage of pin-sharp rack and pinion steering which shades the Fiat's similar system for 'centre feel' and directness. The Escort is the heavier to steer, though. The Fiat

Giant Test

has very good brakes, not over-servoed like so many Fiats of the past but beautifully precise and progressive. And those tyres give the Sport particularly good wet weather retardation, postponing lock-up for an amazingly long time. The Escort's brakes are powerful and precise, too, though the test car had a judder from the servoed front discs which indicated incorrect heat treatment at manufacture and consequent warping. It was annoying in low-effort stops but not noticeable when the brakes were being used hard.

COMFORT

The biggest difference here comes once again from the tyres. Both cars are firmly suspended with flat, controlled rides and well-chosen damper rates. The Fiat has an immediate advantage because of its wider tracks front and rear and longer wheelbase, but the biggest aid lies with its Pirellis. As LJKS has pointed out several times in his various stories about the new wave of tyre development, the old compromises between optimum grip and optimum ride need no longer be struck. The new tyres are designed so that the tread (which must not deform) and the walls (which must, for the best ride characteristics) function in a 'de-coupled' way. The Fiat rides beautifully. It is always in touch with the contours of the road — and in that sense it rides firmly — but minor ripples and harshness are absorbed in a way which is simply outside the experience of a driver who has not experienced P6 or Michelin TRX tyres. This absorption is accompanied by an eery lack of road noise and bump-thump, powerful evidence of how well Fiat have suited the car to Pirelli's tyres. Even when cruising on a wet motorway there is almost no tyre noise; it is the hiss from other cars' tyres you hear.

The Ford's ride is noisier and more choppy than the Fiat's but well-damped and pleasantly free of rolls or lurches. Its compact dimensions make it one of those cars you 'put on', like a track car. It has a comfortable driving position which is aided by its well-bolstered standard Recaro seats. They provide unusually good side and under-thigh support; in fact, they feel so good that it is surprising that more car builders don't try to incorporate the Recaro strong points in their own seats. The Escort suits smaller drivers best because it has fairly narrow, cramped footwells and no surplus shoulder room either. Yet it is comfortable enough for people of 6ft and a little over, thanks to its supportive seats and small high-mounted steering wheel (which gives good knee room) but these people are grateful for opportunities to stop and stretch the limbs every hour or two. Rear seat accommodation is something of a joke in the Escort. The Recaros occupy a lot of the space the designers originally intended for the rear people's legs and the unnecessarily wide rear seat cushion takes up what is left. As a result the Escort has fine rear accommodation for those with large backsides and no legs, or those prepared to assume a lotus position. Everyone else is uncomfortable

The Fiat cabin has more spreading room. Its velour-covered seats look luxurious and are comfortable for most people, although they don't have anything like the firm grip on the body, so helpful for quick driving, of the Escort's Recaros. And drivers with fairly long legs find that the pedals are set too high in relation to the leading edge of the seat; the cushion is also too flat. But there is more footwell and shoulder room and the occupants sit much higher in relation to the bonnet and eyebrow of the dashboard. There is less headroom front and rear than in the Ford, but it is enough. The Fiat's rear passengers aren't luxuriously looked after but at least they can fit in even if knee room is only fair. But one of the more practical things about these cars is the size of their boots. The Escort's is deep and uncluttered — very big for a car of its size — and the Fiat's is nearly 40percent bigger than that. There is stacks of room for the holiday luggage for the two

people who will most often be carried in Fiat or Ford.

DRIVER APPEAL

As the buyer stands and looks at the two cars, the Escort has the more appeal because its styling works better. The shovel nose, the alloy wheels and the plain, compact shape have much more appeal than the businesslike but rather dowdy Fiat. As he sits in the car, the buyer might lean more towards the Fiat because of its panoramic driving position, its luxurious seats and its more impressive dashboard. The Escort is as well-equipped as a sporting saloon needs to be, but the interior has a strong relationship to the Ford Popular which costs almost exactly half as much. In the driving, the Fiat surges ahead in driver appeal because of its fine grip, beautiful handling, amazingly compliant ride and ride silence; the fluency of its gearbox and the fact that there are five speeds. The Escort does have a performance advantage and it is very much a nimble little fun car, but it lacks the Fiat's edge of sophistication. The stalk controls that protrude from either car's steering column are broadly similar — three controls, working the lights, wiper/washers and turn indicators. Neither system is ideal. The Fiat's indicator stalk is on the wrong side and must be worked by the hand that is changing gear. Its lights/flashers switch is too far towards the dash and remote from the steering wheel. The Escort's controls are better sited but they have flimsy, unsatisfying actions and the controls themselves don't fit a hand very well.

The sounds these cars emit are crucial to their appeal and here the Fiat wins again, though not by a big margin. Its twin-cam engine has a willing Italian rasp about it but, as mentioned, it can become a drone (and an annoyance) in high speed, constant throttle cruising. Were it down to us, we'd alter the exhaust system for greater quietness.

The Ford's engine is willing, too, and when being used with verve it has a pleasant, hollow induction noise to accompany its flashy performance. But most of the time it is rather too reminiscent of a Cortina — the kind of car the RS2000's driver would prefer to pretend never happened.

CONCLUSIONS

The Escort would still deserve the superlatives we applied to it in our Giant Test of February 1976 were it not for the existence of the Fiat. The Escort is just as quick, sensitive and appealing as it ever was but the Fiat represents another step up the sporty saloon's scale of evolution. That is not to say it is perfect. The steering could do with more sensitivity at the straight-ahead (and this would seem to be a Fiat engineering shortcoming rather than a Pirelli one since the tyres are claimed to *improve* centre feel), the engine noise is a real problem at times and needs to be reduced, the exterior styling and colour schemes do not work very well and the dashboard has just as many internal buzzes and sizzles as every other 131 we have driven (and complained about). And on a smaller scale, the clutch pedal rubber in each of the three 131 Sports we have driven came adrift after the first half-dozen gearchanges. Annoying and unsafe in wet weather.

The Escort, curiously, has a shorter list of fundamental faults. Of course its rear seat accommodation is a joke, but then it will be used as a coupe most times anyway. It could do with better stalk controls but most of all it needs Pirelli P6 tyres and whatever modifications to suspension geometry, rates and mounting bushes that are necessary to make them work well. That, of course, is the kind of glib remark that makes motor industry engineers see red, shackled as they are by the corporate bean counters. On the other hand, the work may be well under way. Ford are known to be showing great interest in the Michelin and Pirelli tyre developments, in fact it was Ford who made the first bold move to the TRX for the Granada and now the new Mustang. As far as hotshoe saloons go, Ford have been building the best for upwards of five years and it is probably time they were bettered. That, Fiat have duly done.

	FIAT	FORD
Capacity (cc)	1995	1993
Bore (mm)	84	90.82
Stroke (mm)	90	76.95
Compression (to one)	8.9	9.2
Valve gear	DOHC	SOHC
Aspiration	Twin choke Weber	Twin choke Weber
Power (DIN rpm)	115/5800	110/5000
Torque (DIN/rpm)	123lb/ft/3600	116lb/ft/4000
TRANSMISSION		
Type	RWD/five-speed	RWD/four-speed
Ratios/mph per 1000 rpm		
First	3.61/4.8	3.65/5.1
Second	2.04/8.4	1.97/9.4
Third	1.36/12.6	1.37/13.6
Fourth	1.00/17.2	1.00/18.6
Fifth	0.87/19.9	
Final drive ratio	3.9	3.54
CHASSIS AND BODY		
Construction	Unitary	Unitary
Front suspension	Independent, struts and link, coil springs	Struts, lower links, anti-roll bar
Rear suspension	Live axle, coil springs, trailing arms, Panhard rod	Live axle, semi-elliptical springs, radius arm
Steering	Rack and pinion	Rack and pinion
Turns lock to lock	3.5	3.5
Turning circle	33.8ft	29.7ft
Wheels	5.5x14	6x13
Brakes	Servoed discs and drums	Servoed discs and drums
DIMENSIONS (inches)		
Wheelbase	98	94
Front track	54.5	50.8
Rear track	52.2	51.8
Length	166.6	161.8
Width	65.5	61.6
Ground clearance	5	6
Fuel tank capacity	10.9	9.0
Weight (lb)	2359	2035
CABIN DIMENSIONS (inches)		
Front headroom	35.6	37.8
Front legroom (seat back)	39.4	39.3
Rear headroom	33.9	36.9
Rear legroom (seat forward)	28.3	34.0
Front shoulder room	56.7	49.0
Rear shoulder room	54.9	50
Luggage capacity	14	10.3
MAINTENANCE		
Major service time	2.8hrs	2.7hrs
Sump (capacity/oil grade)	10W30	6.6/10W30
Oil change intervals	6000	6000
Grease points	None	None
Time for removing/replacing engine/gearbox	5hrs/2.3hrs	3.4hrs
Time for replacing clutch	2.6hrs	2.4hrs
Time for renewing front brake pads/shoes	0.6hrs	1.4hrs
Time for renewing exhaust system	1.3hrs	0.8hrs
Number of UK dealers	391	82 (Rallye Sport)
MECHANICAL SPARES PRICES		
Engine	£518.06new	£366.53new
Gearbox	568.41new	141.87exch
Differential	131.60	123.50new
Clutch unit	58.80	35.61
Brake disc	8.06	5.60
Set brake pads	6.88	13.53
Set drum linings	14.86	8.39
Fuel pump	7.83	14.56
Damper (front)	22.51	39.04
Exhaust system	90.79	67.40
Oil filter	2.93	3.90
Alternator	74.14	88.11
Starter motor	66.75	59.90
Speedometer	41.49	15.80
BODY PART PRICES		
Front door (primer)	84.85	44.78
Front bumper	38.98	N/A
Bonnet (primer)	75.28	73.21
Windscreen	62.87	32.40
Headlamp unit (each)	12.96	21.66
Grille	32.24	N/A
TOTAL COST, INCLUDING CAR TAX AND VAT		
Price without extras	£4635	£4416
GUARANTEE		
Length and conditions	Mastercover (24 months in 2stages)	12months/unlimited mileage

ACCELERATION	0-30	0-40	0-50	0-60	0-70
Fiat	3.8	5.3	6.5	10.1	13.2
Ford	3.6	5.3	6.6	9.3	12.6

SPEED IN GEARS

	First	Second	Third	Fourth	Fifth
Fiat	0-29	0-51	10-76	15-103	22-108
Ford	0-30	0-56	10-83	20-107	—

FUEL CONSUMPTION (on four-star)

Fiat 21-30mpg   **Ford** 22-30mpg

A fast (but noisy) fun car

THERE IS ONE word that sums up everything about Ford's Escort RS2000 — fun.

The RS2000 is a fun car to drive, a fun car to own, a fun car to have fun in.

And, strangely enough, most of its appeal comes from the image it has. Because when you strip away the plastic nose, bright paint, and tape stripes, the RS2000 is really nothing more than the previous Rally Pack 2.0-litre Escort.

The shovel-nosed model will do a lot to enhance the overall image of the Escort range. It adds some life to an otherwise dull line-up of models.

The RS2000 is probably the closest you'll get to driving a rally car on the road. Its forest racer heritage, the kickback of years of Escort participation in rallying worldwide, is apparent in its sharpness on the road.

It's also a bargain car. The test car, a four-door, retails at just $6513, plus $224 for the optional alloy wheels and $103 for the laminated windscreen — a total of $6840 for one of the most enjoyable cars we've driven for a long time.

The low cost of the RS2000 models — there's a two-door as well — means almost everyone can have a sporty performance car. And when we say performance, we mean performance.

The Australian RS2000, which is different in many ways to the English version, is one of the fastest cars on the road. Its light weight and powerful 2.0-litre, four-cylinder engine give it rapid acceleration.

Out on the highway, where the RS2000 really feels good, it just sings along at between 140 and 160 km/h and gets close to 170 km/h for its top speed. So you can imagine that at the legal 100/110 km/h highway limits around the country it's only loafing along.

The only thing that we didn't like was the noise. It's a very noisy little car. Around town you don't mind that because the growly exhaust is part of its charm. But at high speed, the din — both mechanical and road induced, is very high.

Also, the RS2000 is particularly susceptible to sidewinds, and tends to wander more than you'd expect in blustery conditions.

Otherwise, the Escort RS2000's stability is excellent. Its pin-sharp rack-and-pinion steering is tremendously accurate. Few cars have as much feel and responsiveness through the steering, which is enhanced by the special sports steering wheel that's part of the package.

The RS2000 sits very flat on the road. The uprated shock absorbers and anti-roll bars combine with firmer springing to produce a particularly solid and steady cornering stance.

The ride is very comfortable. There is very little harshness transmitted through to the passenger compartment, and suspension travel is sufficient to stop bottoming on rough roads or over humps.

Handling is generally close to neutral until you start driving enthusiastically through tight corners.

Over our high speed interstate run we averaged 12.1 litres per 100km, which shows the RS2000 combines performance with fuel economy. The best figure we saw during the test was 10 litres for every 100km.

The only drawback of the all-cloth interior trim is that it's available in one color only — black — which gets very hot in warm weather. Also, even in the four-door version, rear space is very cramped — a sign of the age of the Escort design.

Apart from the sports instruments and radio, the RS2000 dash is very bare. In front of the passenger there's just an expanse of black plastic.

The Escort RS2000 is a way of putting fun back into driving. It's the kind of car we should all be driving — responsive, accurate, economical, and fast.

– Mark Fogarty

Ford Escort RS 2000

ENGINE
Cylinders	Four
Bore x Stroke	90.8 x 76.9 mm
Capacity	1998 cc
Carburation	Twin-throat down-draught
Compression Ratio	9.2 to 1
Claimed Power	70 kW at 5200 rpm
Claimed Torque	148 Nm at 3800 rpm

TRANSMISSION
Type	Four-speed manual
Gearbox Ratios	
First	3.65
Second	1.97
Third	1.37
Fourth	1.00
Final Drive Ratio	3.54

SUSPENSION
Front	Independent by MacPherson struts; integral anti-roll bar/tension rod.
Rear	Leaf springs; anti-roll bar.
Wheels	5.0 JJ x 13
Tyres	ZR 70S x 13
Steering	Rack-and-pinion

BRAKES
Front	244 mm discs
Rear	223 mm drums

DIMENSIONS AND WEIGHT
Wheelbase	2405 mm
Front Track	1270 mm
Rear Track	1296 mm
Overall Length	4109 mm
Overall Width	1596 mm
Overall Height	1373 mm
Ground Clearance	146 mm
Kerb Weight	1000 kg
Fuel Tank Capacity	54.6 litres

CALCULATED DATA
Weight to Power	14.29 kg/kW
Specific Power Output	35.04 kW/litre

PERFORMANCE
Fuel Consumption	12.1 litres/100km
Standing 400 Metres	17.9 seconds
0-100 km/h	11.5 seconds
Top Speed	168 km/h
Braking from 100 km/h	46.6 metres

Ford Esc

" The Escort RS-2000 goes from nought to a R100 fine in 10 seconds," is a current quip in motoring circles in South Africa — and nobody tells it with more gusto than the Ford people themselves!

But it does less than justice to the new car, which in road terms is probably the finest performance model Ford has ever put into production here. Almost exactly 15 years after Ford rocked the South African motoring world — and horrified the purists — with the first, immortal Cortina GT, it has launched this brilliant new RS in South Africa: engineered for this country, and in local manufacture as a very special road car with extensive development potential.

LOW-DRAG COACHWORK

The Escort RS-2000 is a well-established concept in Europe, where the first version was produced in 1973 based on the Mk 1 Escort. The present Mk 2 version was launched in 1976, but was not a

A very special model, re-worked for South African conditions, gives top performance without being coarse

KEY FIGURES	
Maximum speed	169,2 km/h
1 km sprint	33,9 seconds
Terminal speed	152,5 km/h
Fuel tank capacity	55 litres
Litres/100 km at 80	7,9
Optimum fuel range at 80	693 km
Engine revs per km	2 120
National list price	R5 680

viable prospect for manufacture in South Africa until the 2-litre "Köln" overhead-cam engine went into manufacture here recently.

SPECIAL EQUIPMENT

It is based on the two-door Escort body shell in heavy-duty form, with reinforcement of suspension mounting points. A special polyurethane nose-cone with front air dam is fitted, which in conjunction with a neat rear decklid spoiler reduces drag co-efficient by 13 per cent to a figure of 0,386 — one of the best available in South Africa. Four halogen headlights are set in this moulded front end, and matt black finish is used for bumpers and other exterior trim features.

The list of special equipment starts with form-fitting Scheel rally-style safety seats with head restraints and inertia-reel seat belts, upholstered in black Beta cloth. Beautiful seats — but not for people with short legs!

The RS instrument cluster includes rev-counter, clock and oil pressure gauge, and an alloy sports-type steering wheel is fitted. The driver's door mirror has remote control from the inside, and the rear window is heated to prevent demisting.

The European version is designed for smooth roads and was found to have a "skitter" tendency on South Africa's corrugations and potholes, so the suspension was revised by the Product Engineering Division of Ford SA — a 22-mm stabiliser bar at front reduced oversteer, a stabliser bar was fitted at rear in place of the radius arms, and South African shockabsorber settings were developed — slightly softer than those used in Europe, to reduce rebound resistance.

ENGINE, TRANSMISSION

The 2-litre Köln engine as used in Cortina and Granada models is used in a mildly-tuned form: a new twin-choke

test Ford Escort RS-2000 Mk 2 sedan

Weber carburettor, low-restriction air-cleaner and free-flow exhaust system are claimed to uprate the engine by 12 per cent, and a cast-aluminium oil pan is used to improve oil cooling and reduce vibration.

Four pre-production prototypes were tested at Port Elizabeth for nearly a year to develop the South African model, and to allow for the Republic's altitude factor it was decided to fit a 3,70 to 1 rear axle ratio in place of Europe's 3,54 to 1. This is a mixed blessing: it gives the car more pull, but also makes it more under-geared than is really necessary. The test car clearly "ran out of revs" in maximum speed tests, going to a full 6 000 both ways on a level road — even though its power peak is listed as 5 500, and permissible maximum as 5 800!

PERFORMANCE

Gearbox is the highly-rated German Ford M3 model with close 2nd and 3rd ratios and a crisp, short selector action.

With its abundant power, performance-style gearing and sporty exhaust note through a big-bore tailpipe, the RS-2000 is a stirring car to drive: ultra-responsive, yet totally controllable.

We found that the big, low-profile radials (175/70) on wide 5,5J rims tended to develop judder in a maximum-effort start, and that best results could be achieved by feeding-in the clutch to avoid sharp engagement. This produced smooth spin and very quick acceleration: to 80 in 7,5 seconds, and to 90 (confirming that joke!) in 9,6 seconds. Maximum speed is restricted by gearing to just under 170 km/h — the car would not go faster, even with a following wind or on a gentle downhill run.

The speedometer overreads by a fair margin (about 8 per cent at middle speeds) but both odometer and rev-counter are reasonably accurate.

ECONOMY, BRAKING

This is a low-geared, 2-litre performance car, and its fuel economy is pretty fair by those standards: 7,9 litres/100 km at 80, and 8,6 at 90. At all speeds up to 100 km/h it keeps on the sunny side of 30 m-p-g — but of course it will chew petrol if a heavy foot is used all the time about town! To obtain the extra fuel capacity, the 55-litre tank is mounted in the luggage trunk above the rear axle, and its protective cover juts into the luggage area, cutting usable space to about 310 dm³.

The uprated brakes with increased boost allow sensitive stopping control within the limits of tyre adhesion: we had a bit of front-wheel locking with the test car, and the engine stalled at times.

Noise levels are fair — performance-style, without being loud.

HANDLING AND RIDE

The RS-2000 is beautifully balanced, and proves that a well-set-up live-rear-axle layout with leaf springs can yield blue-blooded handling.

The factory-recommended tyre pressures (150-170 kPa) are far too low: we are quite sure that a minimum of 200/220 gives superior handling, adhesion and performance — and probably longer tyre life, as well! The car has precise Escort-style handling, with a short turning circle and good control. With all this power on tap the car can be four-wheel-drifted to fine limits, and with a high degree of inherent safety.

SUMMARY

Ride generally is firm and load-capable without being harsh — the Ford people have really done their homework in this department.

This RS-2000 is the basic car, as it comes from the showroom floor at a remarkably low price — well under R6 000. But for owners who want to tweak it, a vast range of bolt-on and build-in parts and accessories is available from Ford dealers: wheel-arch extensions, rear window louvres, stoneguards, rally lights, sunroof and 6J Minilite mag wheels on the cosmetic side, and a twin-carb "Group One" engine kit to boost power by up to 60 per cent. Then there are ventilated brake discs, sumpshield, limited-slip diff and suspension mods — the Ford people assured us that an owner can spend up to R2 000 on goodies without buying any item twice!

The "RS" in its name stands for "Rally Sport", and this new Ford truly earns this accolade as a skilfully-compounded performance model: in many ways, the best of its breed!

Scheel rally seats are great for comfort — but hard on people with short legs because of the high squab.

The enlarged fuel tank set over the rear axle reduces load area slightly.

The Köln 2-litre engine is mildly uprated — but a hot kit is available as an accessory.

SPECIFICATIONS

ENGINE:
Cylinders . . . . 4 in line
Fuel supply . . . . .Weber 36 DCD 7
Bore/stroke . . . . .90,82/76,95 mm
Cubic capacity. . . . . . . 1 993 cm³
Compression ratio. . . . . . 9,2 to 1
Valve gear . . . . . o-h-v, single o-h-c
Ignition. . . . . . coil and distributor
Main bearings . . . . five
Fuel requirement . .98-octane Coast, 93-octane Reef
Cooling. . . . . . . water — 7,1 litres

ENGINE OUTPUT:
Max power I.S.O. (kW). 81
Power peak (r/min). . . . . . 5 500 (see text)
Max permissible r/min . . . . . 5 800 (see text)
Max torque (N.m). 163
Torque peak (r/min) 4 000

TRANSMISSION:
Forward speeds . . . . four
Gearshift . . . . console
Low gear . . . . 3,651 to 1
2nd gear . . . . 1,968 to 1
3rd gear . . . . 1,368 to 1
Top gear . . . . Direct
Reverse gear . . . . 3,66 to 1
Final drive . . . . 3,70 to 1
Drive wheels . . . . rear

WHEELS AND TYRES:
Road wheels . . . . pressed steel discs
Rim width . . . . .5,5 J
Tyres . . . . . . 175/70/SR 13 radials

BRAKES:
Front . . . . .248 mm discs
Rear . . . . .229 mm drums
Pressure regulation . . . dual circuits
Boosting . . . . .vacuum servo
Handbrake position . . .between seats

STEERING:
Type . . . . rack and pinion
Lock to lock. . . . . 3,5 turns
Turning circle . . . . . . 8,9 metres

MEASUREMENTS:
Length overall . . . . .4,140 m
Width overall . . . . .1,596 m
Height overall . . . . .1,398 m
Wheelbase . . . . .2,407 m
Licensing mass. . . . . . . .980 kg

SUSPENSION:
Front. . . . . independent
Type . . . . .MacPherson struts, stabiliser bar
Rear . . . . live axle
Type . . . . . . 3-bladed leaf springs, stabiliser bar

CAPACITIES:
Seating 4/5
Fuel tank. 55
Luggage trunk . . . . . 310 dm³ net

ACCELERATION

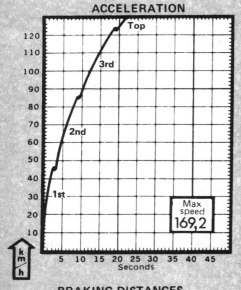

Max speed **169,2**

BRAKING DISTANCES

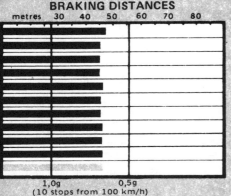

1,0g   0,5g
(10 stops from 100 km/h)

NOISE VALUES

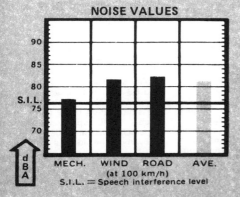

MECH.   WIND   ROAD   AVE.
(at 100 km/h)
S.I.L. = Speech interference level

CALCULATED FUEL RANGE
(km)

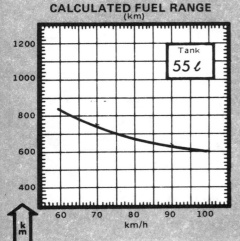

Tank **55 ℓ**

km/h

PERFORMANCE

PERFORMANCE FACTORS:
Power/mass (W/kg) net 82,5
Frontal area (m²) 2,23
km/h per 1 000 r/min (top) . . 28,3

INTERIOR NOISE LEVELS:

	Mech	Wind	Road
Idling	49,0	—	—
60	68,0	—	—
80	73,0	78,0	78,5
100	77,0	81,5	82,5
Average dBA at 100			80,3

ACCELERATION (seconds):
0-60 4,9
0-80 7,5
0-100 11,7
1 km sprint 33,9

OVERTAKING ACCELERATION:

	3rd	Top
40-60	4,0	5,7
60-80	3,4	4,8
80-100	4,1	5,8

MAXIMUM SPEED (km/h):
True speed 169,2
Speedometer reading 180
Calibration:
Indicated: 60 70 80 90 100
True speed: 56 65 74 82,5 91

FUEL CONSUMPTION:
(litres/100 km):
60 6,6
70 7,3
80 7,9
90 8,6
100 9,2

BRAKING TEST:
From 100 km/h:
First stop 3,8
Tenth stop 3,7
Average 3,67
(Measured in seconds with stops from true speeds at 30-second intervals on a good bitumenised surface.)

GRADIENTS IN GEARS:
Low gear . . . . 1 in 2,5
2nd gear . . . . 1 in 3,8
3rd gear . . . . 1 in 5,8
Top gear . . . . 1 in 8,6

GEARED SPEEDS (km/h):
Low gear 46,5
2nd gear 86,4
3rd gear 124,1
Top gear 169,8
(Calculated at engine peak r/min — 6 000.)

TEST CONDITIONS:
Altitude . . . . at sea level
Weather . . . . fine and hot
Fuel used . . . . 98 octane
Test car's odometer . . . . . 2 573 km

WARRANTY:
Six months or 10 000 km.

TEST CAR FROM:
Ford Motor Comapny of SA, Port Elizabeth.

ENGINE SPEED

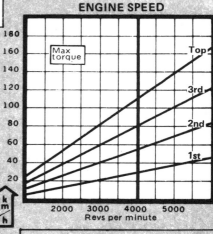

Revs per minute

IMPERIAL DATA

ACCELERATION (seconds):
0-60 11,2
MAXIMUM SPEED (m-p-h):
True speed 105,1
FUEL ECONOMY (m-p-g):
50 m-p-h 35,5
60 m-p-h 31,5

GRADIENT ABILITY

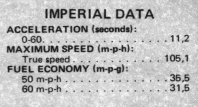

Max torque **4 000** r/min

(Degrees inclination)

CRUISING AT 90

Mech noise level . . . . 75,0 dBA
0-90 through gears . . . . . 9,6 seconds
Litres/100 km at 90 8,6
Optimum fuel range at 90 . . . . 643 km
Braking from 90 . . . . 3,3 seconds
Maximum gradient (top) . . . . 1 in 8,9
Speedometer error . . . . . . 8% over
Speedo at true 90 98
Odometer error . . . . 0,5% under
Rev-counter error . . . . 1,7% over
Engine r/min at 90 . . . . 3 180

STEADY-SPEED FUEL CONSUMPTION
(litres/100 km at true speeds)

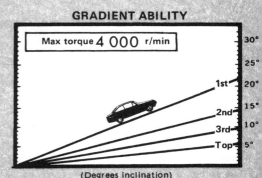

(Miles per gallon)

Ford RS Escorts

WHAT A FASCINATING group of cars is covered by this particular survey. Here is the combination of machinery which invites Walter Mitty-type fantasies, combined with Ford service and parts availability. There is a broad enough spread of prices and performance to give both the impecunious enthusiast and the really serious high-speed saloon car motorist a choice.

But from a *Ford?* How can this possibly be? The answer, of course, is that these secondhand cars are no ordinary Fords, and they are certainly not ordinary Escorts. Grouped together, for want of a better phrase, under the name of "Rallye Sport" Escorts, these are the hand-built machines made and sold to back Ford's enthusiastically-pursued motor sport policies.

Some are potentially faster than others, and some are certainly known to be more reliable than others. All, if found in good condition, are great fun to drive, and the newer ones are potential winners, if suitably prepared, on race track or rally stage.

Ten years ago there wasn't much alternative to a Twin-Cam Escort (the Mini-Cooper S was the obvious rival), but now the hot Escorts are faced by models like the Opel Kadett GT/E, the twin-cam Toyota Celicas, the Vauxhall Chevette 2300HS, the Renault 5 Alpine, and the Fiat 131 Abarth.

In other countries there might be better economic reasons for choosing a rival. In Britain, in terms of availability and spares back-up, an Escort reigns supreme.

What is a "Rallye Sport" Escort?

Every RS Escort ever made has been a 2-door saloon; all but the Twin-Cams and early RS1600s have been specially built in British or West German factories; 4-door saloons and 3-door estate cars have never been sold by Ford — any you find on the secondhand market have been privately converted. There are two types of RS Escort — three models each being based on the original Escort shape of 1968-1974, and the latest three models on the Mark 2 shape still in production. A Mark 2 Escort Sport of 1,297 or 1,599 c.c. is *not* an RS model.

Facia of early RS1600 (below) is retained in similar form in later Mk 1 types such as RS2000 (centre), although steering wheels differed. Mk 2 RS1800 (right) features redesigned facia

Above: RS1600 was initially available only in white

Top right: The Escort Mexico first appeared in 1970. It was really the RS1600 fitted with the 1,599 c.c. Cortina GT/Capri GT engine

Right: Newer Mexico is effectively an RS 1800 with a different engine — the 1,593 c.c. "Pinto" engine

Right: RS1600 gave way to RS1800, rare in road car form. These are built in Germany as the Mexico

Below: The RS 2000 was the next to appear. It had the same body shell, but had 100 bhp "pinto" engine

Below right: RS 2000 in Mk 2 form is splendid machine with distinctive droop-snoot plastic nose cone

Every RS Escort was based on the appropriate heavy-duty structure, and suspensions, but with revised settings. Every RS Escort had larger-than-normal/boosted/completely different engines, and modifications to suit; automatic transmission was never available.

Every RS Escort except the latest Mexico was designed with competition potential in mind, and a whole range of tuning and preparation parts was, or still is, available. In Britain these items, and expertise on all aspects of the cars, is concentrated on Ford Rallye Sport Dealers, of whom there are less than 100 in the mighty Ford network.

Every RS Escort, as catalogued, was a perfectly suitable car for road use, but some — notably the 16-valve RS1600s and RS1800s — were always in extremely short supply. If you were to order a standard RS1800 today, for instance, the chances are that you would have to wait at least six months for delivery, and you could have any colour you liked as long as it was white.

How the Rallye Sport Escorts evolved

In the beginning there was the Escort Twin-Cam, announced in 1968 and built among and alongside the bread-and-butter Escorts at Halewood. This had the stronger "Type 49" body shell, recognisable by its slightly flared wheel arches, and had the Lotus-Cortina 1,558 c.c.2 ohc engine, gearbox and back axle shoehorned neatly into it. This had the basic Escort GT instrument panel and trim, and every car was white. Originally it suffered from rectangular headlamps, but from July 1969 these were replaced by quartz-halogen circular units.

To keep the cars competitive in races and rallies, Ford then replaced the old Lotus engine by the Cosworth-designed 16-valve BDA unit. Thus the Twin-Cam became the RS1600, of which the first few hundred examples were also assembled at Halewood.

However, from the autumn of 1970, a new Rallye Sport production facility was opened at the South Ockendon factory (in space cleared from a spare parts store). Special body shells were shipped down from Halewood, but all assembly operations were carried out on this production line.

RS1600 production was transferred to South Ockendon plant (which has always affectionately been known as "AVO" — the Advanced Vehicle Operation), and from November 1970 it was joined by the Escort Mexico, which was really the RS1600 fitted with the 1,599 c.c. Cortina GT/Capri GT engine (86 bhp instead of the BDA's 120 bhp). Both cars could now be ordered in a choice of colours. The Mexico, being cheaper to buy and much cheaper to insure, was a great success. Like the RS1600 its engine was homologated for competition use at the top-limit figure of 1,601 c.c. which meant that it could be further enlarged into the 2-litre sporting class.

While RS1600 and Mexico production continued, the next RS car to appear was the RS2000 in summer 1973. This retained the usual body shell, but was given a 100 bhp single ohc, "Pinto" engine, and was backed by a gearbox with wider ratios, but with a higher axle ratio. Much work had gone into refining the car, which had different and more compliant suspension settings. Of this trio, the RS1600 was much the rarest, with production dying away in 1974. Both Mexico and RS2000 were homologated into Group 1 for international competition, which meant that Ford claimed to have built at least 5,000 cars of each model in a 12-month period.

With the introduction of Mark 2 Escorts at the beginning of 1975, the AVO plant was closed down (the facility is preserved, in "mothballs"), and RS models temporarily disappeared from the line-up. The new mass-production range included an Escort 1600 Sport, which was superficially like an updated Mexico, but without the old car's character.

New RS models were promised, all to be built at Saarlouis in Germany. There are Mark 2 RS equivalents to each of the originals, but all have important differences. All are based on the Mark 2 heavy-duty body shell.

The RS1600 gave way to the RS1800, and in road car form it is an extremely rare machine. Many

RS1800s, in fact, have come into existence by the re-shelling of RS1600s (for competition use); these form a high proportion of cars on the secondhand market. In catalogue form an RS1800 has an 1,840 c.c. 16-valve engine with a single down-draught dual-choke Weber carburettor, and — like RS1600s built since the autumn of 1972 — rejoices in the use of a light-alloy cylinder block, unique to the RS Escorts. A few RS1800s were assembled at Halewood early in 1975. We must point out, however, that this is a car built and marketed most reluctantly by Ford, who must maintain a presence for sporting homologation purposes. An RS1800 is built as a Mexico (see below) in Germany, then engined and badged in Britain.

Neither the RS Mexico nor the RS2000 became available again until the beginning of 1976, but now sell in fair numbers. The RS2000, indeed, is something of a young businessman's express, with a great deal of status value.

The Mexico, effectively, is an RS1800 with a different engine, in this case the 1,593 c.c. single ohc "Pinto" engine producing 110 bhp. Ford have not promoted the latest cars in any form of competition, so that both in image and in sales the RS Mexico has rather fallen between two stools.

In Mark 2 form the RS2000 is a splendid machine. It has a distinctive droop-snoot nose cone, of plastic, with recessed twin headlamps and built-in bumper. The 1,993 c.c. "Pinto" engine produces 110 bhp. There is a very high standard of trim, fittings and instrumentation, a great deal of sound deadening, and — like all other Mark 2 RS models — a flexible spoiler across the boot lid to aid high-speed stability. An RS2000 as our performance chart shows, combines RS1800 performance with a great deal of refinement.

All three Mark 2 cars, of course, remain in production, though RS1800s are only built to special order.

What to look for?

First, a word of warning. A high proportion of the cars — almost every 16-valve machine, many Mexicos and Twin-Cams, and a good few RS2000s — have been used in some sort of competition work. This means that they have been subjected to maximum stress, they may have been crashed or unduly strained in some way, and they will almost invariably have been considerably modified.

Anyone looking for a secondhand road car should be absolutely sure that the car of his choice has a blameless history. In fact if the car has not been crashed, or is not thoroughly tired from years of rallying, it might be in excellent mechanical condition (careful hand-building of 16-valve engines, for instance, can improve on the standard product to a remarkable degree), but a radically-modified car is probably a most unsuitable road car.

Many RS1600s and RS1800s, for example, are offered with competition fittings still in place — with engines enlarged to 2 litres, with 5-speed ZF gearboxes in place of the standard items, and with entirely different "Atlas" axles instead of the normal "English" axle.

Tell-tale signs of hastily-converted competition cars include non-standard or unusual colour schemes (look for overspray in the usual areas, and for give-away details inside door jambs, or behind trim panels), suspiciously clean patches which might once have been covered by decals or competition numbers, slots, holes or body modifications, extra electrical wiring, non-standard seats, steering wheels, and instruments.

For a road car, however, you should consider the following: The hottest Escorts attract very heavy insurance premiums, both because of their performance and because of spare parts prices and availability problems. Is there any point in buying an RS1800, for instance, when a Mk 2 RS2000 is virtually as quick, and is much cheaper to run? Do you really need a Mk 2 Mexico, when a Mk 2 1600 Sport is nearly as fast, and is as well equipped?

There is a vast spread of prices, and — surprisingly enough — quite a lot of choice, if you concentrate on visiting the Ford Rallye Sport dealer network. Although Twin-Cams were built for more than three years, most seem to have been re-engined as RS1600s, and very few road cars are thought to remain. If you find one, however, remember that Ford do not service the Lotus-type engines, whereas Caterham Car Sales (who still build the Lotus-engined Super Seven) will undoubtedly help.

The cars in greatest supply are Mark 1 and 2 Mexicos and RS2000s. Among Mark 2 cars, at least two RS2000s are sold for every one Mexico, a supply situation mirrored in the last year of Mark 1 production at AVO. Note that in 1975 a fair number of Mark 1 cars were registered from new, even though they had been built in 1974. Since there is a big price jump between 1974 Mk 1s and 1976 Mk 2s, these form a useful buffer stock.

Unless you are a dedicated engine maintenance man, or have the money to keep your car in some luxury, we don't recommend an RS1600 or an RS1800. The 16-valve engines need regular (3,000-mile) and meticulous service, particularly to valve gear and carburation. Both performance and fuel consumption can slump alarmingly if the engine goes off tune, and the Webers must be absolutely right to give the best results.

Performance Comparison

	Escort Twin-Cam (Mk 1) 1,558 c.c.	Escort RS1600 (Mk 1) 1,601 c.c.	Escort RS1800 (Mk 2) 1,845 c.c.	Escort Mexico (Mk 1) 1,601 c.c.	Escort RS2000 (Mk 1) 1,993 c.c.	Escort RS2000 (Mk 2) 1,993 c.c.
Road Tested in *Autocar* of:	6 June 1968	30 April 1970	26 July 1975	10 Dec 1970	11 Oct 1973	17 Jan 1976
Mean maximum speed (mph)	113	113	111	99	108	109
Acceleration (sec)						
0-30mph	3.8	3.4	2.9	3.9	2.9	3.0
0-40mph	5.2	4.8	4.7	5.8	4.8	4.7
0-50mph	7.2	6.8	6.6	7.9	6.9	6.4
0-60mph	9.9	8.9	9.0	10.7	9.0	8.6
0-70mph	13.0	12.4	12.4	14.5	12.8	12.7
0-80mph	16.8	16.1	16.6	20.2	17.2	16.9
0-90mph	24.2	22.6	22.0	30.8	24.2	23.1
0-100mph	33.6	32.3	32.9	—	34.5	33.6
Standing ¼-mile (sec)	17.2	16.7	16.9	18.0	17.1	16.7
Direct top gear (sec)						
10-30	—	—	—	—	—	—
20-40	10.6	—	8.8	9.5	—	8.7
30-50	9.8	10.1	8.2	8.6	7.4	7.8
40-60	9.7	9.2	8.4	8.7	7.9	7.8
50-70	9.9	9.5	8.9	9.4	8.8	8.4
60-80	10.6	10.3	9.6	11.3	8.8	9.1
70-90	12.4	12.5	11.8	16.5	11.0	10.6
80-100	16.5	16.9	17.2	—	16.2	16.9
Overall mpg	21.5	21.5	26.5	27.5	26.6	24.7
Typical mpg	24	22	28	30	28	27

Dimensions:
Length — Mk I and Mk 2 Escorts 13ft 0.6in.
Width — 5ft 1.8in. (Mk I) 5ft 2.7in. (Mk 2)
Height — 4ft 6in. (Mk I), 4ft 7.5in. (Mk 2)

| Unladen weight (lb) | 1,872 | 1,920 | 2,016 | 1,964 | 1,978 | 2,075 |

Milestones and chassis identification

Twin-Cam, RS1600 and RS1800 models

	Series	Chassis No.
Jan 1968: Escort Twin-Cam announced (first 25 cars hand-assembled at Boreham in spring 1968), with 1,558 c.c. Lotus twin-cam engine, Lotus-Cortina gearbox and back axle in two-door "heavy duty" body shell. From:	3026E	49G 01304
July 1969: Circular QI headlamps replaced original rectangular type, from:	3026E	49J 20645
Jan 1970: Escort RS1600 announced, to supplement Twin-Cam. As Twin-Cam but with 16-valve Cosworth-Ford BDA engine. From:	3026E	49K 22435
Oct 1970: Chassis Series sequence changed to:	ATL	
April 1971: Twin-Cam discontinued at:	—	ATLC40214
Oct 1972: Aluminium cylinder block introduced for RS1600 in place of cast-iron block. From:	ATL	ATM00112
November 1974: RS1600 discontinued at:	ATL	ATP 00043
Mar 1975: Escort RS1800 announced, with enlarged (1,845 c.c.) BDA engine and simple carburation, RS1600 transmission and suspension, in Mk 2 Escort shell. From:	ATS	GCATRD23729
Jan 1976: Now produced in Germany (as Mexico) and re-engined in Britain. From:	ATS	GCATS . . . .

Mexico and RS2000 models

	Series	Chassis No.
Nov 1970: Mexico announced, with 1,601 c.c. ohv engine, but Twin-Cam/RS1600 mechanicals and body shell. From:	ATL	ATK 23624
Oct 1972: Battery in boot compartment, sports road wheels, carpets, etc, from:	ATL	ATM·00113
July 1973: RS2000 announced (originally for export, for Britain from October 1973), with RS1600/Mexico body shell, suspension and transmission, but single ohc 1,993 c.c. engine. Reclining seats, carpets, etc, all standard. Opening British numbers:	ATL	BFATNC00066
Jan 1975: Mexico and RS2000 (Mk 1 bodies) discontinued, from: Mexico	ATL	ATR 00442
RS2000	ATL	ATR 00470
Jan 1976: Mexico and RS2000 Mk 2 models available. Mk 2 bodies, standard on Mexico, with four headlamps and "shovel nose" on RS2000. Single ohc engines, 1,593 c.c. on Mexico, 1,993 c.c. on RS2000. Transmissions and suspensions as before. Both cars made completely in Germany. From: RS Mexico	ATS	GCAT . . . .
RS2000	ATS	GCAT . . . .
Jan 1977: Continued basically unchanged, with new vehicle prefix:	—	GXATT . . .

Note: In this period, Ford chassis numbers denote when a car was built. 49G for instance, denotes a 1968 model, 49H a 1969, 49J a 1970, and so on. This system was changed in Autumn 1972.

91

Updating a Mark 2 engine (with a downdraught Weber) to the old RS1600 carburation is expensive, and not recommended, because of the need to move the brake servo, fit a new pedal box, add a new throttle linkage — all of which can cost £400.

The belt-drive should be OK (rumours of belts jumping cogs only really apply to highly-tuned versions), and reliability is excellent as long as the electronic rev-limiter is *not* disconnected. If you used more than 7,000 rpm with a standard engine the results could be catastrophic and expensive.

The 16-valve engines can be oil burners and oil leakers (partucularly from the cam covers and the cylinder head joints). It is also a fact that mildly tuned examples which have been carefully re-prepared are more reliable than the standard units. There appear to be no problems with the aluminium cylinder blocks or heads, though some stretch of standard valves is a known problem. One of our Rallye Sport dealer friends suggested that 1600s were better than 1800s, but that "neither is worth the bother, for road use, compared with an RS2000."

The RS2000 engine is virtually the same as Cortina/Capri units (Mexico units are similarly nearly standard), and they suffer only from the same known problems. The Pinto's engine wears its camshaft lobes quicker than it should, which is a lubrication problem alleviated but not eliminated on later engines, and which shows itself more on "town cars" (where the oil does not heat up enough or often enough) than on long-distance cars. It is not clear why, but RS2000s seem to suffer much less than Cortinas do, probably because they are generally driven harder, and therefore have their oil circulating well. The engines are not temperamental and last very well in all other details.

RS Escorts' transmissions seem to have normal long lives, in spite of the type of car they inhabit. The boxes are fully capable of accepting the power and torque out through them, and are virtually standard in all res-

To keep cars competitive in races and rallies Ford replaced old Lotus engine with Cosworth 16-valve BDA. Thus the Twin-Cam became the RS1600

RS1800 has 1,840 c.c. 16-valve engine with single downdraught dual-choke Weber

The Escort Twin-Cam — the basic hot Escort of 1968 from which the RS cars sprang. The Twin-Cam had the Lotus Cortina 2 ohc engine. Note rectangular headlamps

Pinto 1,993 c.c. engine in RS2000 Mk 2 produces 110 bhp

Approximate selling prices

Price Range	Twin-Cam	RS1600/RS1800	Mexico/RS Mexico	RS2000
£400-£500	1968			
£500-£600	1969			
£600-£700	1970	1970		
£700-£800	1971	1971		
£800-£900			1971	
£900-£1000		1972	1972	
£1100-£1200		1972	1973	
£1300-£1400			1974	1973
£1400-£1500	1974			
£1500-£1600			1975*	
£1600-£1700				1974
£2000-£2100		1975		1975*
£2400-£2500			1976	
£2800-£2900		1976	1977	1976
£3200-£2500		1977		1977

*Mark I model, built in 1974, sold and registered in 1975.

Note: *Values of RS1600s and RS1800s vary a great deal according to their state of tune, their equipment, and their previous history. Supplies, in any case, are very limited. Values shown are top prices for relatively low-mileage road cars. High-mileage machines and those with a competition record should be approached with great caution.*

pects. Standard cars mostly have what we call the latest Cortina 2-litre gearbox, while Mk 1 Mexicos and Twin-Cam/RS1600 models have the "2000E" box of a different but still available type.

All cars have the "English" axle as used in all Escorts and most Capris and Cortinas. There is a big choice of ratios, but the highest (numerically lowest) is the 3.54 found on RS2000s. All RS Escorts, therefore, have to be revved well to give their best performance.

Bodies are based on whatever was the export "heavy duty" shell at the time, and certainly in the case of cars built at AVO there was extra attention given to paintwork and the quality of finish. All the general remarks about Escort body corrosion apply to these cars (our bread-and-butter Escort survey was last published on 6 March 1976) as do comments on suspensions and brakes.

There is an enormous degree of interchangeability of parts between the models, and many are shared with other Escort, Capri or Cortina models. Parts availability, therefore, is very good, and most chassis and transmission items can be sourced from any Ford dealer. Special "RS" parts, however, have to be found at Rallye Sport dealers.

An idea of the number of cars on the market is that at the moment about 2,000 RS Mexicos and RS2000s are being sold in Britain each year. We doubt if there are more than 50 RS1800 *road cars* in Britain.

There is a huge list of optional equipment to improve an RS Escort, which is the good news. The bad news is that buying such items tends to become addictive!

Spares prices

	Mexico	Mark 1 cars RS2000	Twin-Cam	RS1600	RS Mexico	Mark 2 cars RS2000	RS1800
Engine assembly — new	n.a.	n.a.	n.a.	£1,161.20	£320.49	£305.45	n.a.
Short engine — new	£190.25	£263.92	n.a.	£442.11	£257.54	£263.92	n.a.
Gearbox assembly — new	£120.12	£141.91	£120.12	£120.12	£141.91	£141.91	£141.91
Clutch pressure plate — exchange	£13.86	£13.86	£24.62	£13.86	£16.86	£16.86	£20.75**
Clutch driven plate — exchange	£9.31	£11.19	£11.36	£10.70	£11.19	£11.19	£21.44**
Propeller shaft U/J repair kit (each)	£3.25	£3.25	£7.48	£3.25	£5.03	£5.03	£5.03
Crown wheel/pinion set — new	£60.12	£138.34	£60.12	£60.12	£56.81	£56.81	£56.81
Brake pads — front (set, new)	£12.43	£12.39	£12.43	£12.43	£11.84	£11.84	£11.84
Brake shoes — rear (set, exchange)	£13.83	£13.83	£7.34	£13.83	£7.55	£7.55	£7.55
Suspension struts — front (pair)	£69.90	£69.90	£69.90	£69.90	£69.68	£69.68	£69.68
Suspension dampers — rear (pair)	£26.44	£21.72	£26.44	£17.04	£24.00	£24.00	£24.00
Radiator assembly — new	£112.55	£109.13	£39.05	£102.88	£35.45	£35.45	£102.89
Alternator — new (T-C, dynamo)	£55.58	£64.86	£25.24	£55.58	£59.56	£59.56	£59.56
Starter motor — new	£26.63	£97.17	£26.63	£26.63	£80.49	£54.18*	£26.63
Front wing panel	£16.42	£16.42	£16.42	£16.42	£18.19	£23.78	£18.19
Bumper—front—both sides — exchange	£8.73	£8.73	£8.73	£8.73	£15.14	integral	£15.14
Bumper—rear — exchange	£12.70	£12.70	£12.70	£12.70	£16.19	£10.62	£16.19
Windscreen — toughened	£13.80	£13.80	£13.80	£13.80	£14.11	£14.11	£14.11
Windscreen — laminated	£27.97	£27.97	£27.97	£27.97	£28.73	£28.73	£28.73
Exhaust system complete	£35.63	£36.44	£29.60	£35.63	£93.67	£91.42	£85.76

*Exchange **New

Note: *All the above prices include VAT at 8 per cent*